Head First iPhone and iPad Development

Wouldn't it be dreamy if I could get my App idea out there? I think I have the next Angry Birds all figured out...

Tracey Pilone
Dan Pilone

with
Paul Pilone &
Brett McLaughlin

Beijing • Cambridge • Farnham • Köln • Sebastopol • Taipei • Tokyo

Head First iPhone and iPad Development

by Tracey Pilone and Dan Pilone with Paul Pilone and Brett McLaughlin

Printed in the United States of America.

Published by O'Reilly Media, Inc., 1005 Gravenstein Highway North, Sebastopol, CA 95472.

O'Reilly Media books may be purchased for educational, business, or sales promotional use. Online editions are also available for most titles (*safari.oreilly.com*). For more information, contact our corporate/institutional sales department: (800) 998-9938 or *corporate@oreilly.com*.

Series Creators:	Kathy Sierra, Bert Bates
Editor:	Courtney Nash
Design Editor:	Louise Barr
Cover Designer:	Karen Montgomery
Production Editor:	Melanie Yarbrough
Proofreader:	Jasmine Kwityn
Indexer:	Potomac Indexing Services
Page Viewers:	Vinny & Nick

Vinny

Nick

Printing History:

October 2009: First Edition.

June 2011: Second Edition.

December 2013: Third Edition.

The O'Reilly logo is a registered trademark of O'Reilly Media, Inc. The *Head First* series designations, *Head First iPhone and iPad Development*, and related trade dress are trademarks of O'Reilly Media, Inc.

No PCs were harmed in the making of this book.

ISBN: 978-1-449-3165-70

[M]

To my entire family: the Chadwicks, the Pilones, and Element84, who have surrounded me with support both at home and at work. And to my husband who is always there with me, and without whom it wouldn't be fun.

—**Tracey**

To my wife, my cofounder, and best friend. She inspired me to write the first edition, then just handled it for this one. :)

—**Dan**

Authors of Head First iPhone and iPad Development

Tracey

Dan

Tracey Pilone is co-founder (along with Dan Pilone) and operations director at Element 84, a high value outsourcing and consulting company specializing in highly scalable web and mobile software development . In addition to handling the business development work for the company, she works with Element 84's agile development teams to manage and deliver projects to customers.

Prior to starting Element 84, she spent several years working in and around the Washington, D.C., area for two of Engineering News Record's top 20 contractors as a construction manager in commercial construction. This is her fourth *Head First* book, including the two earlier editions of this book and *Head First Algebra*.

She has a civil engineering degree from Virginia Tech and a Master's of Education from the University of Virginia, and holds a professional engineer's license in Virginia. You can follow Tracey on Twitter: @traceypilone.

Dan Pilone is the founder and Managing Partner of Element 84. He has designed and implemented systems for NASA, Hughes, ARINC, UPS, and the Naval Research Laboratory. He currently serves as technical lead for projects with NASA as well as all of Element 84's projects. He speaks frequently in the community most recently at ESIP, AGU, and the DC Ruby Users Group.

He has taught project management, software design, and software engineering at The Catholic University in Washington, D.C. Dan has been an instructor for the D.C. iPhone Bootcamp and has written several books on software development, including *Head First Software Development*, *UML 2.0 in a Nutshell*, and *UML 2.0 Pocket Reference*. You can follow Dan on Twitter: @danpilone.

Coauthors of Head First iPhone and iPad Development

Paul

Brett

Paul Pilone is an iOS and Rails developer with Element 84. He's the author of iHomework, an iPhone, iPad, and Mac app for managing homework assignments. Paul has developed software for the Naval Research Labs, Lockheed Martin, NASA, and Cengage Learning. You can follow Paul on Twitter: @paulpilone.

Brett McLaughlin is a software developer at Element84. He's also a developer who's got his hands into cognitive theory. That means that he sees HTML5, CSS, JavaScript, Java, and Rails as the means to tell interesting stories to users rather than just a load of boring technology and protocols. He's also really interested in the next generation of communication technologies, ranging from ePub to ebooks to mobile devices. And in his free time (what free time?), he's usually playing with video and writing projects and playing guitar... really expensive acoustic ones, if he can manage.

Table of Contents (Summary)

Table of Contents (the real thing)

Intro

Your brain on iOS Development. Here you are trying to learn something, while here your brain is doing you a favor by making sure the learning doesn't stick. Your brain's thinking, "Better leave room for more important things, like which wild animals to avoid and whether naked snowboarding is a bad idea." So how do you trick your brain into thinking your life depends on knowing enough to develop your own iPhone and iPad apps?

getting started

Getting mobile with iOS

1

The iPhone changed everything.

When Steve Jobs said that's what would happen at the unveiling of the iPhone, people were skeptical. Six years later, iPhones and iPads are being used in business and medicine as enterprise devices, and the App Store is a platform for every developer to use, from one-man shows to big-name companies. Apple provides the software and we'll help you with the knowledge—we're sure you've got the enthusiasm covered.

basic iOS patterns

Building from scratch

2

Now that you've gotten your feet wet, it's time to start fresh.

You should have a good idea of the tools you'll be working with and how to get around Xcode a bit. Now it's time to dig a little deeper and start your own project. How do you set up an iOS project, how do the pieces of the app really work together, and what are the interaction patterns you can count on? Turn the page, 'cause you're ready to find out...

interlude

Syntax

It's time to get into some details.

You've written a couple apps and gotten some of the big picture stuff sorted out. Now it's time to get into some line by line details. Why are there @ symbols everywhere? What's the difference between a method and a message? What exactly do properties do? It's time to take a quick dive into the syntax of Objective-C; then we can get back into building apps.

2.5

tables, views, and data

A table with a view

Most iOS apps have more than one view.

We've written a cool app with one view, but anyone who's used a smartphone knows that most apps aren't like that. Some of the more impressive iOS apps out there do a great job of working with complex information by using multiple views. We're going to start with navigation controllers and table views, like the kind you see in your Mail and Contacts apps. Only we're going to do it with a twist...

3

multiview applications

It's all about the details

Most iOS apps have more than one view.

We've gotten this app off to a quick start using built-in templates and doing some really nice updates to the table view. Now it's time to dive into the details, setting up the new view and working with the navigation between them. Because most of the widely used apps up on the store are giving you a good and easy way to work through a lot of data. Spin City is doing just that—giving users an easier way to get through the records than flipping through boxes!

4

The review process, design, and devices

How to live with Apple

5

iOS development comes with some strings.

Everybody has heard the war stories. The Apple review process is famous for being painful and having tons of rules you'll have to follow. Yes, there are some hoops to jump through, but once you know what you're doing, it's not nearly so bad. And besides, once you've gotten your app approved, the massively popular App Store is waiting for you... full of eager device owners with a few bucks to burn. So what's not to love?

6

basic core data and table view cells

Reruns are hard to find

Just sit right back and you'll hear a tale, a tale of a fateful trip.

A challenge faced today is how to work with big data and make it presentable in a more appropriate format for mobile. There are lots of ways to do that, including manipulating the data and presenting it to the users in an easy to navigate and interpret way. TV presents one of those challenges because there are so many showings on the air. What's a Gilligan fan to do?

7
implementing search with core data

Looking for info

It's not enough to just be able to see data anymore.

The era of big data is here and just being able to look at it doesn't get you very far anymore. Now you probably won't have a couple of petabytes on your phone (famous last words), but you will most likely have enough data that you'll need to be able to sort and filter it to make it useful for your users. Core Data comes with some built-in functionality to slice through stacks of data and we're going to show you how to use it!

core data, map kit, and core location

Finding a phone booth

8

Now it's time to get to some goodies.

These devices come with so much in the way of built-in capabilities. iPhones and iPads are part computer, part library, part still and video camera, and part GPS device. The field of location-based computing is in its infancy, but it's very powerful. Fortunately, tapping into those hardware functions is something that iOS makes fairly easy.

how to use this book

Intro

In this section we answer the burning question:
"So why <u>DID</u> they put that in an iOS development book?"

Who is this book for?

If you can answer "yes" to all of these:

 Do you have **previous development experience**?

 Do you want to **learn, understand, remember,** and **apply** important iOS design and development concepts so that you can write your own iOS apps?

 Do you prefer **stimulating dinner party conversation** to dry, dull, academic lectures?

It definitely helps if you've already got some object-oriented chops, too. Experience with Mac development is helpful, but certainly not required.

this book is for you.

Who should probably back away from this book?

If you can answer "yes" to any of these:

 Are you **completely new** to software development?

 Are you already developing iOS apps and looking for a **reference book** on Objective-C?

 Are you **afraid to try something different**? Would you rather have a root canal than mix stripes with plaid? Do you believe that a technical book can't be serious if there's a TARDIS mentioned in it?

Check out Head First Programming for an excellent introduction to object-oriented development, and then come back and join us in iPhoneville.

this book is not for you.

[Note from marketing: this book is for anyone with a credit card.]

We know what you're thinking

"How can *this* be a serious iOS development book?"

"What's with all the graphics?"

"Can I actually *learn* it this way?"

We know what your *brain* is thinking

Your brain craves novelty. It's always searching, scanning, *waiting* for something unusual. It was built that way, and it helps you stay alive.

So what does your brain do with all the routine, ordinary, normal things you encounter? Everything it *can* to stop them from interfering with the brain's *real* job—recording things that *matter*. It doesn't bother saving the boring things; they never make it past the "this is obviously not important" filter.

How does your brain *know* what's important? Suppose you're out for a day hike and a tiger jumps in front of you, what happens inside your head and body?

Neurons fire. Emotions crank up. *Chemicals surge.*

And that's how your brain knows...

This must be important! Don't forget it!

But imagine you're at home, or in a library. It's a safe, warm, tiger-free zone. You're studying. Getting ready for an exam. Or trying to learn some tough technical topic your boss thinks will take a week, ten days at the most.

Just one problem. Your brain's trying to do you a big favor. It's trying to make sure that this *obviously* non-important content doesn't clutter up scarce resources. Resources that are better spent storing the really *big* things. Like tigers. Like the danger of fire. Like how you should never have posted those party photos on your Facebook page.

And there's no simple way to tell your brain, "Hey brain, thank you very much, but no matter how dull this book is, and how little I'm registering on the emotional Richter scale right now, I really *do* want you to keep this stuff around."

Your brain thinks THIS is important.

Great. Only 368 more dull, dry, boring pages.

Your brain thinks THIS isn't worth saving.

We think of a "Head First" reader as a <u>learner</u>.

So what does it take to *learn* something? First, you have to *get* it, then make sure you don't *forget* it. It's not about pushing facts into your head. Based on the latest research in cognitive science, neurobiology, and educational psychology, *learning* takes a lot more than text on a page. We know what turns your brain on.

Some of the Head First learning principles:

Make it visual. Images are far more memorable than words alone, and make learning much more effective (up to 89% improvement in recall and transfer studies). It also makes things more understandable. **Put the words within or near the graphics** they relate to, rather than on the bottom or on another page, and learners will be up to *twice* as likely to solve problems related to the content.

> Wait a second. You promised to explain all this fetching stuff to me...

Use a conversational and personalized style. In recent studies, students performed up to 40% better on post-learning tests if the content spoke directly to the reader, using a first-person, conversational style rather than taking a formal tone. Tell stories instead of lecturing. Use casual language. Don't take yourself too seriously. Which would *you* pay more attention to: a stimulating dinner party companion or a lecture?

Get the learner to think more deeply. In other words, unless you actively flex your neurons, nothing much happens in your head. A reader has to be motivated, engaged, curious, and inspired to solve problems, draw conclusions, and generate new knowledge. And for that, you need challenges, exercises, and thought-provoking questions, and activities that involve both sides of the brain and multiple senses.

> OK, that's cool, but where's the album info?

Get—and keep—the reader's attention. We've all had the "I really want to learn this but I can't stay awake past page one" experience. Your brain pays attention to things that are out of the ordinary, interesting, strange, eye-catching, unexpected. Learning a new, tough, technical topic doesn't have to be boring. Your brain will learn much more quickly if it's not.

Touch their emotions. We now know that your ability to remember something is largely dependent on its emotional content. You remember what you care about. You remember when you *feel* something. No, we're not talking heart-wrenching stories about a boy and his dog. We're talking emotions like surprise, curiosity, fun, "what the...?", and the feeling of "I Rule!" that comes when you solve a puzzle, learn something everybody else thinks is hard, or realize you know something that "I'm more technical than thou" Bob from engineering *doesn't*.

Metacognition: thinking about thinking

If you really want to learn, and you want to learn more quickly and more deeply, pay attention to how you pay attention. Think about how you think. Learn how you learn.

Most of us did not take courses on metacognition or learning theory when we were growing up. We were *expected* to learn, but rarely *taught* to learn.

But we assume that if you're holding this book, you really want to learn how to design user-friendly websites. And you probably don't want to spend a lot of time. If you want to use what you read in this book, you need to *remember* what you read. And for that, you've got to *understand* it. To get the most from this book, or *any* book or learning experience, take responsibility for your brain. Your brain on *this* content.

The trick is to get your brain to see the new material you're learning as Really Important. Crucial to your well-being. As important as a tiger. Otherwise, you're in for a constant battle, with your brain doing its best to keep the new content from sticking.

So just how *DO* you get your brain to treat iOS development like it was a hungry tiger?

There's the slow, tedious way, or the faster, more effective way. The slow way is about sheer repetition. You obviously know that you *are* able to learn and remember even the dullest of topics if you keep pounding the same thing into your brain. With enough repetition, your brain says, "This doesn't *feel* important to him, but he keeps looking at the same thing *over* and *over* and *over*, so I suppose it must be."

The faster way is to do **anything that increases brain activity,** especially different *types* of brain activity. The things on the previous page are a big part of the solution, and they're all things that have been proven to help your brain work in your favor. For example, studies show that putting words *within* the pictures they describe (as opposed to somewhere else in the page, like a caption or in the body text) causes your brain to try to makes sense of how the words and picture relate, and this causes more neurons to fire. More neurons firing = more chances for your brain to *get* that this is something worth paying attention to, and possibly recording.

A conversational style helps because people tend to pay more attention when they perceive that they're in a conversation, since they're expected to follow along and hold up their end. The amazing thing is, your brain doesn't necessarily *care* that the "conversation" is between you and a book! On the other hand, if the writing style is formal and dry, your brain perceives it the same way you experience being lectured to while sitting in a roomful of passive attendees. No need to stay awake.

But pictures and conversational style are just the beginning…

Here's what WE did:

We used *pictures*, because your brain is tuned for visuals, not text. As far as your brain's concerned, a picture really *is* worth a thousand words. And when text and pictures work together, we embedded the text *in* the pictures because your brain works more effectively when the text is *within* the thing the text refers to, as opposed to in a caption or buried in the text somewhere.

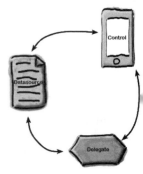

We used *redundancy*, saying the same thing in *different* ways and with different media types, and *multiple senses*, to increase the chance that the content gets coded into more than one area of your brain.

We used concepts and pictures in *unexpected* ways because your brain is tuned for novelty, and we used pictures and ideas with at least *some emotional* content, because your brain is tuned to pay attention to the biochemistry of emotions. That which causes you to *feel* something is more likely to be remembered, even if that feeling is nothing more than a little *humor*, *surprise*, or *interest*.

We used a personalized, *conversational style*, because your brain is tuned to pay more attention when it believes you're in a conversation than if it thinks you're passively listening to a presentation. Your brain does this even when you're *reading*.

BULLET POINTS

We included more than 80 *activities*, because your brain is tuned to learn and remember more when you *do* things than when you *read* about things. And we made the exercises challenging-yet-do-able, because that's what most people prefer.

We used *multiple learning styles*, because *you* might prefer step-by-step procedures, while someone else wants to understand the big picture first, and someone else just wants to see an example. But regardless of your own learning preference, *everyone* benefits from seeing the same content represented in multiple ways.

Fireside Chats

We include content for *both sides of your brain*, because the more of your brain you engage, the more likely you are to learn and remember, and the longer you can stay focused. Since working one side of the brain often means giving the other side a chance to rest, you can be more productive at learning for a longer period of time.

And we included *stories* and exercises that present *more than one point of view,* because your brain is tuned to learn more deeply when it's forced to make evaluations and judgments.

We included *challenges*, with exercises, and by asking *questions* that don't always have a straight answer, because your brain is tuned to learn and remember when it has to *work* at something. Think about it—you can't get your *body* in shape just by *watching* people at the gym. But we did our best to make sure that when you're working hard, it's on the *right* things. That *you're not spending one extra dendrite* processing a hard-to-understand example, or parsing difficult, jargon-laden, or overly terse text.

We used *people*. In stories, examples, pictures, etc., because, well, because *you're* a person. And your brain pays more attention to *people* than it does to *things*.

Here's what YOU can do to bend your brain into submission

So, we did our part. The rest is up to you. These tips are a starting point; listen to your brain and figure out what works for you and what doesn't. Try new things.

Cut this out and stick it on your refrigerator.

1 **Slow down. The more you understand, the less you have to memorize.**

Don't just *read*. Stop and think. When the book asks you a question, don't just skip to the answer. Imagine that someone really *is* asking the question. The more deeply you force your brain to think, the better chance you have of learning and remembering.

2 **Do the exercises. Write your own notes.**

We put them in, but if we did them for you, that would be like having someone else do your workouts for you. And don't just *look* at the exercises. **Use a pencil.** There's plenty of evidence that physical activity *while* learning can increase the learning.

3 **Read the "There are No Dumb Questions" sections.**

That means all of them. They're not optional sidebars, ***they're part of the core content!*** Don't skip them.

4 **Make this the last thing you read before bed. Or at least the last challenging thing.**

Part of the learning (especially the transfer to long-term memory) happens *after* you put the book down. Your brain needs time on its own, to do more processing. If you put in something new during that processing time, some of what you just learned will be lost.

5 **Talk about it. Out loud.**

Speaking activates a different part of the brain. If you're trying to understand something, or increase your chance of remembering it later, say it out loud. Better still, try to explain it out loud to someone else. You'll learn more quickly, and you might uncover ideas you hadn't known were there when you were reading about it.

6 **Drink water. Lots of it.**

Your brain works best in a nice bath of fluid. Dehydration (which can happen before you ever feel thirsty) decreases cognitive function.

7 **Listen to your brain.**

Pay attention to whether your brain is getting overloaded. If you find yourself starting to skim the surface or forget what you just read, it's time for a break. Once you go past a certain point, you won't learn faster by trying to shove more in, and you might even hurt the process.

8 **Feel something.**

Your brain needs to know that this *matters*. Get involved with the stories. Make up your own captions for the photos. Groaning over a bad joke is *still* better than feeling nothing at all.

9 **Write a lot of code!**

There's only one way to learn to program: **writing a lot of code**. And that's what you're going to do throughout this book. Coding is a skill, and the only way to get good at it is to practice. We're going to give you a lot of practice: every chapter has exercises that pose a problem for you to solve. Don't just skip over them—a lot of the learning happens when you solve the exercises. We included a solution to each exercise—don't be afraid to **peek at the solution** if you get stuck! (It's easy to get snagged on something small.) But try to solve the problem before you look at the solution. And definitely get it working before you move on to the next part of the book.

Read Me

This is a learning experience, not a reference book. We deliberately stripped out everything that might get in the way of learning whatever it is we're working on at that point in the book. And the first time through, you need to begin at the beginning, because the book makes assumptions about what you've already seen and learned.

We begin by modifying a completed iOS app by pulling code right from GitHub.

While this book is focused on iOS development, part of what we're hoping to teach is how to use the tools that work not only with iOS development, but with software development in general. So to kick it off, we're going to drop you into completed code that needs some changes, not starting from scratch.

We don't get into app submission.

We used to. But there are two things going on that make that tough. First, once you get into the Apple Developer Program, there are significant chunks that are under NDA, and second, iOS development has gotten more advanced over time. This book is geared toward getting basic knowledge under your belt. You'll need more to get an app ready for submission.

We focus on what you can build and test on the simulator.

The iPhone software development kit (SDK) comes with a great (and free!) tool for testing your apps on your computer. The simulator lets you try out your code without having to worry about getting it on the App Store or on a real device. But it also has its limits. There's some cool iOS stuff you just can't test on the simulator, like the accelerometer and compass. So we don't cover those kinds of things in very much detail in this book since we want to make sure you're creating and testing apps quickly and easily.

The activities are NOT optional.

The exercises and activities are not add-ons; they're part of the core content of the book. Some of them are to help with memory, some are for understanding, and some will help you apply what you've learned. ***Don't skip the exercises.*** The crossword puzzles are the only thing you don't *have* to do, but they're good for giving your brain a chance to think about the words and terms you've been learning in a different context.

The redundancy is intentional and important.

One distinct difference in a Head First book is that we want you to *really* get it. And we want you to finish the book remembering what you've learned. Most reference books don't have retention and recall as a goal, but this book is about *learning*, so you'll see some of the same concepts come up more than once.

The examples are as lean as possible.

Our readers tell us that it's frustrating to wade through 200 lines of an example looking for the two lines they need to understand. Most examples in this book are shown within the smallest possible context, so that the part you're trying to learn is clear and simple. Don't expect all of the examples to be robust, or even complete—they are written specifically for learning, and aren't always fully functional.

We've placed the code on GitHub so you can copy see the full application and all of the code when you need it. The code is available here:

https://github.com/dpilone/Head-First-iPhone-iPad-Development-3rd-Edition

The Brain Power exercises don't have answers.

For some of them, there is no right answer, and for others, part of the learning experience of the Brain Power activities is for you to decide if and when your answers are right. In some of the Brain Power exercises, you will find hints to point you in the right direction.

System requirements

To develop for the iPhone and iPad, you need an Intel-based Mac, period. We wrote this book using OS X version 10.8.5 and Xcode 5.0. If you are running an older version of Xcode, most differences you will see are look and feel based. For some of the more advanced capabilities, like the accelerometer and the camera, you'll need an actual device and to be a registered developer.

In Chapter 1, we point you in the direction to get the SDK and Apple documentation, so don't worry about that for now.

The technical review team

Michael Morrison

Joe Heck

Sean Murphy

Rene Janssen Morrison

Roberto Luis

Eric Shepherd

Rich Rosen

Rich Rosen is one of the co-authors of *Mac OS X for Unix Geeks*. He also collaborated with Leon Shklar on *Web Application Architecture: Principles, Protocols & Practices*, a textbook on advanced web application development.

Sean Murphy has been a Cocoa aficionado for almost 10 years, contributes to open source projects such as Camino, and works as an independent iOS designer and developer.

Joe Heck is a software developer, technology manager, author, and instructor who's been involved with computing for 25 years and developing for the iPhone platform since the first beta release. He's the founder of the Seattle Xcoders developer group, and the author of SeattleBus, an iPhone app that provides real-time arrival and departure times of Seattle public transportation.

Eric Shepherd got started programming at age nine and never looked back. He's been a technical writer, writing developer documentation since 1997, and is currently the developer documentation lead at Mozilla.

Michael Morrison is a writer, developer, and author of *Head First JavaScript*, *Head First PHP & MySQL*, and even a few books that don't have squiggly arrows, stick figures, and magnets. Michael is the founder of Stalefish Labs (*www.stalefishlabs.com*), an edutainment company specializing in games, toys, and interactive media, including a few iPhone apps.

Roberto Luis is a young programmer who loves learning new languages and tools. He's a Computer Science Engineer from Autonoma de Madrid University in Spain, during his career has been involved in desktop, mobile and cloud development.

René Janssen is a multimedia designer from The Netherlands and owner of Ducklord Studio. He started off as a typical graphic designer way, working with Indesign, Photoshop and Illustrator but wanted to learn more, from languages like HTML, CSS, PHP, MySQL to Actionscript. He's worked for years in Flash and Actionscript and evolved to iOS Development, Xcode and Objective-C.

Acknowledgments

Our editor:

Thanks to **Courtney Nash**, who has worked on all three editions of this book (since 2009!), from the beginning to the end. We've had to work around Apple's release cycles and this round was tough to get out the door—thanks to Courtney, we finally did!

Courtney Nash

The O'Reilly team:

To the talented crew over at O'Reilly who prettied up our files after we were done with them and is always there for reachback when we need help with the process and our learners, too.

Our intern:

Thanks to **Jayanth Prathipati**, Element 84's first intern who stepped in to pinch hit and help us finish up with screen shots that had to be updated for iOS7.

Our friends and family:

To all of the **Pilones** and **Chadwicks**, who have helped us with the kids and were understanding of us busting out laptops at various inappropriate times to get this one done.

To all our friends at **Element 84** who ended up helping out here and there when we needed opinions.

To **Paul Pilone**, who helped us write the code for the book and ran through a mess of iOS7 updates pretty quick.

To **Brett McLaughlin**, who worked through storyboarding with us and gave us someone else to help bear the InDesign load.

To **Vinny** and **Nick**, who have been practicing baseball and taekwondo while parts of this book were written, and who we hope are going to be able to help us write the next one!

Safari Books Online

Safari Books Online is an on-demand digital library that delivers expert in both book and video form from the world's leading authors in technology and business.

Technology professionals, software developers, web designers, and business and creative professionals use Safari Books Online as their primary resource for research, problem solving, learning, and certification training.

Safari Books Online offers a range of and pricing programs for organizations, government, and individuals. Subscribers have access to thousands of books, training videos, and prepublication manuscripts in one fully searchable database from publishers like O'Reilly Media, Prentice Hall Professional, Addison-Wesley Professional, Microsoft Press, Sams, Que, Peachpit Press, Focal Press, Cisco Press, John Wiley & Sons, Syngress, Morgan Kaufmann, IBM Redbooks, Packt, Adobe Press, FT Press, Apress, Manning, New Riders, McGraw-Hill, Jones & Bartlett, Course Technology, and dozens more. For more information about Safari Books Online, please visit us online.

1 getting started

Going mobile with iOS

I just don't see what all the iPhone and iPad fuss is about. This phone works just fine and paper does all I need!

The iPhone changed everything.

When Steve Jobs said that's what would happen at the unveiling of the iPhone, people were skeptical. Six years later, iPhones and iPads are being used in business and medicine as enterprise devices, and the App Store is a platform for every developer to use, from one-man shows to big-name companies. Apple provides the software and we'll help you with the knowledge—we're sure you've got the enthusiasm covered.

So you want to build an iOS app...

Mobile development used to be the hip new thing: you were trendy—edgy, even—if you had a mobile app. Those days are gone. Mobile development is everywhere. There are already over 500 million iOS devices out there. By writing an iOS app, you have access to millions of potential users (demanding users, but users all the same).

Back at the beginning of mobile development you could get away with a flashlight application or an app that made noises at the push of a button. Users expect more now. They expect high-resolution graphics that support multiple device orientations, and fast, reliable apps that handle coming in and out of train tunnels without batting an eyelash. Here's the good news, though: jump into this book, work through the exercises, write some code, and you can have your moment of glory on the iTunes App Store right next to names like EA Games and Apple itself!

Welcome to the Apple universe!

You probably know this already, but Apple does things a certain way. iTunes, the storefront for apps, was the first of its kind. To get on the App Store, you need to write your app using Xcode on a Mac, then submit it using iTunes Connect (the portal for submitting and tracking iOS apps) then have it approved by Apple reviewers in California, and then it will appear on the App Store.

There really are live people reviewing these things. We've talked to them... too often.

Xcode

Your app here

There is a lot going on to develop an iOS app, but it all fits together. Let's start with writing the app...

iOS apps are written in Objective-C

You've developed in other languages before, so most of the concepts we'll be dealing with here won't be new. Objective-C is a C-based, object-oriented language. The good news is that the concepts aren't new. The bad news is that the syntax may be confusing because it's somewhat similar to something you've already used. It's probably going to break your brain a little. But that's OK—you'll get over it.

 **It's like Java.**

Object-oriented, with its roots in Smalltalk.

 **The syntax is familiar.**

Since it's a C-based language, all the syntax is the same as that in C for loops, types, pointers, etc. It comes from a long line of Apple heritage, starting with NeXTStep, which led to OpenStep, and finally CocoaTouch.

You'll see NS before a lot of syntax in Objective-C. It comes from the NeXTStep heritage!

 It uses CocoaTouch frameworks.

If you've worked with Mac programming, you already know all about Objective-C, but there's still a lot of iOS-specific things that you need to learn.

☑ **Memory management <u>can</u> be automatic.**

With iOS5, Apple finally introduced some automatic memory mangement tools, like in Java, called automatic reference counting (ARC). That means no more counting references to prevent memory leaks.

It all starts with the SDK ←

Software Development Kit

To write in Objective-C, you'll need Xcode and a Mac. The development tools are free and easy to get your hands on. Just head over to the Mac App Store and search for Xcode. We wrote this book with Xcode 5.0.

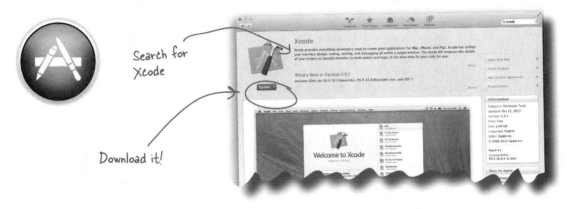

Search for Xcode

Download it!

Once Xcode is downloaded, it'll be dropped into your Applications folder. Xcode is actually a package with a ton of applications, including the compilers, bundled up together. We'll dig into more of what else comes with the Xcode download later, but for now just fire it up. You can get to it by browsing to your Applications folder in Finder or by using Spotlight.

Pin Xcode...you're going to be here a lot

Once you have Xcode up and running for the first time, take a second to add it to your dock. You'll be using it throughout this book. Just right-click (Ctrl-click) on the Xcode icon, select "Options" and then "Keep in Dock."

Meet Sue, your new boss

You've just started working at a new iOS development shop and you need to clean up a Twitter app that's almost finished. We'll make sure you know what you need to know to pull it off, but this is your chance to shine.

Sue's one of those bosses that thinks you should just jump in...

> We keep all our code on GitHub, so go grab InstaTwit and get it set up. I'll let you know what we need to fix before we can ship it. Marketing wants to change a couple of things.

This is GitHub

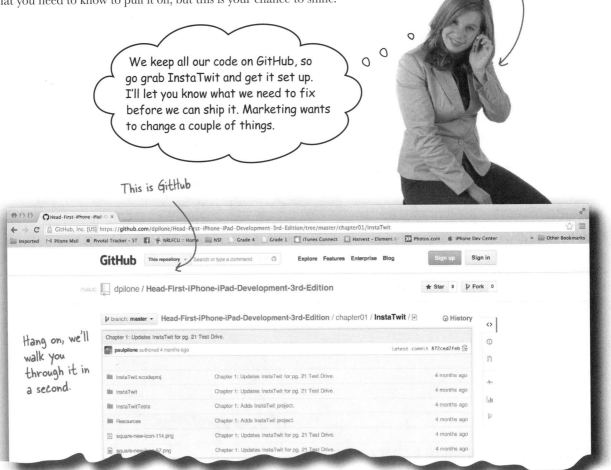

Hang on, we'll walk you through it in a second.

---

there are no Dumb Questions

Q: What is GitHub?

A: GitHub is a place for "social coding." It's an online site that hosts millions of Git code repositories, many of which are publicly available. It's great for distributed teams and open source projects. And code for books. You'll find all the code for this book there, including the example code for this project. GitHub uses Git for its source control, which means you can grab a copy of the code you need for the book and keep track of the changes you make. And if everything falls apart, you can simply revert a change to undo whatever's broken.

Xcode and Git...new best friends

Xcode is the development environment for writing iOS apps. GitHub is an online repository (using Git) for software projects. Together, they can make life easier for development teams. You're working by yourself on this project, but you're using code from the rest of the team. You don't need a GitHub account for this, but if you have one, feel free to fork the code and use it.

 Don't create a new project—we have one in progress.
Xcode's welcome screen gives you the option to start your own project or connect to an existing one. In this case, we'll select "Check out an existing project."

Select this option here.

 Clone the repository.
Next, you need to tell Xcode where to get the code. The URL is *https://github.com/dpilone/Head-First-iPhone-iPad-Development-3rd-Edition.git*. Once you've entered the URL into the repository location box, click Next.

Here there are options.

We have the code for the book set up so that you can pull either the sample code you need for each chapter or the completed code for the book. To get the code for the chapter, you need to check out the branch for the chapter, (in this case, Chapter 1).

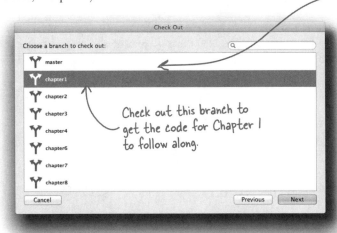

Check out the master branch to pull down the final code for the book. This has everything all finished, so you don't want it yet!

Check out this branch to get the code for Chapter 1 to follow along.

 Pick your project.

This branch contains several different projects, but for now you need only Chapter 1's project, InstaTwit. Select that project and click Open.

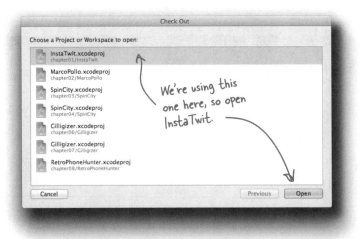

We're using this one here, so open InstaTwit.

Lots of projects, private and open source, use GitHub as their online repository.

Xcode is the hub of your iOS project

Xcode is a full featured integrated development environment (IDE). You use Xcode to edit code and user interfaces (UIs) as well as to look up documentation. There's a full featured debugger, compiler, contextual editing support for code implementation, static code analyzer, code quality suggestions and warnings, and full version control support using Git or Subversion.

You can configure build destinations here; the simulator for now, an actual device later.

Xcode is showing the GUI editor here.

These controls can configure the view, including adding the console and assistant editors to show companion code.

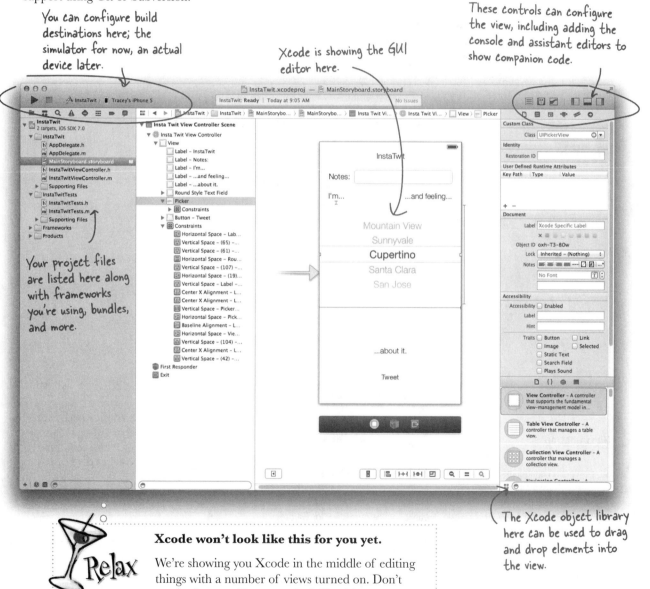

Your project files are listed here along with frameworks you're using, bundles, and more.

The Xcode object library here can be used to drag and drop elements into the view.

Relax
Xcode won't look like this for you yet.

We're showing you Xcode in the middle of editing things with a number of views turned on. Don't worry about making yours look like this yet.

TEST DRIVE

1 **Go ahead and build and run the new code.**
Confirm that the schema listed is "InstaTwit" iPhone Retina (4-inch) simulator.

All you need to do to make it go is click the play button!

2 **Click Build and Run.**
It looks like a play button.

3 **Enable Developer Mode.**
You may get a pop up at this time to enable developer mode. Go ahead and do it now—it means you won't have to enter your password all the time!

there are no Dumb Questions

Q: Git is what, again?

A: Git is a version control management system originally developed for Linux development. It works differently than Subversion or CVS, in that every local copy of the repository is in itself a complete repository. That makes it more robust for distributed, asynchronous development teams. For more information about Git and its commands, see *http://git-scm.com/about*.

Q: And how is Git related to GitHub?

A: Git is a type of version control that can be installed locally on one machine or on a private server for remote access. GitHub is a public, online repository for Git projects.

Q: What about Subversion?

A: Subversion is also supported under Xcode. If you are working in an environment using Subversion, you can check out code using the same workflow (and URL supported by GitHub), but we don't have a Subversion workflow for the book; you'll need to use Git for InstaTwit code.

Q: What else does Xcode do with Git?

A: Xcode uses Git to keep track of changes to files. It can tell you with a little icon which files you've modified, let you commit your changes right from inside Xcode, and even compare the old files versus the new ones.

The iOS simulator

The simulator will launch automatically when you build and run the app for the first time. The simulator supports basic interactions besides just tapping on the screen, including rotating views, taking screenshots for app submission, and shaking the device for accelerometer support.

This is the view you'll get in the iOS simulator—it's a separate app that opens automatically.

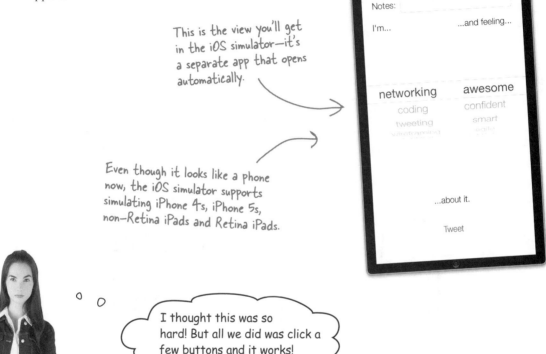

Even though it looks like a phone now, the iOS simulator supports simulating iPhone 4s, iPhone 5s, non-Retina iPads and Retina iPads.

I thought this was so hard! But all we did was click a few buttons and it works!

Xcode just did some major heavy lifting.

Even though Xcode makes it look like a simple play button a lot just happened. Even though we didn't write any new code, you have a fully working project in front of you with a good bit of code. Xcode compiled, linked, processed, packaged, installed, and ran your app when you hit that button. Let's take a closer look...

An Xcode Build Up Close

1   **Xcode pulled the project from GitHub**
This one you walked through, but Xcode pulled the original code from GitHub. Xcode pulled more than just the Objective-C source, though. It pulled a full project description, workspace layout, and icons and UIs we use in the app. These are all part of an Xcode project.

Technically this isn't part of the build process, but we didn't want to skip where the code came from...

2   **Classes in your project are compiled**
Time to talk files a little. An Objective-C class typically has a *.h* and a *.m* file, used as the header and the implementation, respectively. A header file describes the public interface to a class—its API. The implementation file is just that, where the meat goes that makes the class do what it does. Those two get combined and compiled into binary form during the build process.

3   **Your UIs are processed and converted to a binary form**
UIs in Xcode are usually built as storyboards and are XML documents that describe what goes where. Xcode compiles those down into a binary format along with optimizing any images, icons, etc. that your app uses to a format that's easily renderable by the target device.

4   **Framework code is linked in**
There's lots of shared library code in an iOS app: UI drawing code (UIKit), mapping support (MapKit), low-level drawing code (CoreGraphics), etc. Apple calls these shared libraries frameworks. Frameworks are more than just shared compiled code like JARs or *.so* files from other languages. In Objective-C, frameworks can include header files, graphics resources, and more. Some frameworks, like MapKit, are optional and needed only if your application uses them, whereas others, like CoreGraphics, are required because every application relies on the code they contain.

An Xcode Build Up Close (cont.)

⑤ Your compiled code, images, etc. get packaged up
If you've never worked with OS X or iOS applications before, *SomeApp.app* is actually just a directory with specific contents. An iOS application is a folder with a compiled executable, a number of configuration files, and any resources the app needs to run. We'll talk more about the directory structure later.

⑥ If you're installing on a device, the code is signed
Installation onto devices—everything from just testing on your personal device to posting on the App Store—is controlled with certificates based on your developer credentials. This is how the iOS ecosystem controls what can be installed on devices. Certificates are managed in the organizer and you use provisioning profiles to match up applications with devices.

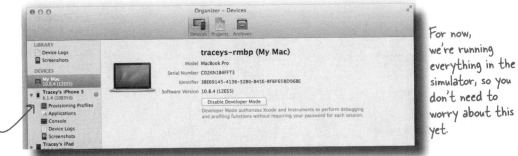

Here are all the profiles in your installation.

For now, we're running everything in the simulator, so you don't need to worry about this yet.

⑦ Your app is installed on the simulator
The simulator acts a lot like a real device. It has a directory where your data is stored, apps get their own directories by IDs, etc. We'll talk more about that later, but it's all happening right now when you hit Play...

⑧ Your app is launched and the debugger is attached
Xcode will start up your application in the simulator and then attach the debugger to it if you chose to debug the app (versus just running it without debugging). We'll see more of this shortly, but the console will start logging events in the app and you can monitor it through a panel in Xcode.

Oh. I guess that is a lot...

OK, good, you're all set up. We need to change the text of the tweets—marketing wants to pitch this app to the startup community as a time saver.

Sometimes search is your best friend.

It's a minor change (we're changing static content that's hardcoded into the app). Let's just be real: the easiest way to figure out where the code for that text lives is to use search. Since "awesome" is one of the labels, search for that.

Here's the search term

Click here to reveal the search dialog.

Here it is!

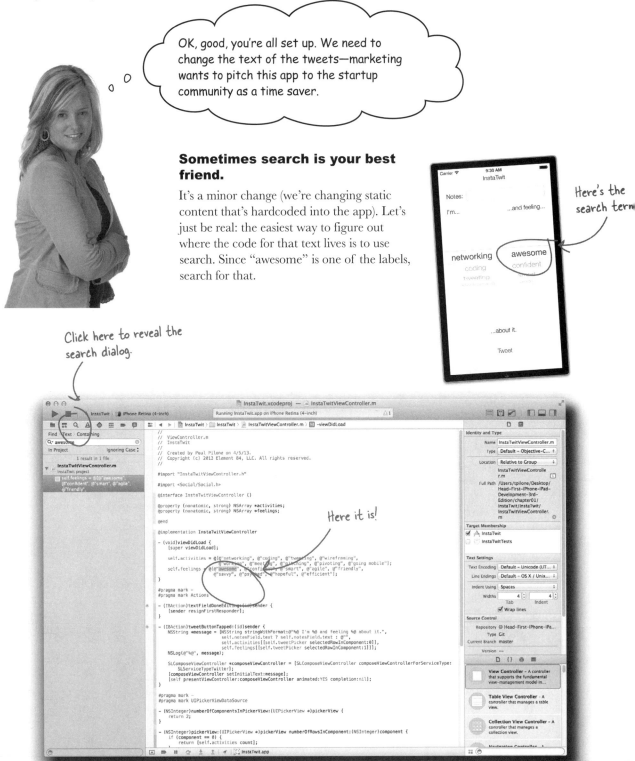

Your code is stored in source files

The actual code for the application is broken up into classes and each class is made up of two files, a header (*.h*) file and an implementation (*.m*) file. The header file (*.h*) is the public API to the class, whereas the implementation file (*.m*) has all the meat. Our problem has to do with the data our app is showing, not some issue with a class's API.

This is one of the methods in your implementation, the viewDidLoad method.

This method is called by the frameworks right after the view is loaded. It's used to set up the view before it's shown. Here we set up two arrays with the values we see in the spinner.

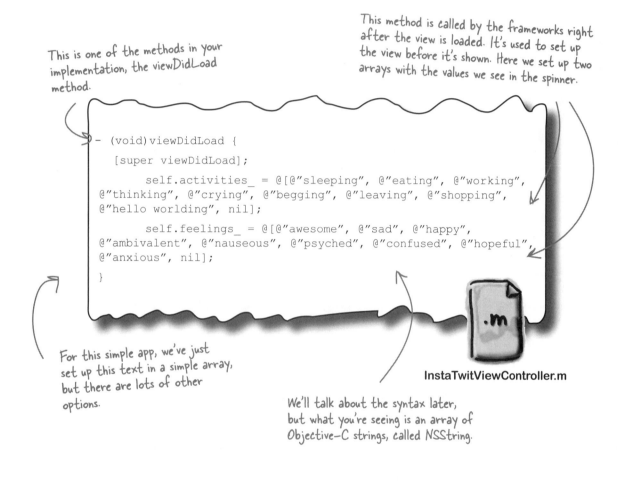

```
- (void)viewDidLoad {

    [super viewDidLoad];

        self.activities_ = @[@"sleeping", @"eating", @"working",
    @"thinking", @"crying", @"begging", @"leaving", @"shopping",
    @"hello worlding", nil];

        self.feelings_ = @[@"awesome", @"sad", @"happy",
    @"ambivalent", @"nauseous", @"psyched", @"confused", @"hopeful",
    @"anxious", nil];

    }
```

For this simple app, we've just set up this text in a simple array, but there are lots of other options.

InstaTwitViewController.m

We'll talk about the syntax later, but what you're seeing is an array of Objective-C strings, called NSString.

BRAIN BARBELL

InstaTwitViewController.h is the header file for this class; it declares the public interface, meaning the public properties and actions for this class. Navigate over to the header file and take a look if you're curious.

Do this!

Throughout the book, we'll cross out code that we need you to delete.

Make the following edits to the existing code base.

Sticky from Sue with your new terminology

Text to change:

Get rid of sleeping and all those other things...

Activities – networking, coding, tweeting, wireframing, working, meeting, pitching, pivoting, going mobile

Feelings – awesome, confident, smart, agile, friendly, savvy, psyched, hopeful, efficient

```
- (void)viewDidLoad {
  [super viewDidLoad];
    self.activities_ = @[@"sleeping", @"eating", @"working", @"thinking",
@"crying", @"begging", @"leaving", @"shopping", @"hello worlding",
@"networking", @"coding", @"tweeting", @"wireframing", @"working",
@"meeting", @"pitching", @"pivoting", @"going mobile", nil];
    self.feelings_ = @[@"awesome", @"sad", @"happy", @"ambivalent",
@"nauseous", @"psyched", @"confused", @"hopeful", @"anxious", @"awesome",
@"confident", @"smart", @"agile", @"friendly", @"savvy", @"psyched",
@"hopeful", @"efficient", nil];

}
```

Bold code is new code to add.

InstaTwitViewController.m

there are no Dumb Questions

Q: Do I always have to build and run the app to test things?

A: Yes—some languages like Ruby and Javascript do away with the compilation step, but Objective-C is a compiled language. In order to test changes, you need to build the app, install it on the simulator (or a real device), and run it there. Xcode does have good support for unit and functional tests and you can use a tool called Instruments to do full application interaction tests. Using automated tests speeds up the testing cycle and avoids having to build and run the full app and run it, but that's no substitute for full application testing.

Q: How important is it to run on a real device? Can I just do everything on the simulator?

A: You can do a lot in the simulator. Depending on what you're doing, you can probably do most of your testing there. But there are differences between running in the simulator and running on a real device. Ultimately you'll need to test things on a real device, and depending on what features you use, you might need to do it sooner rather than later. We'll talk about device-specific capabilities in later chapters. Regardless of what features you trust, you **really really** have to test performance on real devices—never test simulator performance when testing your application.

Sharpen your pencil

What does this do? Now that you know what `viewDidLoad` does, look at some other methods from the *.m* file and write what you think those methods do.

```
- (IBAction) textFieldDoneEditing: (id)
sender {
      [sender resignFirstResponder];
}
```

....

....

....

....

```
- (NSInteger)pickerView:(UIPickerView *)pickerView
numberOfRowsInComponent:(NSInteger)component {
      if (component == 0) {
            return [activities_ count];
      }
      else {
            return [feelings_ count];
      }
}
```

....

....

....

....

```
- (IBAction) tweetButtonTapped: (id) sender {
      NSLog(@"%@", @"Tweet button tapped!");
NSstring...
```

This isn't the whole method. To see the rest, jump back into Xcode.

....

....

....

Relax

It's OK if the Objective-C still looks a little weird...

We're throwing a bunch of Objective-C at you here. Hopefully you can guess what's going on, but we're going to talk a lot more about Objective-C throughout this book. Nothing to fear yet..

Sharpen your pencil
Solution

Here are some of the other methods that were in the *InstaTwitViewController.m* file.

```
- (IBAction) textFieldDoneEditing: (id)
sender {
        [sender resignFirstResponder];

}
```

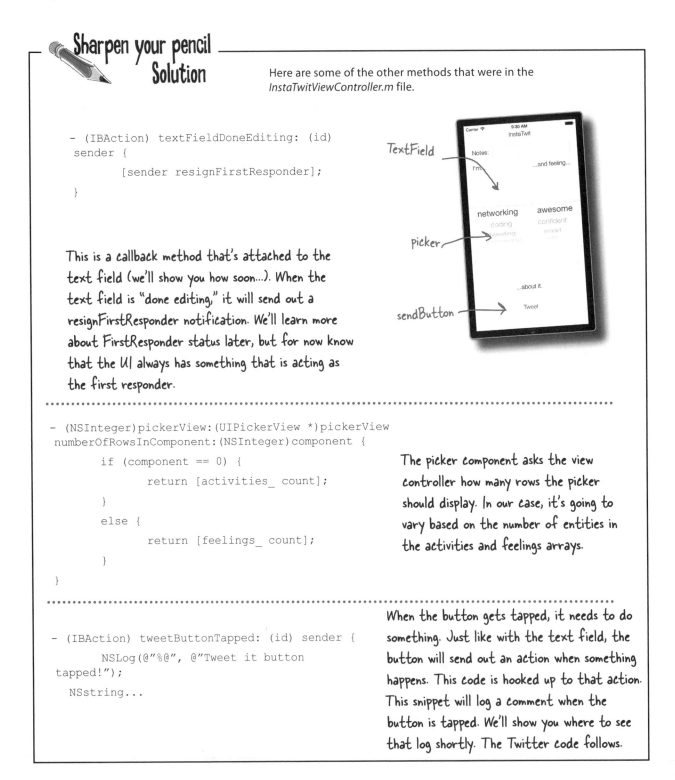

TextField

picker

sendButton

This is a callback method that's attached to the text field (we'll show you how soon....). When the text field is "done editing," it will send out a resignFirstResponder notification. We'll learn more about FirstResponder status later, but for now know that the UI always has something that is acting as the first responder.

```
- (NSInteger)pickerView:(UIPickerView *)pickerView
numberOfRowsInComponent:(NSInteger)component {
        if (component == 0) {
                return [activities_ count];
        }
        else {
                return [feelings_ count];
        }
}
```

The picker component asks the view controller how many rows the picker should display. In our case, it's going to vary based on the number of entities in the activities and feelings arrays.

```
- (IBAction) tweetButtonTapped: (id) sender {
     NSLog(@"%@", @"Tweet it button
tapped!");
   NSstring...
```

When the button gets tapped, it needs to do something. Just like with the text field, the button will send out an action when something happens. This code is hooked up to that action. This snippet will log a comment when the button is tapped. We'll show you where to see that log shortly. The Twitter code follows.

TEST DRIVE

Now that you've found the code to update for this app, make the changes and rebuild the app.

 Go into Xcode and make the text changes.
Flip back a couple of pages to the *InstaTwitViewController.m* file and make the edits on that page.

 Save and rebuild the app.
After changing the text, go back and build and run the app.

3 **Configure your Twitter account in the simulator**
If you want these tweets to show up live in the Twitter-verse, press the home button on the simulator, go into settings, and add your account details. Then go back into the app and send a tweet!

Xcode can provide lots of help with debugging if your app didn't quite build right....

Code Editor, Hub...and debugging, too

Unless you are the most perfect typist and you've not been paying attention when
your code is incomplete, you've probably noticed the warnings and errors coming
in and out of the editor. Xcode tries to keep up while you write code and provides
you inline warnings and errors before you build anything.

Warnings —

Errors

Click here to switch the
navigator to the thread view.

Warnings and build errors
will show up here...

...and here

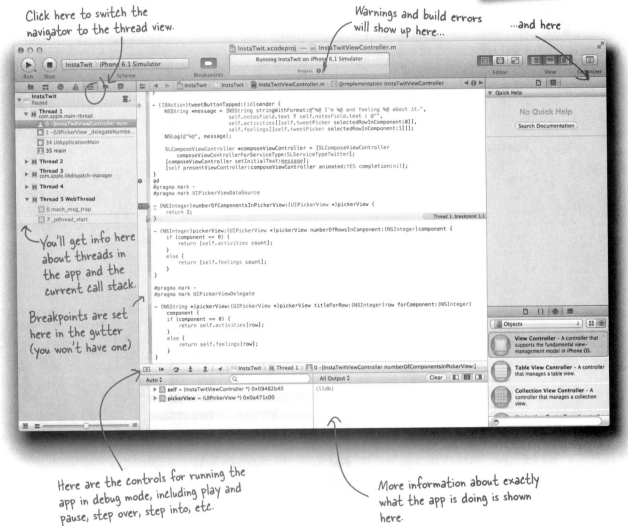

You'll get info here
about threads in
the app and the
current call stack.

Breakpoints are set
here in the gutter
(you won't have one)

Here are the controls for running the
app in debug mode, including play and
pause, step over, step into, etc.

More information about exactly
what the app is doing is shown
here.

Once you get your code running, Xcode also has a full debugger to help you
figure out what's going on. You can set breakpoints by clicking in the gutters,
set watches on variables, and, once things hit one of your breakpoints, inspect
variable values and step through code.

Excellent! Almost done. We just need the new icon from marketing and it's ready for review.

Did you notice the old icon?

It was kinda lame, really just a boring bird, (since it's Twitter). To be more startup/tech friendly, marketing has this new retro 8-bit looking @.

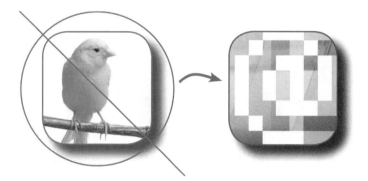

Changing the app icon is easy with Xcode

Xcode treats graphics as application resources. Every app has some resources associated with it (even this one), varying from icons all the way up to high-res images and embedded video.

Xcode helps you organize all your images (you can view most image types), and then packages and preprocesses the images for use within the application.

One iPhone, two iPhones, red iPhone, blue iPhone...

In Xcode, click on the main project name and bring up the summary page. This page is a high-level overview of your app including deployment info, some images, and version numbers. It also allows you access to the Asset Catalog for the app.

OK, not yet, but we heard from a guy who has a friend who knows this woman who says that Apple is working on glow-in-the-dark ones...

Select the project here.

Use this arrow here to get into the Asset Catalog file and see the icons.

Asset catalogs are specialized files that help you keep all the images straight for your app. This page lets you use a nice graphic interface to organize the icons. You'll see similar interfaces for the launch images and other graphics.

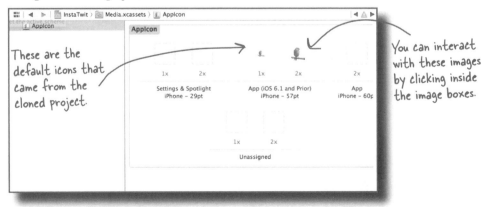

These are the default icons that came from the cloned project.

You can interact with these images by clicking inside the image boxes.

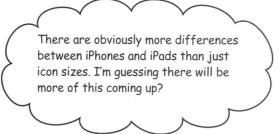

Absolutely! We'll be dealing with device capabilities as we go.

Different devices and different generations of the same device have different capabilities. iOS generally does a good job of hiding these things from you. For example, when you lay out your user interface, iOS will automatically draw it at the higher resolution on a Retina display. There are some parts you need to know about, though, such as different icon sizes, whether or not the device has a camera, etc. We'll point them out as we go.

TEST DRIVE

 Find the icons from cloned project.
The code you cloned from GitHub has alternate icons in it. Use Finder and navigate to where you cloned the code.

 Drag onto dialogs in the Asset catalog.
Take the new images and drag them in from Finder. The files are *square-new-icon-60.png* and *square-new-icon-120.png*.

Delete the app from the simulator.
To make sure that the old icon doesn't persist, go into the simulator, hit the home button, and then click and hold on InstaTwit. Once the icon starts vibrating and a little x appears, click the x to delete the app.

 Build and run from Xcode.
Click play again. The app will rebuild and reinstall in the simulator with the new icon. If you press the home key, you'll see it!

TEST DRIVE

You should see that fancy new icon on the springboard!

BULLET POINTS

- Xcode is the hub of your iOS development.

- Xcode is a powerful IDE with documentation support, debugging, and user interface editors.

- The simulator is good for testing, but it has its limitations; you'll need to test on a real device.

- To get an app on a device, you'll need to be a paid Apple Developer.

- Git support is built into Xcode.

- You'll need to care about different device capabilities as you build your app.

Wouldn't it be dreamy if I could get this on an iPhone instead of the simulator? But I know it's just a fantasy...

You can. Just pay $99 to Apple.

Seriously. To get an app on a device, there are some
security things that need to be taken care of, certificates
and profiles that need to be set up. To get access to those
signing mechanisms, you have to be a registered and paid
Apple iOS developer. To find out more information about
the program, head over to *http://www.apple.com/iosdeveloper*.

For the purposes of this book, we're going to stay in the
simulator, so you won't need to buy the program to keep
up here.

You are here.

Your app on
your device
(only)

Want more? Check out the Developer Site!

Just saw the app changes—they look great. Ship it!

Great job!

You got your feet wet with Xcode and started navigating around the Apple Developer universe. Using the standard controls and Xcode, you can get some pretty good apps going fairly quickly. There's nothing like seeing people actually using your app...we're just getting warmed up.

iPhone Development Cross

Take some time to exercise the other half of your
brain and check your terminology.

Across

2. The higher resolution screen name
4. Used to sign applications to put them on physical devices
5. Something that the simulator cannot reliably test
7. The language used to write iOS apps
8. The framework used to write iPhone apps
9. The term to describe each screen of an iPhone app
10. This is used on a desktop to test an app
11. These are used in Xcode to provide classes to be accessed.

Down

1. The name for the IDE for iPhone Apps
2. The folder used to organize the images for the app
3. This is the name of the editor used for Objective-C
6. The iPhone is a _____ device.

Your iPhone Development toolbox

You've got Chapter 1 under your belt and now you've added some basics to your toolbox.

iOS applications

- Must follow Apple's guidelines and constraints
- Go through a review process before being allowed in the App Store
- Must be signed before they can be put on physical devices
- Are written in Objective-C

Xcode

- Full featured IDE for iOS and Mac development
- Manages your code, frameworks you link to, and resources for your application
- Built in UI design tool to layout your views and link things together

Simulator

- Great for quick testing
- Has limited support for accelerometer, memory, performance, GPS, and camera testing

BULLET POINTS

- Xcode is the hub of your iOS development.

- Xcode is a powerful IDE with documentation support, debugging and user interface editors.

- The simulator is good for testing, but it has its limitations; you'll need to test on a real device

- To get an app on a device, you'll need to be a paid Apple Developer.

- Git support is built into Xcode.

- You'll need to care about different device capabilities as you build your app.

iPhone Development Cross Solution

Take some time to exercise the other half of your brain and check your terminology.

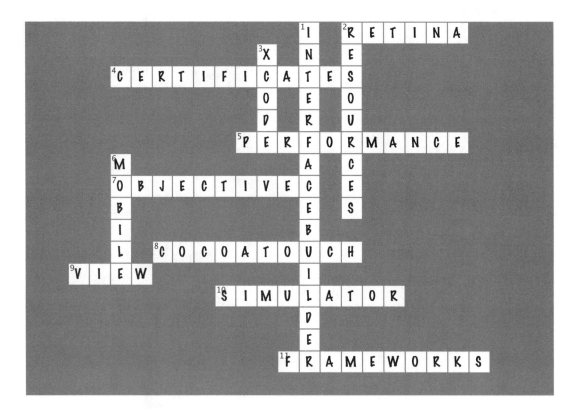

Across

2. The higher resolution screen name [RETINA]
4. Used to sign applications to put them on physical devices [CERTIFICATES]
5. Something that the simulator cannot reliably test [PERFORMANCE]
7. The language used to write iOS apps [OBJECTIVEC]
8. The framework used to write iPhone apps [COCOATOUCH]
9. The term to describe each screen of an iPhone app [VIEW]
10. This is used on a desktop to test an app [SIMULATOR]
11. These are used in Xcode to provide classes to be accessed. [FRAMEWORKS]

Down

1. The name for the IDE for iPhone Apps [INTERFACEBUILDER]
2. The folder used to organize the images for the app [RESOURCES]
3. This is the name of the editor used for Objective-C [XCODE]
6. The iPhone is a _____ device. [MOBILE]

2 basic iOS patterns

Building from scratch

It didn't take me long to whip this together. Couple of days prep time is all...

Now that you've gotten your feet wet, it's time to start fresh.

You should have a good idea of the tools you'll be working with and how to get around Xcode a bit. Now it's time to dig a little deeper and start your own project. How do you set up an iOS project, how do the pieces of the app really work together, and what are the interaction patterns you can count on? Turn the page, 'cause you're ready to find out...

iOS apps run full screen, but there's a lot going on

One of the big things that separates working on an iOS device (i.e., an iPhone or iPad) from desktop or laptop computers is always working in full screen. In fact, when iPhone first came out, there wasn't any multitasking on the device at all. That has changed, although it's not multitasking in the sense that desktops do it. The user interacts with one app at a time through a particular view the app is showing on the screen.

Behind the scenes a view is splitting up responsibilities for responding to the user over a couple different pieces, as illustrated below.

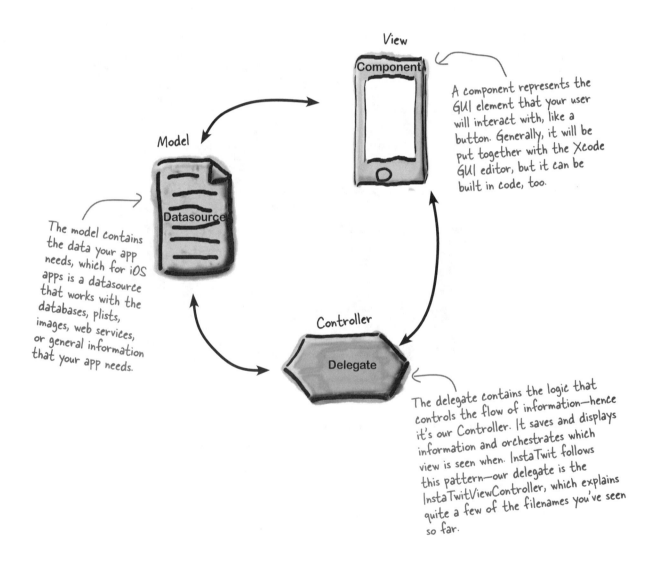

View

Component

A component represents the GUI element that your user will interact with, like a button. Generally, it will be put together with the Xcode GUI editor, but it can be built in code, too.

Model

Datasource

The model contains the data your app needs, which for iOS apps is a datasource that works with the databases, plists, images, web services, or general information that your app needs.

Controller

Delegate

The delegate contains the logic that controls the flow of information—hence it's our Controller. It saves and displays information and orchestrates which view is seen when. InstaTwit follows this pattern—our delegate is the InstaTwitViewController, which explains quite a few of the filenames you've seen so far.

Model-View-Controller is a design pattern

Model-view-controller (MVC) is a pattern that is discussed at length in *Head First Design Patterns*. You see it used a lot with GUI applications, and it's all over the CocoaTouch framework. In MVC, we separate responsibilities into showing information to the user (the view), management of the underlying data (the model), and responding to interactions with the user (the controller).

Breaking things up using the model-view-controller pattern helps keep the complexity down in your application and lets you reuse large parts of code regardless of the device you're using (e.g., an iPhone versus an iPad).

MVC is a standard design pattern and makes an appearance in a lot more than just iOS development. Ruby on Rails, for example, is loaded with it.

WHO DOES WHAT?

Match each MVC item to what it does in an iOS application.

Thing	What the thing does
Model	The user interacts with this. It contains the buttons, images or other media, text, etc. that are being consumed by the user at any given time.
View	This is responsible for the data. It can be stored locally or in the cloud, use plists, databases, web services, etc.
Controller	This is responsible for coordinating responses to user interaction or things happening inside the application. Think of this as the traffic cop directing the flow of the application.

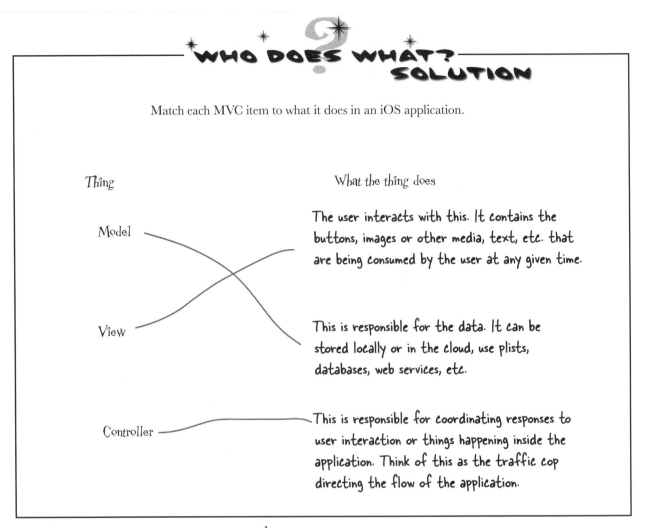

WHO DOES WHAT? SOLUTION

Match each MVC item to what it does in an iOS application.

Thing

What the thing does

Model

View

Controller

The user interacts with this. It contains the buttons, images or other media, text, etc. that are being consumed by the user at any given time.

This is responsible for the data. It can be stored locally or in the cloud, use plists, databases, web services, etc.

This is responsible for coordinating responses to user interaction or things happening inside the application. Think of this as the traffic cop directing the flow of the application.

there are no Dumb Questions

Q: Does every iOS app have a model, view, and controller?

A: Yes and no. You'll almost certainly have at least one view and corresponding view controller. Depending on your application, you might not have model backing things, but that will make for a pretty simple application.

Q: I don't see anything called a model in the InstaTwit code. Does it not have one?

A: One of the challenges with iOS code and a lot of the sample code is that it squashes model responsibilities with the controller.

You end up with a gigantic ViewController that's doing a little bit of everything. This becomes a maintenance nightmare. Can you see where InstaTwit has this problem?

Q: No...

A: InstaTwit has the array of feelings and activities stored in the view controller. We did this on purpose to keep the code short in the first project, but if InstaTwit was a bigger project it would become a problem. Our later projects will be better about splitting that out. You've been warned.

> Listen, I need some help here. I've got to get my restaurant on this social media thing, but I don't even have a computer at work, just my iPhone. Help!

Marco, chef and restaurant owner. Not a tech guy.

Marco needs a mobile social media app.

Fortunately, iOS makes Twitter and Facebook easy. It's no secret that everyone assumes most restaurants will have some social media presence and a website. It's also no secret that chefs are crazy busy and don't have time to mess around. Here's what Marco wants to be able to do with his app.

Things I want:

1. Easy tweets

2. Easy updates to my Facebook page, too

3. All my tweets to say #marcos

Sharpen your pencil

You have a rough idea of what the app needs to do. We're only going to use one view; it needs to have a status update and it can post to Twitter, Facebook, or both. Sketch up what you think it should look like.

This is a major part of iOS development. You should spend a ton of time doing sketches and designs for apps you're going to write. The code should always come second.

Get started with Xcode and Git

We're on the road to professional iOS development here, so we're going to set up a new project with Git enabled. As soon as we have the empty project ready to go, we can agree on a final design.

 Create a new Xcode project.
When you launch Xcode, on the welcome screen "Create a new Xcode project" is an option, front and center. If you already have Xcode started, select File→New→Project...

 **Select a Single View Application.**
Then click Next.

Select the options for the new project.
Set the product name as "MarcoPollo" and leave the Class Prefix as the default. Select iPhone as the device and click Next.

Select where you want to save the app. Make sure the Source Control box is checked!

The checkbox for "Create git repository on My Mac" is on this dialog. Make sure it's checked before you click Create.

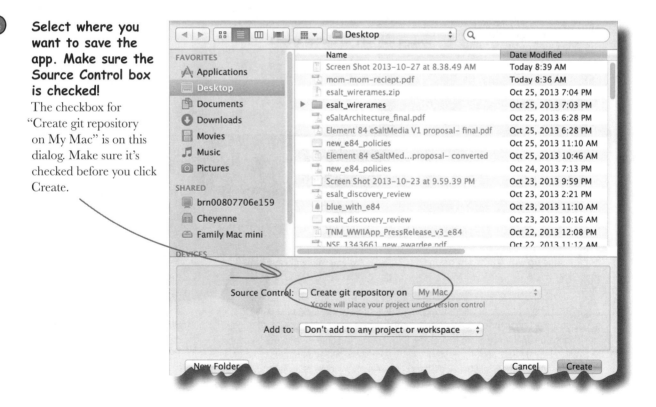

Sharpen your pencil Solution

Here's what we came up with for the final design for Marco's app. It needs to have space for status updates and a way to publish those updates.

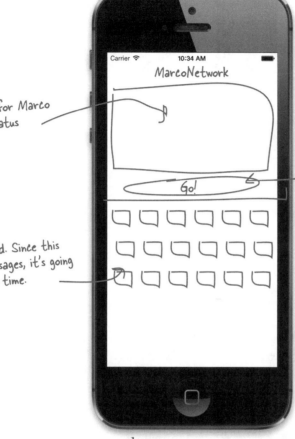

This is the area for Marco to type up his status messages.

This button makes his messages go live to Facebook and Twitter.

Here is the keyboard. Since this app is all about messages, it's going to be visible all the time.

MarcoNetwork

Go!

---

there are no Dumb Questions

Q: I came up with a different design. Is that OK?

A: Sure! There are lots of different ways to design these things. If you go looking at similar apps up on the App Store (Hootsuite, Seezmic, even the Facebook App), you'll see similar designs. Now that the App Store has matured, it's always a good idea to look at apps that are accomplishing similar tasks to yours to get a sense of good designs.

Q: Do you really always start with design?

A: User interaction on a small, mobile device is critical. It's really hard to get it right the first time. As you get feedback from users and add features, your designs will evolve. Figure out what's absolutely necessary, get rid of everything else, and build from there.

Q: Should we limit the length of text in the text box?

A: Yes! Twitter only allows 140 characters. We'll add a check in for that later. It's definitely worth noting in the design comps though.

Design time!

Now it's time to get in Xcode and start building this view. Xcode has a really nice editor for GUI work: to edit the view, all you have to do is click the *Main. storyboard* file.

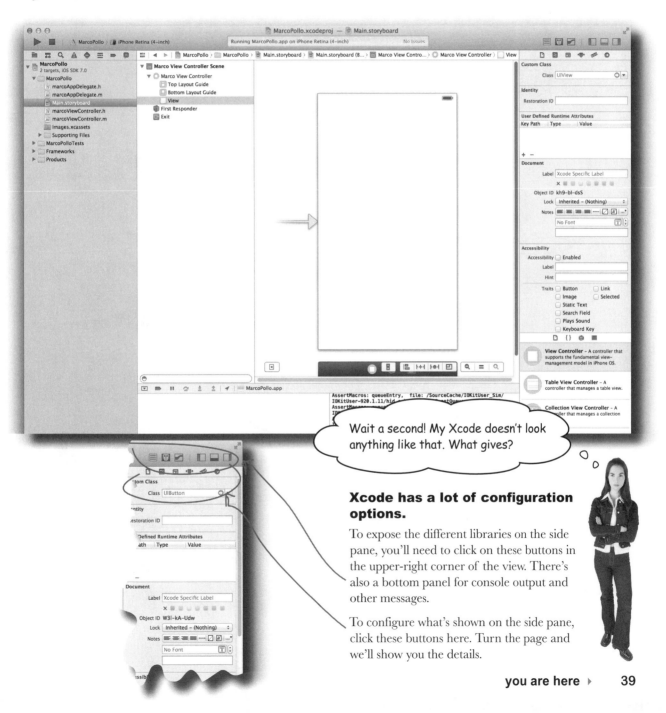

Wait a second! My Xcode doesn't look anything like that. What gives?

Xcode has a lot of configuration options.

To expose the different libraries on the side pane, you'll need to click on these buttons in the upper-right corner of the view. There's also a bottom panel for console output and other messages.

To configure what's shown on the side pane, click these buttons here. Turn the page and we'll show you the details.

Dŏ thîs!   To edit the views in Xcode, you'll need to open up the *.storyboard* file and change some settings in the workspace.

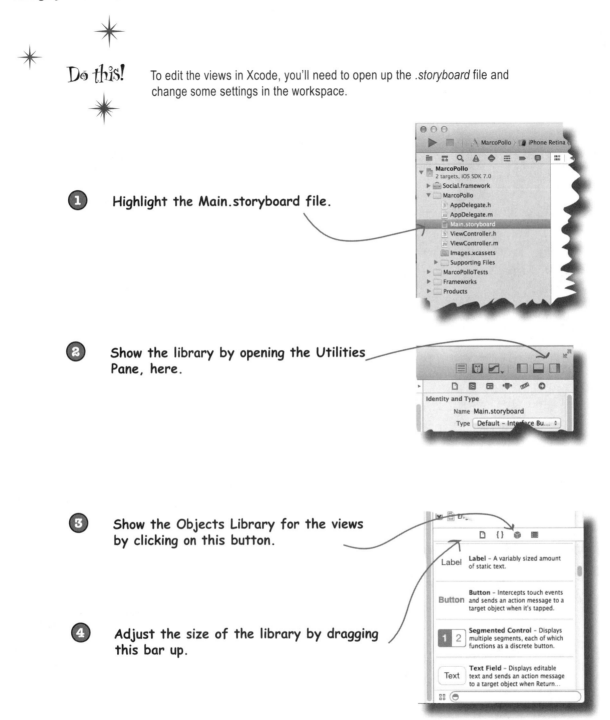

①   Highlight the Main.storyboard file.

②   Show the library by opening the Utilities Pane, here.

③   Show the Objects Library for the views by clicking on this button.

④   Adjust the size of the library by dragging this bar up.

Design time...redux

Storyboards were new with iOS 5 and provide an easier way for editing iOS UI. There is a drag-and-drop interface for the components themselves, which is a great way to speed up layout, but as your apps grow to more than one view, the transitions and flow between the views are also represented here. Since we already have a good idea of how the view will look, it's a matter of dragging and dropping the pieces into place.

When you drag the elements into the view, they will not be sized this way. Grab the little boxes at the corners of the component when they're highlighted and size them to fit.

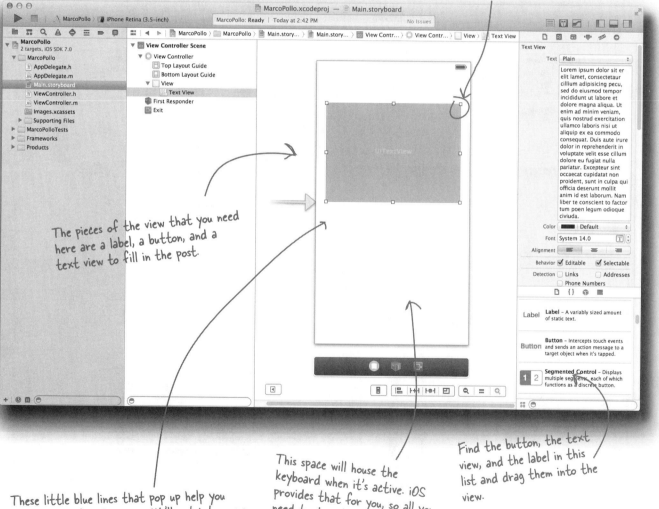

The pieces of the view that you need here are a label, a button, and a text view to fill in the post.

These little blue lines that pop up help you with alignment and spacing. We'll get into more detail later about some of that; when you start worrying about supporting iPhone 5 and iPhone 4, you'll use relative spacing.

This space will house the keyboard when it's active. iOS provides that for you, so all you need to do is leave room.

Find the button, the text view, and the label in this list and drag them into the view.

Let's get started!

STORYBOARD CONSTRUCTION

We'll go through each view component to add and configure them. We'll start with the UILabel at the top of the view.

Grab a label and drag it into the upper-left corner of the view. When you do that, you'll see some constraints pop up under the view controller. These guidelines are based on Apple's Human Interface Guidelines (HIG) spacing recommendations and, in general, you should respect them and leave the recommended space.

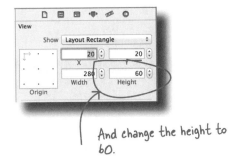

Both constraints should show up with the "standard" box checked in the inspector.

Next, change the text of the label and fix the height. All of this work can be done in the Attributes Inspector on the righthand side of the editor.

In the inspector, change the title of the label to MarcoNetwork.

Select the Size pane of the Attributes Inspector...

And change the height to 60.

STORYBOARD CONSTRUCTION (CONT.)

We need to do similar configurations for the other two elements of the view, the
UITextView and the UIButton.

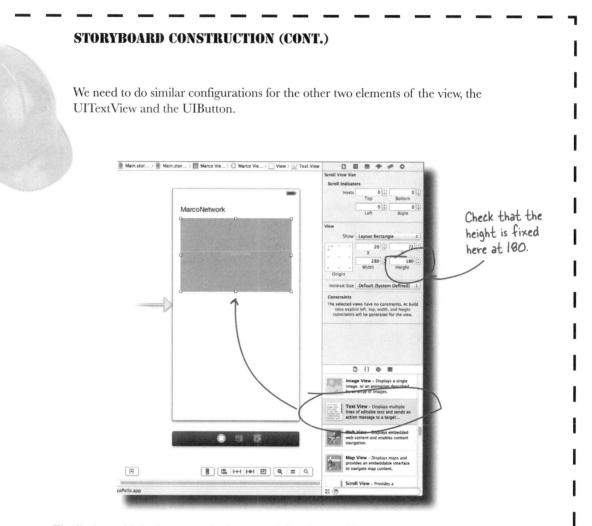

Check that the
height is fixed
here at 180.

Finally, just add the button to the bottom of the view, making sure that the default
spacing from the edges stays in place.

TEST DRIVE

 Here's your storyboard in Xcode.
Right now you should have three elements: the label at the top of the screen, the text field for the post, and the button to complete the action.

We used Interface Builder to tweak some of the layout and fix some control heights to get things where we want them.

 Click run. Here's what's in your simulator!
It should look just like what you have in your *.storyboard* file.

> What's all that text—is that Latin? Italian, maybe, but Latin? I'm gonna need that fixed. The button isn't going to actually say "button," is it? And I was hoping that the title could be a little nicer...

The stock controls are...stock controls.

Out of the box, the stock controls aren't very exciting. There are lots of knobs we can twist, though, to spruce up our application. Most controls support custom images as well, so you can theme your application with color, button styles, etc. Be deliberate when you style controls—usability is critical, and while you might think a blinking neon green button is the shizzle, your users might not.

BRAIN BARBELL

Write up a list of your to-dos to handle Marco's requirements. Check them at the bottom of the page.

....

....

....

1. Adjust the font for the title. 2. Remove the Latin and replace with default text that says "<your message here>." 3. Change the text of the button to say "Post it!"

Cosmetic changes are easy in Xcode

We've used the inspector a little bit so far, but let's get into some more details. First, we'll fix the default text and the labels.

Using the attributes inspector, you can change the font for MarcoNetwork to Zapifino 17.0.

Center the text too, it'll look better.

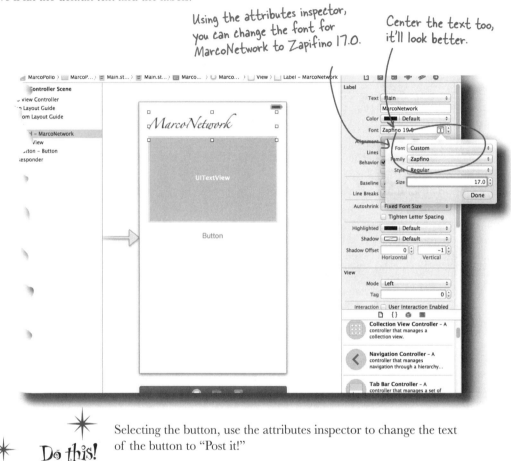

Do this!

Selecting the button, use the attributes inspector to change the text of the button to "Post it!"

Then select the text view, in the attributes inspector, delete the giant block of Latin text and replace it with "<your message here>."

You could code this if you're into that kind of thing...

When you make changes like font size or default text in Interface Builder, Xcode is storying that information in the storyboard so that it's set when the storyboard is loaded by your application. Everything it's doing, and even more, can be done in code in your application instead. Whether you make UI changes in code or through Interface Builder is somewhat a matter of personal preference and obviously depends on whether Interface Builder exposes what you want to change.

iOS controls are more than skin deep

We changed the button to say what we want, but it still doesn't do
anything when the user taps it. We need to wire that button up to some
code to get it to do anything meaningful.

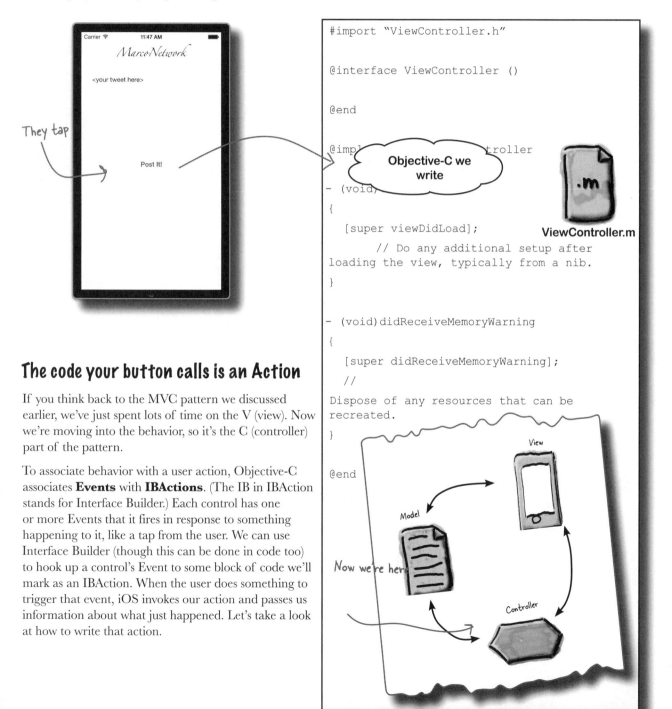

They tap

Post It!

Objective-C we
write

ViewController.m

```
#import "ViewController.h"

@interface ViewController ()

@end

@impl                    troller

- (void)
{
    [super viewDidLoad];
        // Do any additional setup after
loading the view, typically from a nib.
}


- (void)didReceiveMemoryWarning
{
    [super didReceiveMemoryWarning];
    //
Dispose of any resources that can be
recreated.
}

@end
```

The code your button calls is an Action

If you think back to the MVC pattern we discussed
earlier, we've just spent lots of time on the V (view). Now
we're moving into the behavior, so it's the C (controller)
part of the pattern.

To associate behavior with a user action, Objective-C
associates **Events** with **IBActions**. (The IB in IBAction
stands for Interface Builder.) Each control has one
or more Events that it fires in response to something
happening to it, like a tap from the user. We can use
Interface Builder (though this can be done in code too)
to hook up a control's Event to some block of code we'll
mark as an IBAction. When the user does something to
trigger that event, iOS invokes our action and passes us
information about what just happened. Let's take a look
at how to write that action.

View

Model

Now we're here

Controller

Geek Bits

Xcode has a mode called the assistant editor that can show you both parts of a class at once (.*h* and .*m*), or a view with its associated view controller. You can also use it to graphically link Events and IBActions. To turn on that editor, you'll need to close the righthand pane of the editor and turn on the assistant editor.

Open up the assistant editor in here.

Close the righthand pane here.

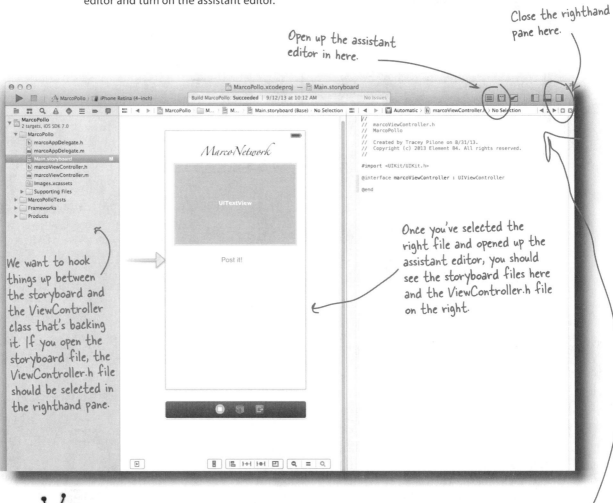

We want to hook things up between the storyboard and the ViewController class that's backing it. If you open the storyboard file, the ViewController.h file should be selected in the righthand pane.

Once you've selected the right file and opened up the assistant editor, you should see the storyboard files here and the ViewController.h file on the right.

The Assistant Editor doesn't always grab what you need.

If you see the .m file on the righthand pane, then click the arrows in the upper-right corner, here, to make sure ViewController.h *is visible.*

Watch it!

You'll create the action using the Xcode GUI editor

The Xcode GUI editor lets you graphically set up the action for any component that needs it (in this case, the "Post it!" button).

 Select the "Post it!" button in the storyboard.

 Ctrl-click (or use the right mouse button) and drag over to the *ViewController.h file* on the righthand pane, landing between the **@interface** and the **@end** in that file.

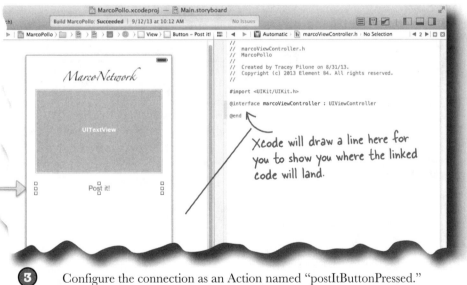

Xcode will draw a line here for you to show you where the linked code will land.

Configure the connection as an Action named "postItButtonPressed." To commit the connection, click Connect.

4 Xcode will add a declaration of the action in the header file and an empty implementation in the *.m*. Just to make sure it works, let's update the implementation in the *.m* to log message to the action. Here's the code:

```
- (void)didReceiveMemoryWarning
{
    [super didReceiveMemoryWarning];
    // Dispose of any resources that can be recreated.
}
- (IBAction)postItButtonPressed:(id)sender {
    NSLog(@"Post It button was pressed!");
}
@end
```

Look for the IBAction that was generated in the .m file with the IBAction.

Put the logging code between the braces.

ViewController.m

TEST DRIVE

Wait a sec...I have no idea what just happened there. I know we created an action...what was the rest of it?

Post it!

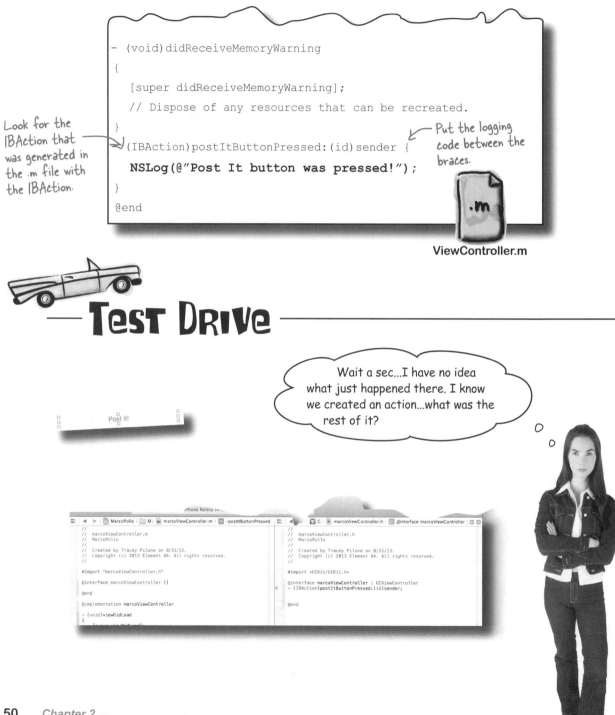

```
//
// marcoViewController.m
// MarcoPollo
//
// Created by Tracey Pilone on 8/31/13.
// Copyright (c) 2013 Element 84. All rights reserved.
//

#import "marcoViewController.h"

@interface marcoViewController ()

@end

@implementation marcoViewController

- (void)viewDidLoad
{
```

```
//
// marcoViewController.h
// MarcoPollo
//
// Created by Tracey Pilone on 8/31/13.
// Copyright (c) 2013 Element 84. All rights reserved.
//

#import <UIKit/UIKit.h>

@interface marcoViewController : UIViewController
- (IBAction)postItButtonPressed:(id)sender;

@end
```

Connect your controls to your actions

This is your control

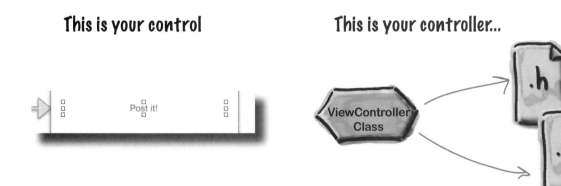

The control represents the view. It has visual information, font, text color, pressed and unpressed images, background colors, etc. It's responsible for rendering some information to the user and collecting input back. Controls are used in all sorts of different places so rather than put application specific code in them, they simply fire off events saying "Hey! This just happened to me..."

This is your controller...

Application logic lives in the code you write in your application. But, by design, it's a step removed from what the user sees. You don't need to write code to draw a button for every app you write. You focus on behavior—what your application should do if the user wants to send out a message for Marco, for example.

Your control has events...

When we configured the connection in the dialog box in Xcode, there was a default event selected. If you go back in and click the drop-down box for that dialog, you can see all the different events a button can raise.

You can only see all the options with a new event, not one that is already set up.

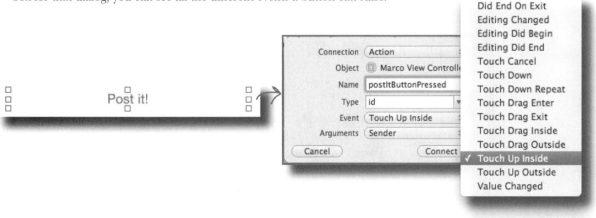

...and those events can connect to Actions

Different controls can raise different events, but, in general, events are raised to let the system know the user has done something. For example, we linked "Touch Up Inside" to our action so that we know when the user lifts their finger off the screen inside the button. You generally won't use all of the events available on a control; 99% of the time you only need Touch Up Inside on a button, for example.

When you link an event to an action, iOS will pass along which control sent the event, which means you can use the same action for multiple events on different controls if you want to, as long as you check the sender. This can make your code a little more complicated than just using separate actions, though, so you usually just create an action for each event you want to respond to.

Linking Events to Actions is what ties user actions in your user interface to code in your application.

Did End On Exit
Editing Changed
Editing Did Begin
Editing Did End
Touch Cancel
Touch Down
Touch Down Repeat
Touch Drag Enter
Touch Drag Exit
Touch Drag Inside
Touch Drag Outside
✓ Touch Up Inside
Touch Up Outside
Value Changed

Different controls have different events, but they're all documented in Apple's UIKit documentation.

ViewController Class

.h

.m

It's coming along! You've got a control, an event, and an action. But there's a lot more still to do....

① Get the text that Marco types.

② Add the marketing stuff to the text.

③ Tweet out Marco's message.

④ Eat at Marco's for free!

Don't worry if you don't know what all of these mean! You'll know in a few pages, but try this out!

WHO DOES WHAT?

Match each thing from iOS development to what it does.

Thing

What the thing does

Control

View element that can react to user interactions and raise events for anyone who cares to listen.

iBAction

An object that acts as the backing logic for an iOS view. This object typically has references to elements on in the view, code to respond to user interactions, and logic to transition to other views.

iBOutlet

An event that can be raised by a button to indicate that the user has lifted their finger inside the button—in other words, the button was tapped.

View Controller

An indicator on a class property that tells Interface Builder it should point to a UI control.

Touch Up Inside

Code (Objective-C) that is invoked in response to an associated Event being raised.

Q: I've heard of nib files. What are they?

A: Before storyboard files, there were nibs, which are really *.xib* files. Those files now make up the *.storyboard* files and represent just one view. You can still work in specific nibs if you want, but for the purposes of this book we're going to use the recommended Apple practice.

Q: What kind of files are *.storyboard* files?

A: They are actually XML files. They contain information about how to draw the views and how to transition between them.

As iOS development matured, it became clear that most apps support multiple views and that working between them was becoming a bigger and bigger pain point for developers. Storyboards are a great way to view the application as a whole and see exactly how your views are working together.

Q: This is our second app for iPhone, what about all the other devices?

A: We'll get there! For purposes of teaching, we're keeping it simple for now. This is also a great opportunity to think about usability concerns. There are apps for which just an iPhone implementation makes sense. Running apps, transit apps, and anything that nobody is going to want to use on their iPad.

Q: What if I want to add iPad later?

A: Good question. There are a couple of things that you can do. First off, you can choose the Universal app option, rather than iPhone only. We've also been taking care of something else in the views. Our view design hasn't been fixed, we've been focusing on the spacing in the view.

iOS development now has much more in common with web or even - gulp- Android development. With the iPad mini and the various Retina displays, there are a number of sizes to support and it's only going to expand going forward. One way to insulate your application long term is to have the views based on spacing, not fixed locations.

Q: I really prefer the command line to GUI editors. What can I do?

A: That works too. That being said, we really recommend you get over that. Apple has spent a lot of time and effort to improve the GUI editor and make it as useful as possible. Try to stick with it for a little while!

Q: You started talking about Actions. But we haven't even talked about any syntax really...

A: We're getting there soon, we promise! Keep moving into the next page...

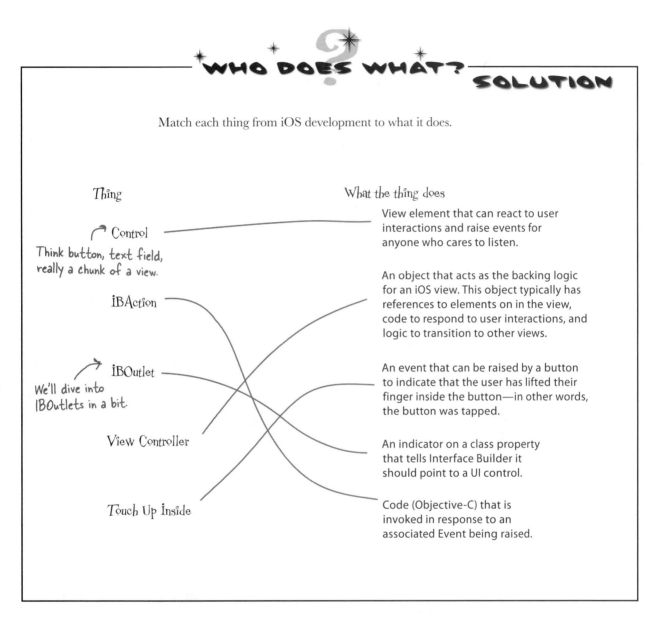

WHO DOES WHAT? SOLUTION

Match each thing from iOS development to what it does.

Thing

What the thing does

Control
Think button, text field, really a chunk of a view.

View element that can react to user interactions and raise events for anyone who cares to listen.

IBAction

An object that acts as the backing logic for an iOS view. This object typically has references to elements on in the view, code to respond to user interactions, and logic to transition to other views.

IBOutlet
We'll dive into IBOutlets in a bit.

An event that can be raised by a button to indicate that the user has lifted their finger inside the button—in other words, the button was tapped.

View Controller

An indicator on a class property that tells Interface Builder it should point to a UI control.

Touch Up Inside

Code (Objective-C) that is invoked in response to an associated Event being raised.

So about these classes and interfaces we keep writing...

We keep talking about View Controllers and User Interfaces, but we really haven't spent much time talking about how classes and class interfaces work. We added a method (our IBAction) to our View Controller's interface, but that's about it. Let's spend a couple minutes looking at classes in a little more detail. We're going to spend the rest of the book writing them, so you may as well get comfortable...

Classes... Up Close

Objective-C is loaded with Classes

Everything in an iOS app is defined as a class somewhere in the code you write.

Post it!

Xcode you write

```
#import "ViewController.h"

@interface ViewController ()

@implementation ViewController

- (void)viewDidLoad
{
    [super viewDidLoad];
        // Do any additional
    r loading the view,
       rom a nib.

-          eceiveMemoryWarning

           t
    [super
didReceiveMemoryWarning];
    // Dispose of any resources
that can be recreated.
}

@end
```

.h

foo.h

.m

foo.m

Interface is what your class does.

Your interface declares what your class can do and how it's intended to be used by other objects.

Implementation is how your class does it.

The implementation file is how your class does what your interface claims it can do. Other objects don't care how you implement something, as long as they know you can do it!

Your code is written in <u>classes</u>. A class has an interface and an implementation.

Hey, I've done interfaces before. Like in Java, right? An implementation class implements an interface.

Not really...

In Objective-C the *.h* simply declares the public interface of a class, including any properties, methods, and optionally any private ivars (though these you usually move into the *.m* and keep out of the public interface). A Java interface is often compared to an Objective-C protocol, which we'll talk more about later.

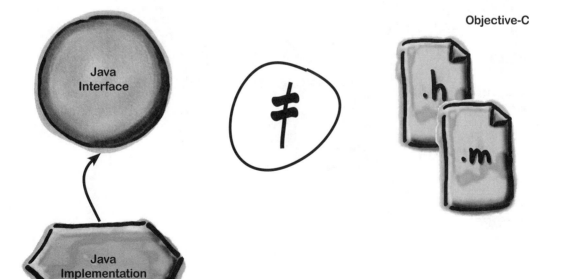

Objective-C

Java Interface ≠ .h .m

Java Implementation

there are no Dumb Questions

Q: Those events are kinda hard to understand?

A: There are actually a ton of events that iOS can respond to for the different controls; the button is actually one of the easier ones. The words used to describe events are carefully chosen. "Touch up inside" is used because the iOS should be responding to the end of the button selection, the "click," not the beginning.

For more information about the events with descriptions, see the Event Handling Guide in the iOS Developer Documentation.

Q: I'm seeing compile errors?

A: Well, that happens. Xcode is pretty good about warning you before you run the app. Some things you should look for in the top of the window: if you see little red exclamation points or yellow triangles, then you know something's up.

You can click on them anywhere you see them to get taken to the offending code, and once you're there, to get an explanation of what Xcode is unhappy about.

Q: How do you hide or show the debugger?

A: If the app stops while running in the simulator, you'll dump right back into Xcode with the debugger view.

To get back to the normal file navigation view, just click here:

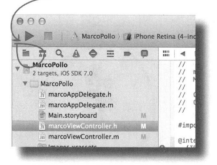

Q: @ in front of strings?

A: Remember that Objective-C is an object-oriented language. The string class commonly used in Objective-C is NSString and since strings are used all over the place, Objective-C provides a shorthand for initializing an NSString object: the '@' symbol.

This is all fascinating... how's my app coming? I need customers to come to my restaurant!

So how do we get to that text?

Now that we have an action that will be called when the button is tapped, we need a way to access the text so that we can tweet it!

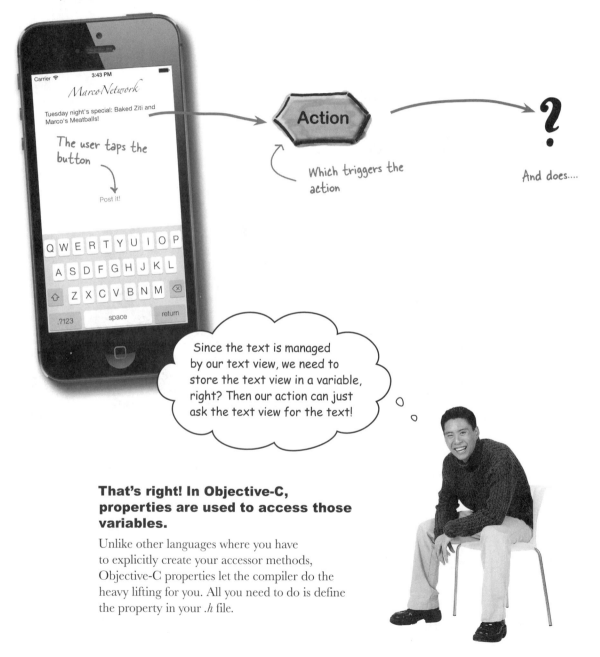

The user taps the button

Which triggers the action

And does....

> Since the text is managed by our text view, we need to store the text view in a variable, right? Then our action can just ask the text view for the text!

That's right! In Objective-C, properties are used to access those variables.

Unlike other languages where you have to explicitly create your accessor methods, Objective-C properties let the compiler do the heavy lifting for you. All you need to do is define the property in your *.h* file.

Properties handle creating getters and setters

Using @property in the header file lets the compiler know we have a property. In modern Objective-C, these properties are automatically synthesized—you no longer need to write @synthesize in the implementation file. With a synthesized property, the compiler will generate a getter and, if it's a read/write property, a setter, and implement it based on the @property attributes declared in the *.h* file.

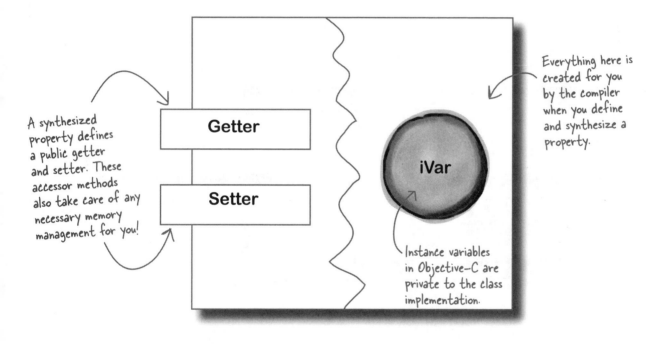

A synthesized property defines a public getter and setter. These accessor methods also take care of any necessary memory management for you!

Everything here is created for you by the compiler when you define and synthesize a property.

Instance variables in Objective-C are private to the class implementation.

Now, what does that all look like in Objective-C?

Sharpen your pencil

Of the code snippets below, only one will store the text view for the tweet. Circle the one that will work!

```
    NSLog(@"Post It button
was pressed: %@", self.tweetTextView.text);
```

```
@property (weak, nonatomic) IBOutlet UITextView *tweetTextView;
```

```
    self.tweetTextView.
font=[UIFont fontWithName:@"Helvetica" size:15.f];
```

```
NSString *buttonTitle=[sender titleForState:UIControlStateNormal];
```

Create a property for that text field

We'll need a property to wrap up everything for the tweet, and a way to get the
information out. Using the storyboard editor again, we'll create everything we
need in one move to get the text set up and used in our app.

Do this!

Select the text field and then hit Control and drag over to
between the `@interface` and `@end` of the *ViewController.h*
file.

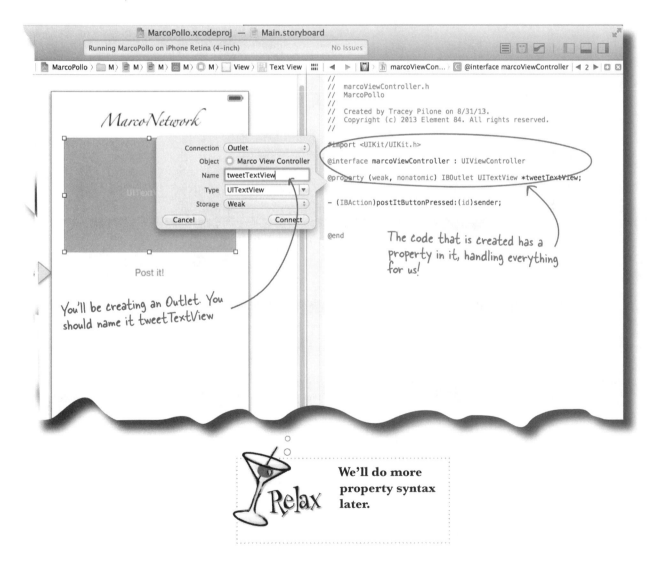

You'll be creating an Outlet. You
should name it tweetTextView

The code that is created has a
property in it, handling everything
for us!

Relax We'll do more
property syntax
later.

Sharpen your pencil
Solution

We gave you some options for which code snippet to use for the tweet. What did you come up with?

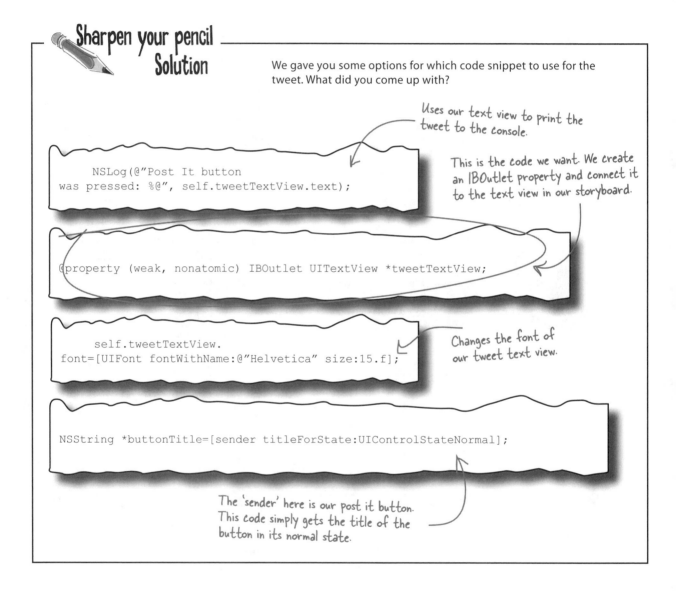

Uses our text view to print the tweet to the console.

```
    NSLog(@"Post It button
was pressed: %@", self.tweetTextView.text);
```

This is the code we want. We create an IBOutlet property and connect it to the text view in our storyboard.

```
@property (weak, nonatomic) IBOutlet UITextView *tweetTextView;
```

```
    self.tweetTextView.
font=[UIFont fontWithName:@"Helvetica" size:15.f];
```

Changes the font of our tweet text view.

```
NSString *buttonTitle=[sender titleForState:UIControlStateNormal];
```

The 'sender' here is our post it button. This code simply gets the title of the button in its normal state.

You connect your controls to outlets

Creating the outlet was the last piece so that we can interact with the text view. Since our text view stores the text for our tweet, we needed some way to access it in our code. In this case, we're interacting with a control in our UI, not just responding to an event.

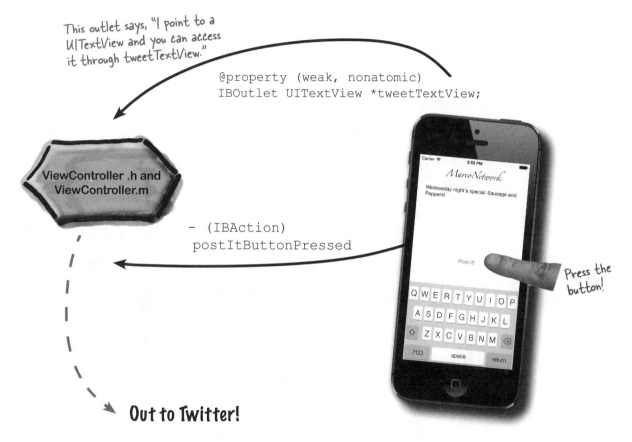

This outlet says, "I point to a UITextView and you can access it through tweetTextView."

```
@property (weak, nonatomic)
IBOutlet UITextView *tweetTextView;
```

ViewController .h and ViewController.m

```
- (IBAction)
  postItButtonPressed
```

Press the button!

Out to Twitter!

An IBOutlet references something in the UI

Since the user is interacting with the interface, we need a way to access and update that interface through code. In order to tweet, we need to respond to a button press (IBAction) and access the text the user has typed (IBOutlet).

Test Drive

1 **Connect to your outlet.**
If you didn't do this already, go back and Ctrl-drag in the storyboard to the *ViewController.h* file.

2 **Log the message.**
Once the outlet is set up, you have everything except a way to see that it's working. Go ahead and edit the NSLog message in the `postItButtonPressed` method in the *ViewController.m* file like this:

```
- (IBAction)postItButtonPressed:(id)sender {
  NSLog(@"Post It button was pressed: %@", self.tweetTextView.
text);
}
```

ViewController.m

3 **Run the app in the simulator.**
Build and run the app. Once it's up and running, go ahead and replace the <your tweet here> text with something interesting and tap the "Post It" button...

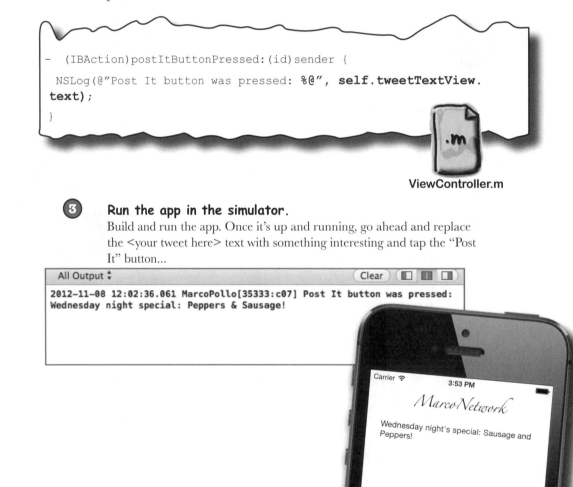

```
All Output ⬍                                              Clear  ▢ ▢ ▢
2012-11-08 12:02:36.061 MarcoPollo[35333:c07] Post It button was pressed:
Wednesday night special: Peppers & Sausage!
```

Carrier 🖗 3:53 PM

MarcoNetwork

Wednesday night's special: Sausage and Peppers!

Post it!

Q: **What is an event again?**

A: UI controls trigger events when things happen to them. You can "wire" these events to methods so that your method is called when an event is triggered. Most of the time, you can wire events to methods using Interface Builder, but you can also do it in code (we'll do this later in the book).

Q: **So in one line of auto-generated code, we handle like eight things?**

A: Yes! Control+drag to create an Outlet in the storyboard editor gets you a line of code that starts with an @property, and

so it declares the variable, creates the setter and the getter for the variable, and also has the outlet for the UI to get the text out of the text field. All in one tiny line of code.

Q: **Didn't there used to be @ synthesize?**

A: Yes, but not anymore. With the implementation of ARC (Automatic Reference Counting), Apple moved a lot of the memory management work involved in iOS development out of the code and into the compiler. The @synthesize was used to create the variable in the implementation file and start that process. Now the compiler handles all that for you.

Q: **Does declaring an @property always generate a setter and getter?**

A: Not always! You can define a property to be read/write or read-only. When a property is defined as read-only, the compiler will only generate the getter. A read-only property ensures that a property can not be changed via a setter method.

BULLET POINTS

- Actions respond to events.

- Outlets are used to work with the interface and present or receive information from the user.

- The storyboard editor can be used to auto-create much of the code that you need to create Actions and Outlets.

- Properties are used to create instance variables as well as the getters and setters for them.

Twitter, the easy way...

For the first time, iOS 6 gave you frameworks for talking to Twitter and Facebook. Instead of having to worry about figuring out both sites' APIs and authentication, Apple is doing it for you—which is great, because these things change a bit.

This is way easier—just ask your local Android Developer what a pain this is to do...

☐ You'll need to get the framework installed on your project to take care of messaging (frameworks are like libraries in Java).

☐ You'll need to implement code within your app to fire off the tweet.

Ready Bake Framework

With the project highlighted, make sure the general tab is highlighted, then scroll down to the expand the Linked Frameworks and Libraries section, and push the + button. Then select Social Framework from the list and click Add.

This is the project highlighted.

Here is the new framework installed.

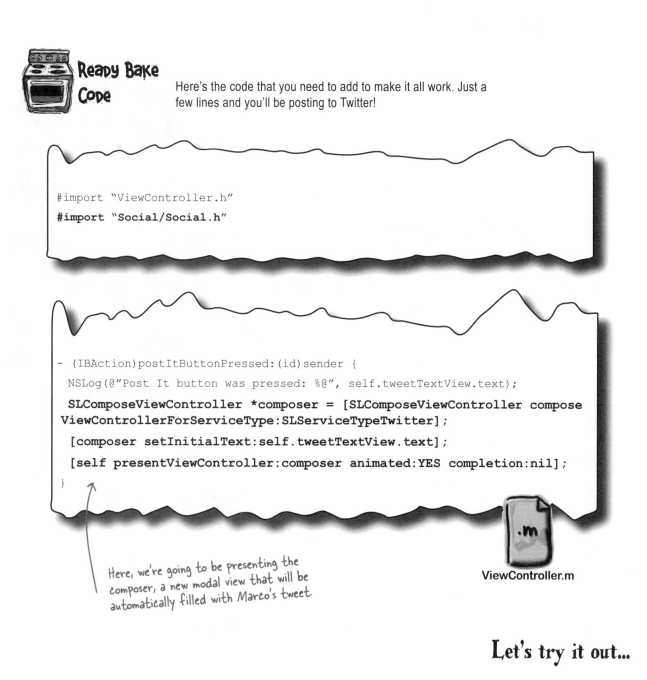

Ready Bake Code

Here's the code that you need to add to make it all work. Just a few lines and you'll be posting to Twitter!

```objc
#import "ViewController.h"
#import "Social/Social.h"
```

```objc
- (IBAction)postItButtonPressed:(id)sender {
  NSLog(@"Post It button was pressed: %@", self.tweetTextView.text);
  SLComposeViewController *composer = [SLComposeViewController compose
ViewControllerForServiceType:SLServiceTypeTwitter];
  [composer setInitialText:self.tweetTextView.text];
  [self presentViewController:composer animated:YES completion:nil];
}
```

ViewController.m

Here, we're going to be presenting the composer, a new modal view that will be automatically filled with Marco's tweet.

Let's try it out...

TEST DRIVE

 Make sure you've added the Social framework and the ready bake code.

 Build and run the app.
Go ahead and put a new tweet in for Marco.

 Set up your Twitter account in the simulator.
When you hit "Post it!" you'll be prompted to go into settings and set up your account. Once that's done, these tweets will be live!

Nice work! Marco is gonna be overwhelmed with new clients...

---

there are no
Dumb Questions

Q: So what's the difference between an IBAction and a method?

A: Nothing! An IBAction is no different than any other method in your implementation file. By declaring it an 'IBAction', the method is exposed to IB so you can wire it up to control events.

#MarcoPollo

Where's my hashy tag? How can I know when people are tweeting?

Marco wants his tweets to be post-processed.

Marco is looking for efficiency and consistency. And also maybe some trending with #MarcoPollo. We need to add some more logic to the app so that it'll add his hash tag...

iOS Magnets

We need to add the code to add Marco's hashtag. Since that's going to happen in the message formatting, it's back into the action for the `postItButtonPressed` action again...

```
- (IBAction)postItButtonPressed:(id)sender {
  NSLog(@"Post It button was pressed: %@", self.tweetTextView.text);

  NSString _____ = [ _____ stringWithFormat:@"    ", _____ ];
  _____

  SLComposeViewController *composer = [SLComposeViewController composeViewControllerForServiceType:SLServiceTypeTwitter];
  [composer setInitialText:tweetText];
  [self presentViewController:composer animated:YES completion:nil];
}
```

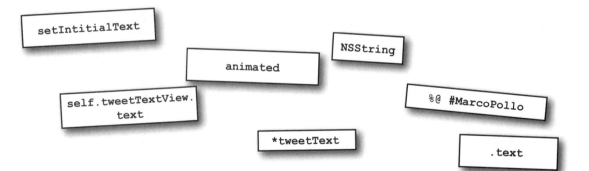

setIntitialText

animated

NSString

self.tweetTextView.
text

*tweetText

%@ #MarcoPollo

.text

iOS Magnets Solution

We need to add the code to add Marco's hashtag and check the post for 135 characters (for Twitter, Facebook doesn't care).

```
- (IBAction)postItButtonPressed:(id)sender {
  NSLog(@"Post It button was pressed: %@", self.tweetTextView.text);

  NSString  *tweetText  st NSString Format:@"        ,    %@ #MarcoPollo
       self.tweetTextView.
              text

  SLComposeViewController *composer = [SLComposeViewController compos
  eViewControllerForServiceType:SLServiceTypeTwitter];
  [composer setInitialText:tweetText];
  [self presentViewController:composer animated:YES completion:nil];

}
```

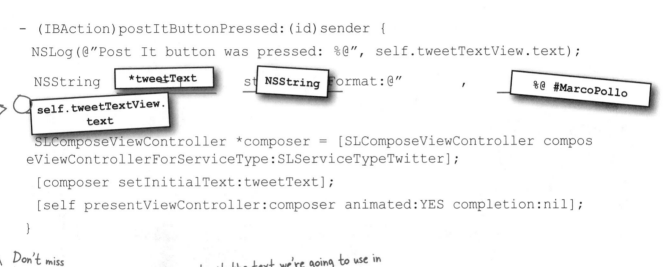

Don't miss
this comma!

We need to construct the text we're going to use in
our tweet. We initialize a new NSString object to
combine the hashtag with the text from the user.

animated

.text

setIntitialText

TEST DRIVE

 Enter the magnet code.

② **Build and run the app.**
Go ahead, plug another tweet in there and my check it out!
You'll have a nice #MarcoPollo at the end.

③ **Eat some chicken!**

iOS Basics Cross

Let's work on some of that left brain now and check your terminology.

Across

3. What your class does
5. Something in a view that a user can interact with.
6. _____ files are used to design views.
9. _____ is how your class does it.
12. Touch up _____ is usually used as a button click.

Down

1. Getters and setters make up _____.
2. The "C" in the MVC pattern
4. An IB_____ responds to an event.
7. The type of version control we're using
8. The "V" in the MVC pattern
10. The "M" in the MVC pattern
11. This basic pattern is used in iOS app design.

Your iOS Basics toolbox

You've got Chapter 2 under your belt and now you've added some basic patterns and syntax to your toolbox.

Storyboards

- Hold all the views for your application.

- The storyboard editor is where you work with all your view layout

- Xcode now supports some relative dimensions for iOS development in the storyboard.

Controls

- At the elements that you interact with in the view.

- Are controlled by controllers that are a class.

- Those classes are made up of .h and .m files.

BULLET POINTS

- Actions respond to events.

- Outlets are used to work with the interface and present or receive information from the user.

- The storyboard editor can be used to auto-create much of the code that you need to create Actions and Outlets.

- Properties are used to create instance variables as well as the getters and setters for them.

 # iOS Basics Cross Solution

Let's work on some of that left brain now and check your terminology.

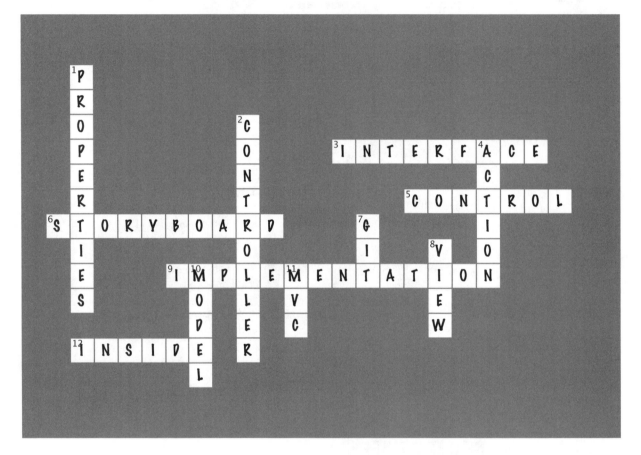

Across

3. What your class does [INTERFACE]
5. Something in a view that a user can interact with. [CONTROL]
6. _____ files are used to design views. [STORYBOARD]
9. _____ is how your class does it. [IMPLEMENTATION]
12. Touch up _____ is usually used as a button click. [INSIDE]

Down

1. Getters and setters make up _____. [PROPERTIES]
2. The "C" in the MVC pattern [CONTROLLER]
4. An IB_____ responds to an event. [ACTION]
7. The type of version control we're using [GIT]
8. The "V" in the MVC pattern [VIEW]
10. The "M" in the MVC pattern [MODEL]
11. This basic pattern is used in iOS app design. [MVC]

2.5 interlude

Syntax

I know these are letters and all, but I have no idea what you're saying...

It's time to get into some details.

You've written a couple apps and gotten some of the big picture stuff sorted out. Now it's time to get into some line by line details. Why are there @ symbols everywhere? What's the difference between a method and a message? What exactly do properties do? It's time to take a quick dive into the syntax of Objective-C; then we can get back into building apps.

Classes: Interface and Implementation

In Objective-C, a class is split into separate files, the *.h* and *.m* files. The *.h* file defines
how other objects should interact with your class. It defines the properties, methods,
and other attributes.

The *.m* file, which imports the *.h*, implements the internal behavior of your class.
The compiler will check to make sure what is defined in your interface file has an
implementation in the *.m*.

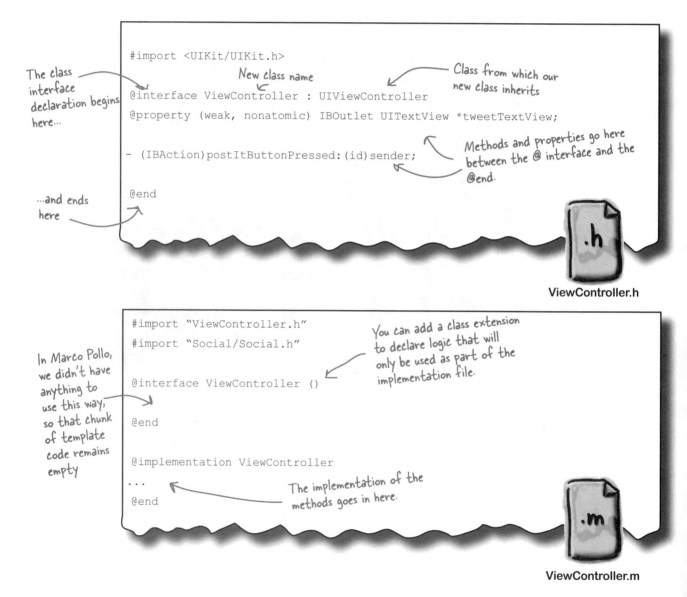

The class interface declaration begins here...

New class name

Class from which our new class inherits

```
#import <UIKit/UIKit.h>

@interface ViewController : UIViewController

@property (weak, nonatomic) IBOutlet UITextView *tweetTextView;


- (IBAction)postItButtonPressed:(id)sender;


@end
```

Methods and properties go here between the @ interface and the @end.

...and ends here

ViewController.h

In Marco Pollo, we didn't have anything to use this way, so that chunk of template code remains empty

```
#import "ViewController.h"
#import "Social/Social.h"


@interface ViewController ()


@end


@implementation ViewController

...

@end
```

You can add a class extension to declare logic that will only be used as part of the implementation file.

The implementation of the methods goes in here.

ViewController.m

Header files describe the interface to your class

In Objective-C, classes are defined with interfaces in the header file. It's where you declare whether your class inherits from anything, as well as your class's instance variables, properties, and methods.

As Objective-C matured, more code has been moved into the implementation file as a class extension. This is the only way to define truly "private" properties and methods.

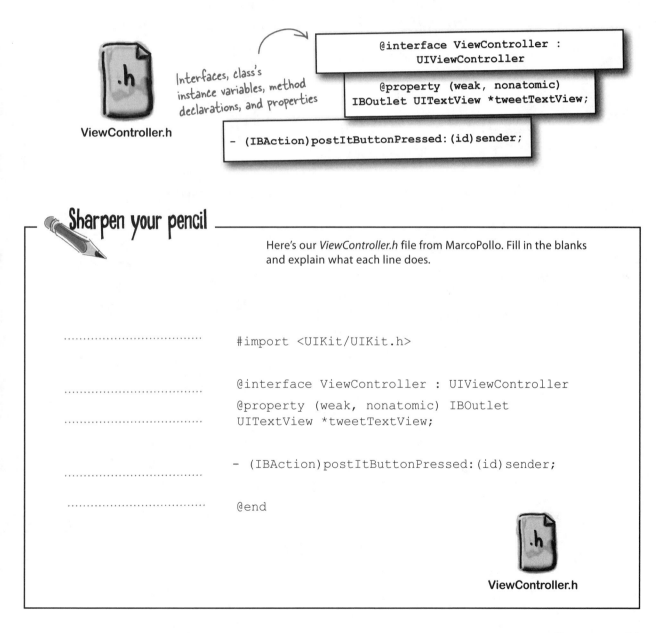

ViewController.h

Interfaces, class's instance variables, method declarations, and properties

```
@interface ViewController :
    UIViewController
```

```
@property (weak, nonatomic)
IBOutlet UITextView *tweetTextView;
```

```
- (IBAction)postItButtonPressed:(id)sender;
```

Sharpen your pencil

Here's our *ViewController.h* file from MarcoPollo. Fill in the blanks and explain what each line does.

....

```
#import <UIKit/UIKit.h>
```

....

```
@interface ViewController : UIViewController
```
```
@property (weak, nonatomic) IBOutlet
UITextView *tweetTextView;
```
....

```
- (IBAction)postItButtonPressed:(id)sender;
```
....

....

```
@end
```

ViewController.h

Sharpen your pencil
Solution

Here's our current *ViewController.h* file. Let's see how you explained what each line does.

```
#import <UIKit/UIKit.h>
```

It's almost identical to C's #include, except that it automatically prevents including the same header multiple times (so no more #ifndef MY_HEADER).

import incorporates another file (almost always a header file) into this file when it's compiled. It's used to pull in classes, constants, etc. from other files.

@interface indicates you're going to declare a class.

Next comes the class name and, if it inherits from something, then a colon and the super class's name.

Objective-C doesn't support multiple inheritance...

Here, we specify what we inherit from and what protocols we conform to.

```
@interface ViewController : UIViewController {
```

```
    UITextField *notesField_;
```

The syntax for instance variables is just like in C++: Basic types like int and float are used as is; pointer types use an asterisk. By default, all fields are given protected access, but you can change that with @private or @public sections similar to C++.

This is where we can declare instance variables of our class; this one wasn't in Marco Pollo, but you get the idea.

```
}
```

Once you've closed the field section of your interface, you can declare properties. @property tells Objective-C that there will be accessor methods for the given property and lets you use the '.' notation to access them.

ViewController.h

Sharpen your pencil
                    Solution

The @property keyword tells the compiler
this is a property that will be backed by
getter and (maybe) setter methods.

These are property attributes; we'll
talk more about these shortly...

`@property (weak, nonatomic) IBOutlet UITextView *tweetTextView;`

IBOutlet allows Interface Builder to recognize
properties that you can attach to controls (like
our notes property in InstaTwit).

Here are our type and
property name, just like the
field in the class.

The minus sign means it's an instance
method (a + means it's a class method).
All methods in Objective-C are public.

These are the method declarations.

`- (IBAction)postItButtonPressed:(id)sender;`

IBAction lets Interface
Builder identify methods
that can be attached to
events.

IBAction method signatures can have no arguments, one
argument of type ID (which is like an Object reference
in Java), or two arguments where one is the id of the
sender and one is a UIEvent*.containing the event that
triggered the call.

`@end`   @end: ends your class interface declaration.

.h

ViewController.h

Properties are about efficiency

To work with an object, properties allow you to create the setter and getter methods; they also provide some other help. By putting creation of those methods on the compiler, it can also check to make sure that all your properties are used and to handle synthesizing the accessor methods. All for one line of code.

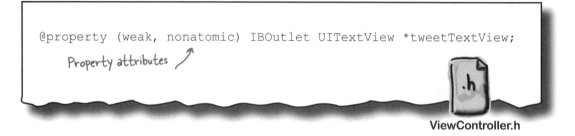

```
@property (weak, nonatomic) IBOutlet UITextView *tweetTextView;
```

Property attributes ↗

ViewController.h

Property attributes talk to the compiler

To dictate exactly how the accessor methods work, you declare attributes of the property. They are broken into three categories: write-ability, setter semantics, and atomicity. Properties are atomic by default. This means that those accessor methods that are synthesized always return or set a value in a mulithreaded environment.

If you dive into the list of attributes in the Apple Developer documentation, you can see the complete list.

> So it's safe because we're controlling access to our variables, right?

That's right! Properties protect your variables.

By defining a property, we restrict the way other objects interact with our class's data. This promotes good encapsulation and ensures our class manages how we manage the data.

WHO DOES WHAT?

Below is a list of the most commonly used property attributes and definitions. Match each attribute with its definition.

read-only

strong

read/write

copy

weak

When you want the property to be modifiable by people. The compiler will generate a getter and a setter for you. This is the default.

This attribute does not keep the referenced object alive. It's set to nil when there are no strong references to the object. With this reference, you don't take ownership of the object.

When you're dealing with object values. The object remains "alive" as long as there is a strong pointer to it. With this reference, you claim ownership to the object.

When you don't want people modifying the property. You can still change the field value backing the property, but the compiler won't generate a setter.

When you want to hold onto a copy of some value instead of the value itself; for example, if you want to hold onto an array and don't want people to be able to change its contents after they set it. This sends a copy message to the value passed in, then keeps that.

WHO DOES WHAT?
SOLUTION

Below is a list of the most commonly used property attributes and definitions. Match each attribute with its definition.

read-only

strong

read/write

copy

weak

When you want the property to be modifiable by people. The compiler will generate a getter and a setter for you. This is the default.

This attribute does not keep the referenced object alive. It's set to nil when there are no strong references to the object. With this reference, you don't take ownership of the object.

When you're dealing with object values. The object remains "alive" as long as there is a strong pointer to it. With this reference, you claim ownership to the object.

When you don't want people modifying the property. You can still change the instance variable value backing the property, but the compiler won't generate a setter.

When you want to hold onto a copy of some value instead of the value itself; for example, if you want to hold onto an array and don't want people to be able to change its contents after they set it. This sends a copy message to the value passed in, then keeps that.

there are no Dumb Questions

Q: How does the compiler know what field to use to hold the property value?

A: When a property is automatically synthesized for you, an ivar is automatically generated for you by the compiler. This ivar is named the same as the property with a preceding _. For example, a property named `superSecretField` will have a backing ivar named `_superSecretField`. You can change this by adding a custom @synthesize, but we suggest sticking with best practices.

Q: What about that nonatomic keyword?

A: By default, generated accessors are multithread safe and use mutexes when changing a property value. These are considered **atomic**. However, if your class isn't being used by multiple threads, that's a waste. You can tell the compiler to skip the whole mutex thing by declaring your property as nonatomic. Note that just making your properties atomic doesn't mean your whole class is thread safe, so be careful here.

Message passing: How Objective-C gets around

When you want to interact with another object in Objective-C, you pass it a message. The **message** may or may not include arguments, and the combination of the method name and arguments is called the **selector**. Remember, messages are sent to another object, where it's handled by a **method** implementation.

Below is a message used with the UIPickerView controller (we used it in InstaTwit; it's the controller that spins like a dial). This method returns the number of rows for a given component in a picker view. It's declared like this:

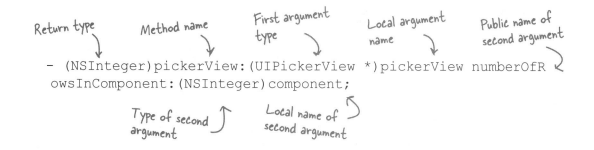

```
- (NSInteger)pickerView:(UIPickerView *)pickerView numberOfRowsInComponent:(NSInteger)component;
```

Return type · Method name · First argument type · Local argument name · Public name of second argument · Type of second argument · Local name of second argument

Objective-C Magnets

This is a message from the Marco Pollo *ViewController.m* file; it tells this composer view to set the initial text. Build the message itself and then add the description of the pieces of the message too.

[_____ _____] ; _____

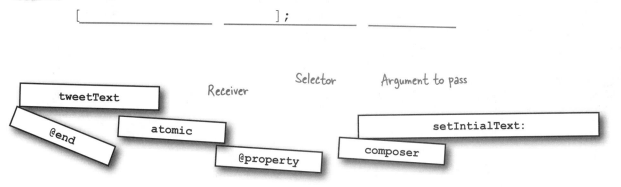

Receiver · Selector · Argument to pass

tweetText
@end
atomic
@property
composer
setIntialText:

Objective-C Magnets Solution

Here's how you built the message from the MarcoPollo ViewController.m file; it tells this composer view to set the initial text. Build the message itself and then add the description of the pieces of the message too.

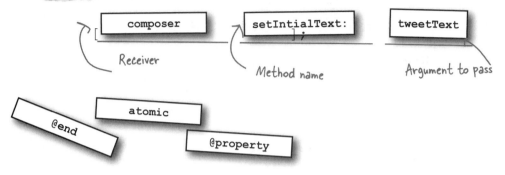

```
composer          setIntialText:          tweetText
```

Receiver   Method name   Argument to pass

```
@end        atomic
                    @property
```

there are no
Dumb Questions

Q: So about those arguments to methods...what's the deal with the name before the colon and the one after the type?

A: In Objective-C, you can have a public name and a local name for arguments. The public name becomes part of the selector when someone wants to send that message to your object. That's the name before the colon. The name after the type is the local variable; this is the name of the variable that holds the value. In Objective-C, they don't have to be the same, so you can use a nice friendly public name for people when they use your class and a convenient local name in your code.

Q: You mentioned selectors, but I'm still fuzzy on what they are.

A: Selectors are unique names for methods when Objective-C translates a message into an actual method call. It's basically the method name and the names of the arguments separated by colons. For instance, look at the code using the selector `pickerView:numberOfRowsInComponent`. You'll see them show up again in later chapters when we do more interface connecting in code. For now, Interface Builder is handling it for us.

Q: When we send the `resignFirstResponder` message to sender, the sender type is "id". How does that work?

A: "id" is an Objective-C type that can point to any Objective-C object. It's like a void* in C++. Since Objective-C is a dynamically typed language, it's perfectly OK with sending messages to an object of type "id". It will figure out at runtime whether or not the object can actually respond to the message.

Q: What happens if an object can't respond to a message?

A: You'll get an exception. This is the reason you should use strongly typed variables whenever possible—it will generate warnings at compile time, not just runtime problems. However, there are times when generic typing makes a lot of sense, such as callback methods when the sender could be any number of different objects.

Q: So seriously, brackets for message passing?

A: Yes. And indexing arrays. We all just have to deal with it.

This is dumb. You say this is a message, but it sure looks like a method call to me. Isn't this all a little silly?

A message is a request for a particular named method with particular arguments. In Objective-C, you send messages to objects and they respond.

The Objective-C runtime turns your message into a method call, which returns a value. So, generally you talk about sending some receiver a message, but if you're implementing what it does in response, you're implementing a method.

Objective-C tries to match your message to an existing method... and it might not be successful!

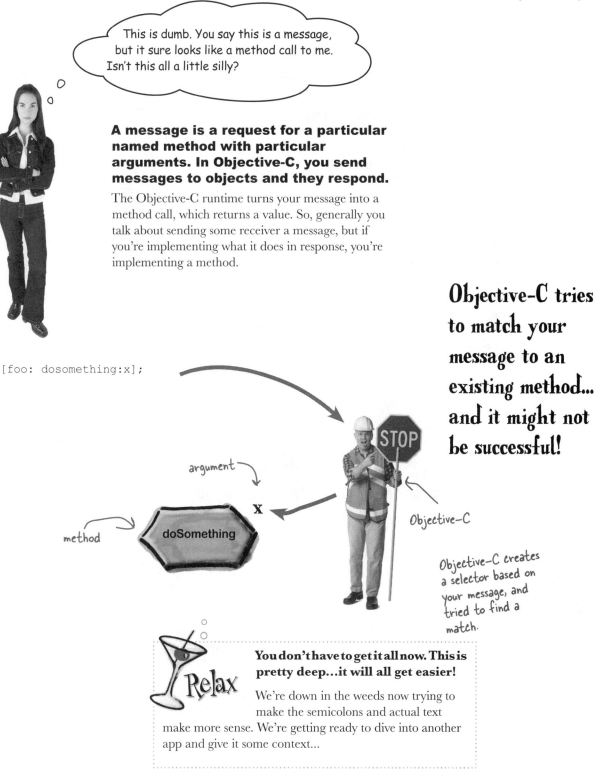

`[foo: dosomething:x];`

argument

x

method

doSomething

Objective-C

Objective-C creates a selector based on your message, and tried to find a match.

You don't have to get it all now. This is pretty deep...it will all get easier!

Relax

We're down in the weeds now trying to make the semicolons and actual text make more sense. We're getting ready to dive into another app and give it some context...

This is pretty complicated, isn't it? I'm not sure I get why this matters.

Messages let you define message receivers at runtime, not just compile time.

Sending a message is the way objects interact with each other. It's how you instruct an object to perform a task or compute a value. Even accessing a property is turned into a message by the compiler.

Apple's documentation uses the message terminology throughout.

BULLET POINTS

- In Objective-C, you send messages to receivers. The runtime maps these to method calls.

- Method declarations go in the header (*.h*) file after the closing brace of an interface.

- Method implementations go in the implementation (*.m*) file between the `@implementation` and the `@end`.

- Method arguments are usually named, and those names are used when sending a message.

- Arguments can have an internal and external name.

- Use a "-" to indicate an instance method; use "+" to indicate a static method.

Speaking of messages....

I own this great vinyl record store, and I think I need an app...

It's time to get back to work...

Syntax Cross

Let's make sure you learned your terms! It makes
reading Apple documentation way easier.

Across

8. In Objective-C, a _____ is made up of a .h and a .m file.
9. You send messages to _____.
11. This incorporates another file.
12. Signals that the compiler will retain the object.

Down

1. This tells the compiler to skip mutexes.
2. Automatic methods
3. Unique names for methods after Objective-C translation are _____.
4. Arguments can have an _____ and external name.
5. This property creates a setter for the basic types.
6. _____ management is important for iPhone apps.
7. This is sent between objects.
10. Objective-C tries to match your message to an existing _____.

Your Syntax toolbox

You've got Chapter 2.5 under your belt and now you've added some syntax to your toolbox.

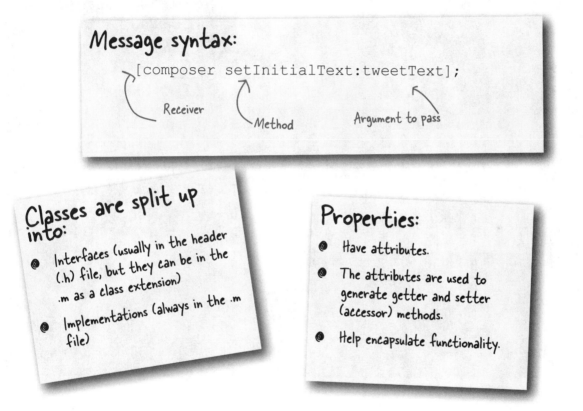

Message syntax:

```
[composer setInitialText:tweetText];
```

Receiver

Method

Argument to pass

Classes are split up into:

- Interfaces (usually in the header (.h) file, but they can be in the .m as a class extension)

- Implementations (always in the .m file)

Properties:

- Have attributes.

- The attributes are used to generate getter and setter (accessor) methods.

- Help encapsulate functionality.

BULLET POINTS

- In Objective-C, you send messages to receivers. The runtime maps these to method calls.

- Method declarations go in the header (*.h*) file after the closing brace of an interface.

- Method implementations go in the implementation (*.m*) file between the @implementation and the @end.

- Method arguments are usually named, and those names are used when sending a message.

- Arguments can have an internal and external name.

- Use a "-" to indicate an instance method; use "+" to indicate a static method.

Syntax cross solution

Let's make sure you learned your terms! It makes reading Apple documentation way easier.

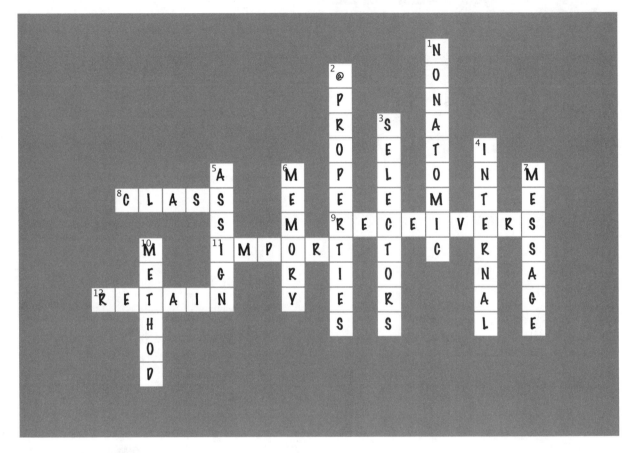

Across

8. In Objective-C, a _____ is made up of a .h and a .m file. [CLASS]
9. You send messages to _____. [RECEIVERS]
11. This incorporates another file. [IMPORT]
12. Signals that the compiler will retain the object. [RETAIN]

Down

1. This tells the compiler to skip mutexes. [NONATOMIC]
2. Automatic methods [@PROPERTIES]
3. Unique names for methods after Objective-C translation are _____. [SELECTORS]
4. Arguments can have an _____ and external name. [INTERNAL]
5. This property creates a setter for the basic types. [ASSIGN]
6. _____ management is important for iPhone apps. [MEMORY]
7. This is sent between objects. [MESSAGE]
10. Objective-C tries to match your message to an existing _____. [METHOD]

3 tables, views, and data

A table with a view

I like my coffee with two sugars, cream, a sprinkle of cinnamon, stirred twice, then...

Most iOS apps have more than one view.

We've written a cool app with one view, but anyone who's used a smartphone knows that most apps aren't like that. Some of the more impressive iOS apps out there do a great job of working with complex information by using multiple views. We're going to start with navigation controllers and table views, like the kind you see in your Mail and Contacts apps. Only we're going to do it with a twist...

Congratulations!

You've just landed the development gig for Spin City, a hit new underground record store. The owner, Rob, is listening to his customers and has a request...

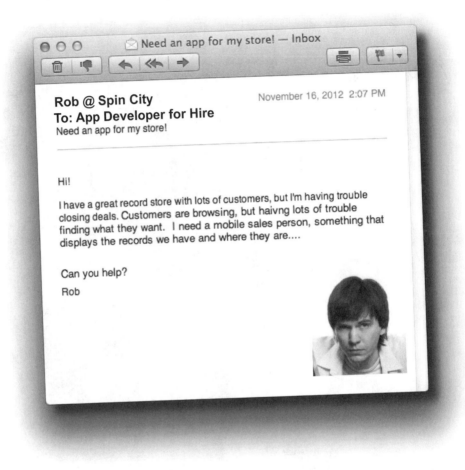

○ ○ ○   ✉ Need an app for my store! — Inbox

Rob @ Spin City   November 16, 2012 2:07 PM
To: App Developer for Hire
Need an app for my store!

Hi!

I have a great record store with lots of customers, but I'm having trouble closing deals. Customers are browsing, but haivng lots of trouble finding what they want. I need a mobile sales person, something that displays the records we have and where they are....

Can you help?

Rob

SpinCity browsing app overview

The app needs to keep track of the data for the store inventory and then display it in a way that customers can search. This way, all of Rob's vintage records are easier to find and he can start converting all that foot traffic into sales.

All these records have locations in the store.

Salesperson entering all that data.

Hi-Fi App being used by a happy customer!

Your job is to create an iPhone app that displays the record location, price, and description. The app needs to list all of the records.

The way iOS apps work

There's a lot of information that we need to get across to users. Location and price aren't so bad, but any kind of detailed listing or description and that row is going to get crowded.

Each record has a cell, but there's not room for all the info you need! You'll have to build out another view with some details.

Using the touch screen....

iOS applications were one of the first interfaces to work through touch. That, coupled with a small screen being used for a single task, leads to multiview apps being the norm. Spin City is going to need to respond to user touch by presenting more information.

Multiview iOS applications typically have some kind of overview display (called the master view), and one or more views that drill in on specific pieces of information (called detail views). Our table view acts as our master view; we need a detail view to show all of the information we want to convey.

UI Design Magnets

We've already shown you a little about what the first view will look like.
What are you thinking for the detail view?

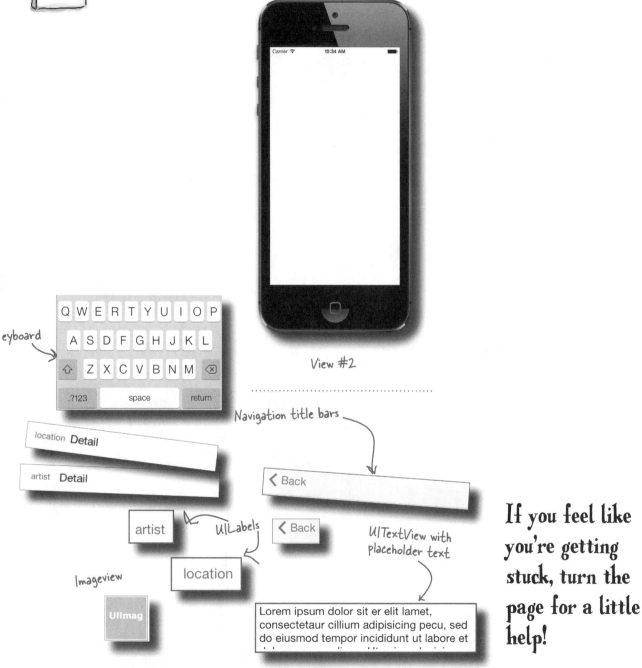

View #2

eyboard

Navigation title bars

location **Detail**

artist **Detail**

< Back

artist

UILabels

< Back

*UITextView with
placeholder text*

location

Imageview

Lorem ipsum dolor sit er elit lamet,
consectetaur cillium adipisicing pecu, sed
do eiusmod tempor incididunt ut labore et

UIImag

**If you feel like
you're getting
stuck, turn the
page for a little
help!**

Hierarchical data—get out your table view

Data frequently falls into the category of being organized into parent-child relationships, where there is a high-level piece of data with further details to follow. It happens with contacts and calendars, for example. In our case, the record data fits nicely into this model.

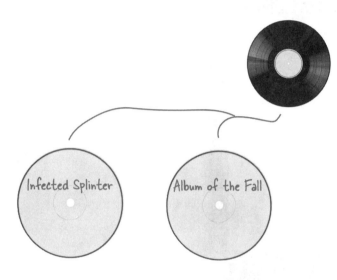

The top-level piece of data is the record name.

The detailed data is all the info on the label: the track names, description, and location of the record.

Infected Splinter

Album of the Fall

Use table and detail views together to represent hierarchical data

The table view/detail view combination is perfect for this type of data. The table view shows all of the top-level items (in this case, records) and then each detail view shows the information for each individual record.

When you build applications, give a lot of thought to how each view should be used: What's it trying to convey to the user? How will they interact with it? Different views frequently support different use cases, so you might want to place buttons or eliminate access to some functions entirely depending on which view the user is in and what they're trying to do.

How would I even know that? And is there a template for this type of app? Don't programs get to make up their own rules?

Apple has a lot to say about iPhone apps in the HIG.

The iOS Human Interface Guidelines (HIG) is a document maintained by Apple that gives both best practices and App Store guidelines for app interaction patterns.

When you start going through the introduction, check out the note about using navigation for hierarchical data (using a detail view). Since it's such a common pattern, one of the app templates in Xcode is the master-detail template.

The HIG can be found online at https://developer.apple.com/library/ios/documentation/userexperience/conceptual/mobilehig/ or through the Organizer window in Xcode, search for "iOS Human Interface Guidelines."

there are no Dumb Questions

Q: Do I have to follow the HIG?

A: Yes and no. It's a good idea to make sure that your app behaves the iOS way; it will keep the user experience consistent for the user and will make it easy for the Apple reviewers when you submit the app.

Of course, you want to keep some originality for your app. For basic things, like drilling down into data, it's best to keep things uniform with user expectations. For things that are more unique to your app, that's a good place to differentiate yourself.

Q: Why switch views instead of changing the view to present more information?

A: This is one of those times when the small screen and basic interaction patterns used in iOS become important. With limited screen space, iOS apps are very task centric. One of the most challenging parts of building a good application is effectively presenting the information you need to communicate without overloading the user or making overly complicated interactions. Each view should have a specific purpose and be

designed to get the user the information they need in a way that makes it easy (and fun!) to understand and use.

Q: What other ways does touch influence the interface?

A: Designing for a touch interface means that some things need to be completely different from web development; the biggest one being that the space for interaction needs to be the size of a fingertip, not a mouse pointer. Other things like hover don't really work as a design paradigm either.

UI Design Magnets Solution

Here's what we came up with for the detail view just to give you an idea. We'll get into implementing it later!

These are both just labels populated with the right data.

Navigation bar

The image will go here (when you have data...otherwise, it'll be blank)

These are actually table cells, but we'll explain that later.

Here is the text view with functioning text.

Detail View

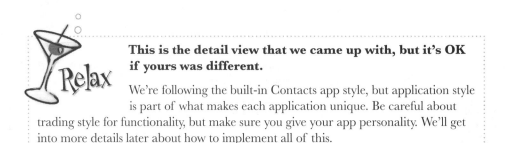

This is the detail view that we came up with, but it's OK if yours was different.

We're following the built-in Contacts app style, but application style is part of what makes each application unique. Be careful about trading style for functionality, but make sure you give your app personality. We'll get into more details later about how to implement all of this.

We need to hook these views together...

You have the two views, but there's nothing linking them. We need to set up when each should be used, how we transition between them, and what kind of information each one needs in order to do its thing.

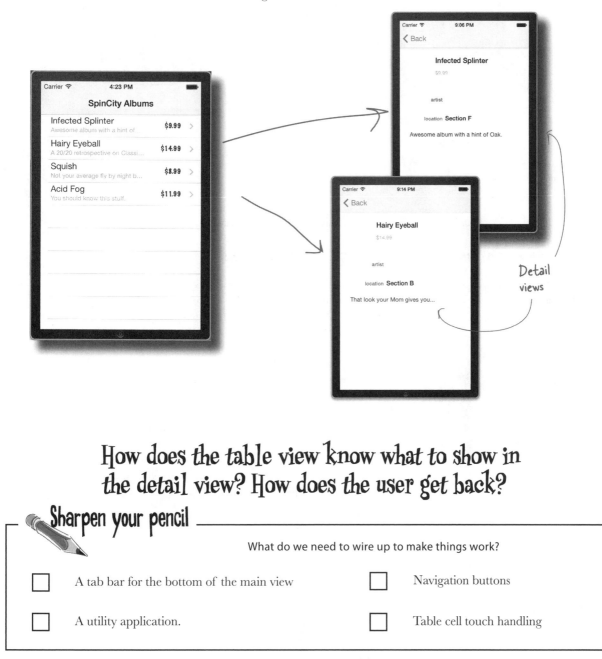

Detail views

How does the table view know what to show in the detail view? How does the user get back?

Sharpen your pencil

What do we need to wire up to make things work?

☐ A tab bar for the bottom of the main view

☐ Navigation buttons

☐ A utility application.

☐ Table cell touch handling

Sharpen your pencil
Solution

What do we need to wire up to make things work?

☐ A tab bar for the bottom of the main view.

A tab bar is used when you have views of equal importance that don't necessarily relate to each other. Useful, but not here!

☐ A utility application.

A utility application is a term used to describe a straightforward app that's usually one or two views only. Think the weather app that comes on iOS or a stock app.

☑ Navigation buttons

View transitions and back buttons come as part of the navigation controller

☑ Table cell touch handling

Table cells can be tapped by the user and shoot off an event to let us know what happened. We can take advantage of that to hook our views together.

The navigation controller gets you around in your views

The navigation controller can handle transitions between views. There are several view transitions built in, we just need to wire things up. It provides things like back buttons, title bars, and view history so that the user can move between data without getting lost. The navigation controller handles things like sizing the views and maintaining a view stack; we just need to tell it which views we're working with.

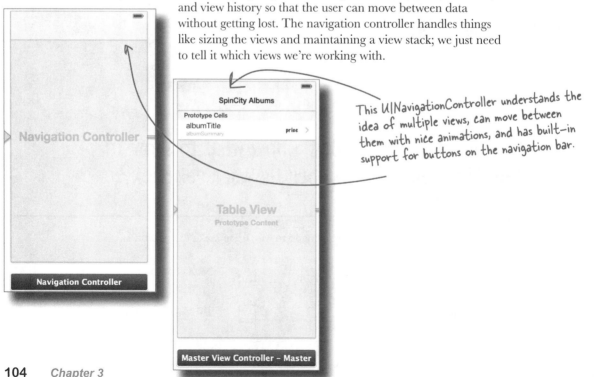

This UINavigationController understands the idea of multiple views, can move between them with nice animations, and has built-in support for buttons on the navigation bar.

Q: What built-in apps on iOS use the navigation controller?

A: For examples on how the navigation controller works, check out the Mail app on both iPhone and iPad. The iPad uses the split view controller, which is similar to the iPhone but it allows for the presentation of the master view and the detail view at the same time. That allows iPads to leverage the additional screen space without really changing the navigation pattern of the app between devices.

Another good example is the Calendar app on the iPhone. Although it supports several different views (the month, day, list or week view), it still is fundamentally driven by the navigation controller.

Q: Do I have to use a table view for my root view?

A: No, it's just the most common, since it provides a natural way to show an overview of a lot of data and have the user drill down for more information. Table views are very

easily customized, too, so some apps that might not seem like table views really are, like Notes or the iTunes Store, for example.

Q: How does the navigation controller relate to view controllers?

A: We'll talk a lot more about this in a minute, but the navigation controller coordinates the transition between view controllers. Typically, each top-level view is backed by a view controller, and as views transition on screen, the corresponding view controller starts getting events from its view. There's a whole view lifecycle that we'll work through that lets a view controller know what's going on with its view.

Q: What if I want buttons, like the Edit button in the iPhone Mail app, up in the top? Is that a problem with navigation controllers?

A: Nope, not at all. The navigation controller has the idea of button in that top navigation bar; you just tell it what to put up there. It also supports the back navigation button to the previous view.

Q: You mentioned that on the iPad you can see the master and detail view side by side. Does that make things complicated?

A: Not really. On the iPad, you'll use a split view control which takes a master view and a detail view. These could be the same master and detail views you use on your iPhone application. They're wired together with the SplitViewController on the iPad instead of a navigation controller like on the iPhone or a Touch. Sometimes on the iPad you actually see the master view wrapped in its own navigation controller. Check out the Mail app on the iPad to see that in action. The master view (when in landscape mode) can show accounts, then drill down to folders, then down to actual messages. Those are all different views inside a navigation controller. When you actually tap an email, the detail view (bigger view on the right) shows the details of the selected message.

Three views in one template

Now that we have a good understanding of what the app is going to do (show records and some details about them) and how it's going to do that (using a navigation controller and a table view), we can get started. Go ahead and open up Xcode.

 Choose the template.

Start a new project and choose the "Master-Detail Application." That one comes with the basic views and the navigation controller. Change the product name to "SpinCity" and do not add a class prefix. Leave the "Use Core Data" box unchecked.

② Click "Next" and save your project.
Save your new project somewhere you can find it later and Xcode will
create a new iOS application with a table view master view and a blank
detail view.

③ Open up the storyboard.
The template includes a storyboard that has all the project's views on it,
including transitions. Click on the storyboard and Xcode will open it up
in the storyboard view. Let's dig into what we get out of the box...

Storyboards Up Close

The storyboard is a view within Xcode that was introduced with Xcode 4.2 and allows you to work graphically with all the views and transitions used in your app. Now that we're moving into an app with multiple views, it's important to see how those views are related.

Each view in an app is called a "scene" on a storyboard.

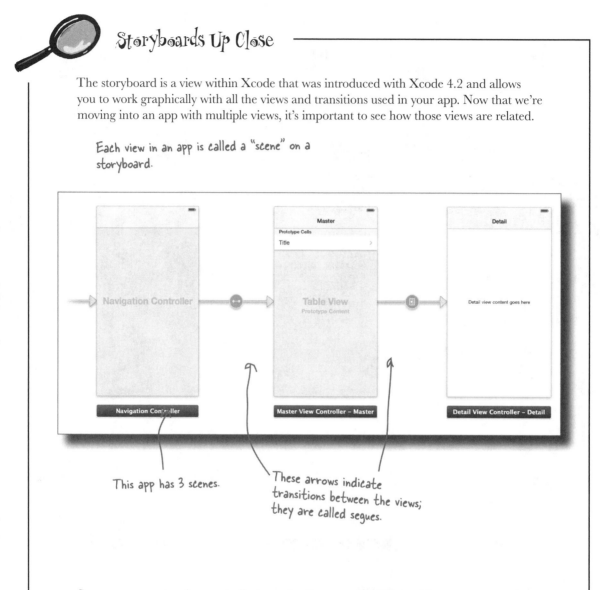

This app has 3 scenes.

These arrows indicate transitions between the views; they are called segues.

Scenes represent a view controller's worth of content. On iPhone it's on one screen, but on iPad there can be more than one view controller (and its view) present on the screen at one time. You can also see **segues** above. They represent the different types of transitions between views. Some different segues include modal or push transitions and can be customized. The segue itself is an object that is created to prep the new view and is also used to pass data between views.

TEST DRIVE

 Create the app.

Using the instructions on the previous page, dive into Xcode and get Spin City set up. This will give you a generic template app to work with.

 Set the title of the master view.

In the storyboard view, click on the navigation item in the master view controller. In the property editor on the right, change the title to "Spin City Albums." Make sure to check the "is initial view controller" box under the title.

 Build and Run!

You don't need to do anything else to get the app to run—the template comes ready to go. Click the Play button to build and run, and you're off!

Now that you have the basic views and transitions between them, we need to start working with real data.

Jim

Frank

Joe

So we have three views..but no data! How do we populate that table view and the details?

Joe: The TableView view controller knows about the table view, so we can stick the data there.

Jim: We need more than just the title of the album though, we need everything that goes on that detail view too.

Joe: We need to store that somewhere....

Frank: ...but data doesn't belong in the view controllers.

Jim: Why not? The view controller knows everything that's going on, shouldn't it have the data too?

Frank: What happens when we need to add new albums or edit albums in a different view? Should all of our views know about the master view controller?

Joe: No, I see your point. Hey, is this a place to use MVC?

Jim: What's MVC?

Frank: MVC is the model-view-controller pattern. It's used in web apps all the time with things like Ruby on Rails. It means we keep the visual presentation (the view) separate from the business logic (the controller) separate from the underlying data (the model).

Joe: But so far everything we've done has put the logic and the data in the same class.

Frank: Well, I think it's time that we changed that. We need a separate class for an album and some place for them to live.

Jim: That's fine, I guess, but what's going in that class?

Frank: We need to define the fields for the data, build up the data model...

Use MVC to separate your concerns...

The MVC pattern is a common pattern in a number of frameworks and it's all over CocoaTouch. The MVC pattern pushes you to separate the various concerns in an application into their own class or classes to help reduce the complexity in each one. iOS development blurs the view and the view controller a little, but generally you describe the view in the storyboard and keep the business logic in the view controller.

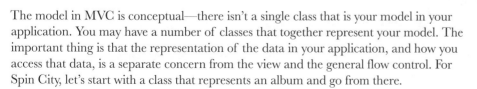

The model represents the data in your application. It usually contains not only the actual data, but whatever's actually holding too, like a database connection, a web service, or just an array of simple objects.

A view is described in a storyboard (though can be built-in code, too) and represents the GUI elements your user will interact with, like buttons and text fields.

The controller, or delegate depending on what we're working on, contains the business logic that controls the flow of the application. It's used to respond to user events and transition to different views (in conjunction with segues).

The model in MVC is conceptual—there isn't a single class that is your model in your application. You may have a number of classes that together represent your model. The important thing is that the representation of the data in your application, and how you access that data, is a separate concern from the view and the general flow control. For Spin City, let's start with a class that represents an album and go from there.

Behind the Scenes

Adding a new class

We've only worked with the classes that have come with the template so far, so we need to get into some nuts and bolts for adding a new class in Xcode. When you create a new class with Xcode, it will generate the header and implementation files for you using a wizard. This is probably also a good time to mention the folders in the Xcode file tree. They're really just groups to help you organize things in Xcode; they don't necessarily have any bearing on where the files actually live on disk. We're going to stick our new class in the Spin City group.

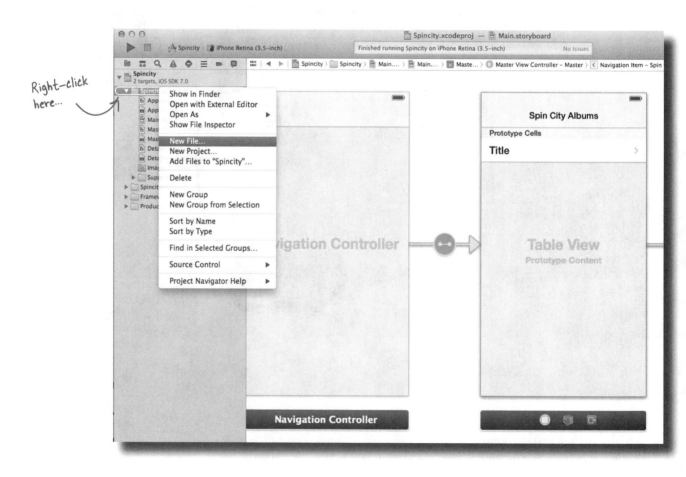

Right-click here...

1 **Get the class generated.**

Right-click on the folder for Spin City in Xcode and then select **New File....** From there you'll go through a dialog to create the new class. Make sure that Cocoa Touch is selected under iOS and you should see Objective-C class as a file option. Click **Next**. Name the class **Album**, select **Next**; save it in Spin City, in the Spin City group, and make sure that the Spin City **Target** is still selected. Then click **Create**.

BRAIN
BARBELL

Now we have a class to represent an album. Take a minute here to list the properties we need to capture the various pieces of information we want. Think about what type each property should be, too. There's also one method that we need in the Album Class. Take a guess for extra credit!

Class properties

....

....

....

....

....

Method for the
Album class

....

Properties expose class attributes

We have album information that we want to be accessible to users of our Album class. To do that, we'll declare a set of properties which the Objective-C compiler will turn into accessor methods for us to let people get to the information we want to expose. Update our Album class with a property for title, artist, summary, location in store, and price. We're also going to tack on a method to initialize a new Album so we can set everything the way we want it whenever we create a new Album.

Do this!

Here's how we flesh out the new data model. Open up the Album header and implementation file and update them to look like this.

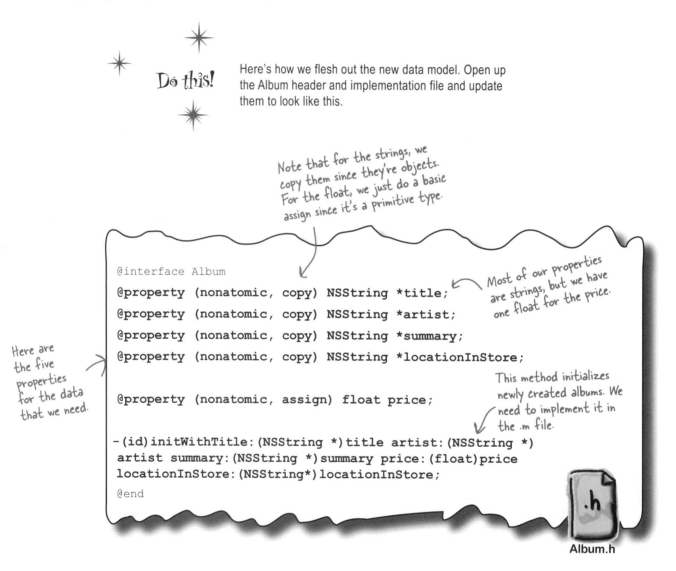

Note that for the strings, we copy them since they're objects. For the float, we just do a basic assign since it's a primitive type.

```
@interface Album

@property (nonatomic, copy) NSString *title;

@property (nonatomic, copy) NSString *artist;

@property (nonatomic, copy) NSString *summary;

@property (nonatomic, copy) NSString *locationInStore;


@property (nonatomic, assign) float price;


-(id)initWithTitle:(NSString *)title artist:(NSString *)
artist summary:(NSString *)summary price:(float)price
locationInStore:(NSString*)locationInStore;

@end
```

Most of our properties are strings, but we have one float for the price.

Here are the five properties for the data that we need.

This method initializes newly created albums. We need to implement it in the .m file.

Album.h

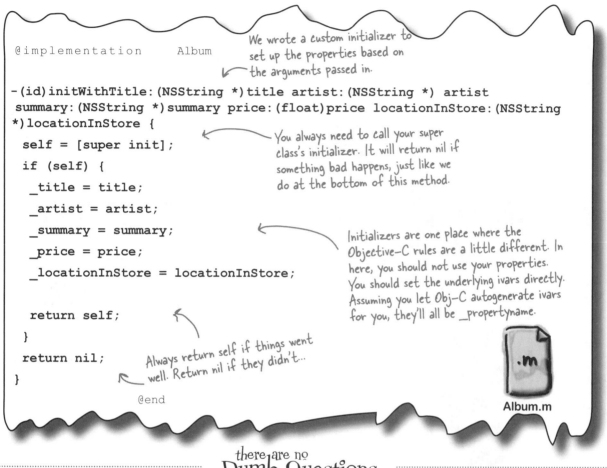

We wrote a custom initializer to set up the properties based on the arguments passed in.

```objc
@implementation    Album

-(id)initWithTitle:(NSString *)title artist:(NSString *) artist
summary:(NSString *)summary price:(float)price locationInStore:(NSString
*)locationInStore {
  self = [super init];
  if (self) {
  _title = title;
  _artist = artist;
  _summary = summary;
  _price = price;
  _locationInStore = locationInStore;

  return self;
  }
  return nil;
}
                          @end
```

You always need to call your super class's initializer. It will return nil if something bad happens, just like we do at the bottom of this method.

Initializers are one place where the Objective-C rules are a little different. In here, you should not use your properties. You should set the underlying ivars directly. Assuming you let Obj-C autogenerate ivars for you, they'll all be _propertyname.

Always return self if things went well. Return nil if they didn't...

Album.m

there are no Dumb Questions

Q: Where are we going to get this data?

A: We're going to add it as an array to start, but other options include plists, SQL databases, and more. Just about every app out there has some kind of data store and we're going to be talking about several different kinds as we work through the book.

Some data sources are purely web-based and just do local caching. Anybody using DropBox APIs or iCloud is working with a web service to move data in and out of the app. Those types of services are often used as a mechanism to keep data synced across devices.

Q: What happens if we return nil from an initializer?

A: If this happens, it's indicating to the caller that initialization failed. The caller should then handle this properly and recover. In practice, that's a pretty bad situation to be in and doesn't happen very often. You need to follow convention properly here though, as CocoaTouch frameworks assume (and provide) this pattern.

Q: How do we display this data to the user?

A: First we need to actually get some data together to use and figure out how to create all those little Album objects we need. Let's work on that next...

How are we going to load/save the actual data to put in these objects?

So now we have a class that neatly encapsulates the idea of an album, but we still don't know where we're getting this data from. We already talked about why we don't want to just jam it into a view controller, so where are we going to put it and how are we going to get to it?

This is a common problem/question in iOS development. We're getting into an important pattern here...

Data Access Objects hide low-level data access

Just like the view has a controller, we'll use a class to hide how we're actually fetching the data we're stuffing into instances of our album class. By hiding the actual retrieval, we avoid splattering SQL or web service calls all over our view controllers. We can encapsulate the data access into a **Data Access Object** or DAO.

Our DAO needs to take requests like "I need album 12" and translate that into a request that works with the data, gets the information back out, and passes it in some meaningful way back to the view controller.

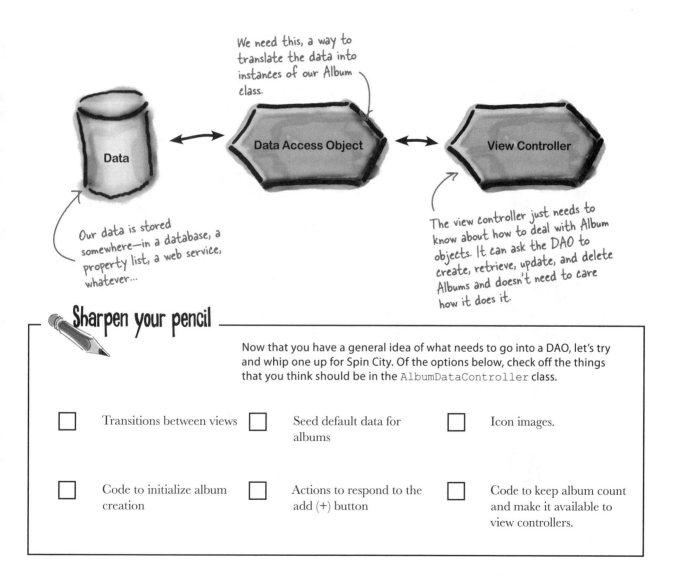

We need this, a way to translate the data into instances of our Album class.

Our data is stored somewhere—in a database, a property list, a web service, whatever...

The view controller just needs to know about how to deal with Album objects. It can ask the DAO to create, retrieve, update, and delete Albums and doesn't need to care how it does it.

Sharpen your pencil

Now that you have a general idea of what needs to go into a DAO, let's try and whip one up for Spin City. Of the options below, check off the things that you think should be in the `AlbumDataController` class.

☐ Transitions between views

☐ Seed default data for albums

☐ Icon images.

☐ Code to initialize album creation

☐ Actions to respond to the add (+) button

☐ Code to keep album count and make it available to view controllers.

Sharpen your pencil
Solution

Now that you have a general idea of what needs to go into a DAO, let's try and whip one up for SpinCity. Of the options below, check off the things that you think should be in the AlbumDataController class.

☐ Transitions between views

☑ Seed default data for albums

The class will have a default array created with some seed data.

☐ Icon images

↑ *These go in the plist for the app.*

☑ Code to initialize album creation

☐ .Actions to respond to the add (+) button

☑ Code to keep album count and make it available to view controllers

↗ *To populate the table view, it needs to know how many albums there will be...*

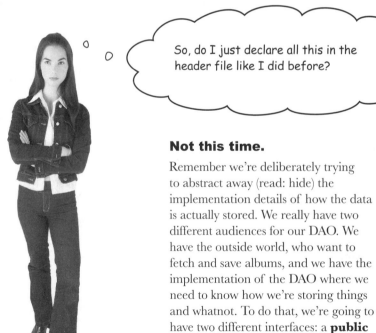

So, do I just declare all this in the header file like I did before?

Not this time.

Remember we're deliberately trying to abstract away (read: hide) the implementation details of how the data is actually stored. We really have two different audiences for our DAO. We have the outside world, who want to fetch and save albums, and we have the implementation of the DAO where we need to know how we're storing things and whatnot. To do that, we're going to have two different interfaces: a **public interface** and a **private interface**.

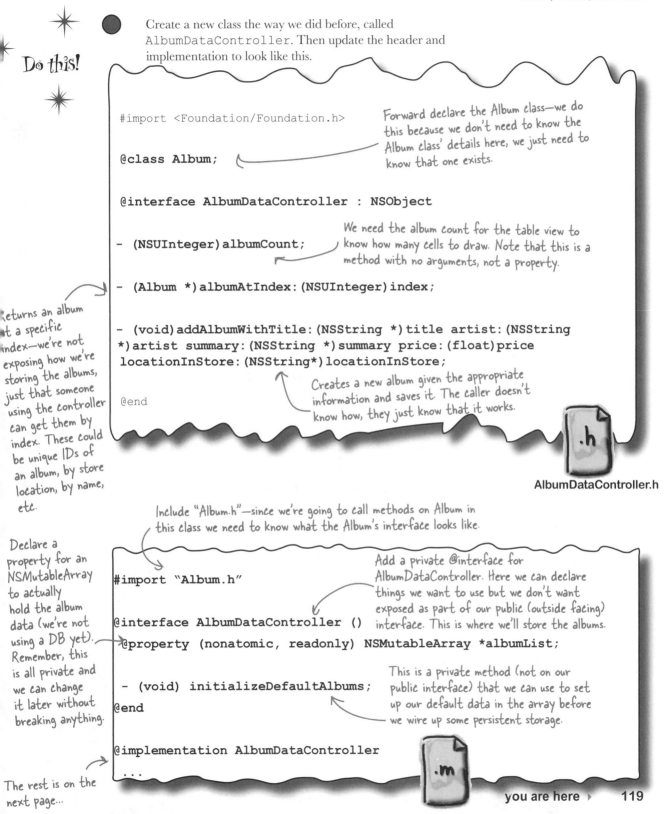

Create a new class the way we did before, called
AlbumDataController. Then update the header and
implementation to look like this.

Do this!

```
#import <Foundation/Foundation.h>

@class Album;

@interface AlbumDataController : NSObject

- (NSUInteger)albumCount;

- (Album *)albumAtIndex:(NSUInteger)index;

- (void)addAlbumWithTitle:(NSString *)title artist:(NSString
*)artist summary:(NSString *)summary price:(float)price
locationInStore:(NSString*)locationInStore;

@end
```

Forward declare the Album class—we do
this because we don't need to know the
Album class' details here, we just need to
know that one exists.

We need the album count for the table view to
know how many cells to draw. Note that this is a
method with no arguments, not a property.

Returns an album
at a specific
index—we're not
exposing how we're
storing the albums,
just that someone
using the controller
can get them by
index. These could
be unique IDs of
an album, by store
location, by name,
etc.

Creates a new album given the appropriate
information and saves it. The caller doesn't
know how, they just know that it works.

AlbumDataController.h

Include "Album.h"—since we're going to call methods on Album in
this class we need to know what the Album's interface looks like.

Declare a
property for an
NSMutableArray
to actually
hold the album
data (we're not
using a DB yet).
Remember, this
is all private and
we can change
it later without
breaking anything.

```
#import "Album.h"

@interface AlbumDataController ()

@property (nonatomic, readonly) NSMutableArray *albumList;

- (void) initializeDefaultAlbums;

@end

@implementation AlbumDataController

...
```

Add a private @interface for
AlbumDataController. Here we can declare
things we want to use but we don't want
exposed as part of our public (outside facing)
interface. This is where we'll store the albums.

This is a private method (not on our
public interface) that we can use to set
up our default data in the array before
we wire up some persistent storage.

The rest is on the
next page...

AlbumDataController.m

```objc
- (id) init {
  self = [super init];

  if (self) {
  _albumList = [[NSMutableArray alloc] init];
  [self initializeDefaultAlbums];
  return self;
  }
  return nil;
}

- (void)initializeDefaultAlbums {

  [self addAlbumWithTitle:@"Infected Splinter" artist:@"Boppin'
Beavers" summary:@"Awesome album with a hint of Oak." price:9.99f
locationInStore:@"Section F"];

  [self addAlbumWithTitle:@"Hairy Eyeball" artist:@"Cyclops"
summary:@"A 20/20 retrospective on Classic Rock." price:14.99f
locationInStore:@"Discount Rack"];

  [self addAlbumWithTitle:@"Squish" artist:@"the Bugz" summary:@"Not
your average fly by night band." price:8.99f locationInStore:@"Section
A"];

  [self addAlbumWithTitle:@"Acid Fog" artist:@"Josh and
Chuck" summary:@"You should know this stuff." price:11.99f
locationInStore:@"Section 9 3/4"];

}

- (void)addAlbumWithTitle:(NSString *)title artist:(NSString *)
artist summary:(NSString *)summary price:(float)price
locationInStore:(NSString *)locationInStore {

  Album *newAlbum = [[Album alloc] initWithTitle:title artist:artist
summary:summary price:price locationInStore:locationInStore];

  [self.albumList addObject:newAlbum];

}

- (NSUInteger)albumCount {

  return [self.albumList count];

}

- (Album *)albumAtIndex:(NSUInteger)index {

  return [self.albumList objectAtIndex:index];

}

@end
```

Update the init method to create the array we'll use to hold the data and call our new initializeDefaultAlbums method when the data controller is created.

Implement the initializeDefaultAlbums method to use our public addAlbumWith... method to create a handful of default albums.

Implement the addAlbumWith... method to create a new album from the given information and add it to the array.

Implement the albumCount and albumAtIndex methods to simply use the underlying array.

AlbumDataController.m

You've built your DAO!

That's it! Check that you don't have any warnings or errors and you should be all set. The app isn't quite ready to show you any new tricks (we need to wire it up with the table view), but we have a lot to work with now.

there are no Dumb Questions

Q: Why did we just do all that? Couldn't we just add an array to the view controller?

A: You could have, but the view controller already has stuff to do. In iOS, view controllers tend to become dumping grounds for code that really belongs somewhere else. We've set this up with a standard pattern that's going to make it easier to update later if we want to add a database or core data to the app.

Using the DAO storage pattern is much more maintainable and it will match up with Apple's sample code that's out there for download if you look at other sample apps.

Q: I'm still a little fuzzy on the public/private interface thing. Why did we put an `@interface` in our implementation file?

A: Objective-C uses the `@interface` keyword to define a place to declare properties and methods for a class. You typically think of `@interface` being used in header files to declare a public interface for a class. Other classes include the header file and know what that class has to offer.

There are lots of times, however, where you want to set up internal properties or methods that are implementation specific and you don't want other people to call. You still want to use the nice property notation, etc., you just don't want people all up in your class's business. To do that, we can declare a private interface by putting an `@interface` section in your implementation file. Since the only code that sees that file is the actual class implementation, that's the only code that knows that interface even exists.

Q: So no other code could call my private methods?

A: Well, sorta. Since private methods aren't declared in the header file, no other code should know they're there. Objective-C allows for runtime invocation of methods through message passing and won't prevent other code from inspecting your class at runtime and sending it a message it thinks your class might respond to. Their compiler will yell at them (with a warning) and puppies will shiver, but they technically could still do it.

Q: OH! So is that what Apple talks about with "don't use private APIs"?

A: YES! Exactly. Pull some private method invocation madness on a CocoaTouch class and you'll be rejected from the App Store post haste!

On to wiring this up to the view!

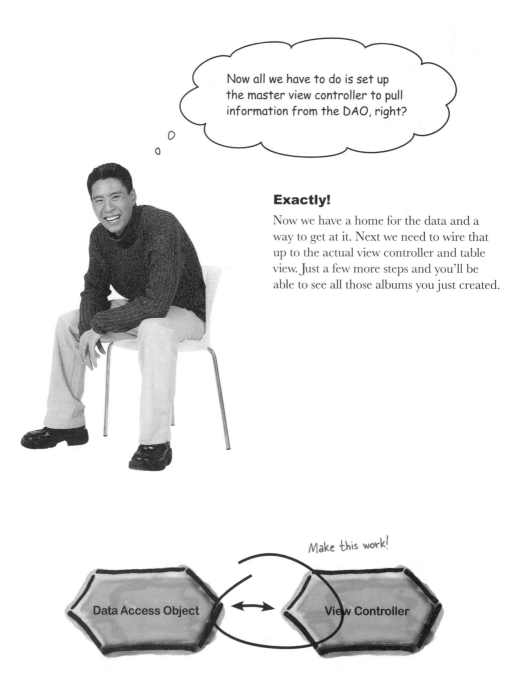

Now all we have to do is set up the master view controller to pull information from the DAO, right?

Exactly!

Now we have a home for the data and a way to get at it. Next we need to wire that up to the actual view controller and table view. Just a few more steps and you'll be able to see all those albums you just created.

Make this work!

Data Access Object ↔ View Controller

Exercise

Let's get the `MasterViewController` working with the `AlbumDataController` class. The template code obviously isn't set up to use it, so some edits are needed...

1 **Remove some of the template code in MasterViewController.m.**

We're building this out past the template now, and so need to make some modifications. Remove the `NSMuteableArray` declared in the private `@interface`, the button creation from `viewDidLoad`, the `insertNewObject` method, and `commitEditingStyle`. Finally, change `canEditRowAtIndexPath` to return NO instead of YES.

2 **Add the code to work with the `AlbumDataController` in MasterViewController.m.**

Add the imports for the `AlbumDataController` and `Album` classes at the top of the file, declare a property to hold our `AlbumDataController`, and initialize the `AlbumDataController` property in `awakeFromNib`.

Exercise Solution

Let's get the MasterViewController working with the AlbumDataController class. Let's see the changes that we needed to make to the template code to get this all working.

1 **Remove some of the template code in MasterViewController.m.**
We're building this out past the template now, and so need to make some modifications. Remove the NSMuteableArray declared in the private @interface, the button creation from viewDidLoad, the insertNewObject method, and commitEditingStyle. Finally, change canEditRowAtIndexPath to return NO instead of YES.

```
- (void)viewDidLoad
{
  [super viewDidLoad];
  self.navigationItem.leftBarButtonItem = self.editButtonItem;
  UIBarButtonItem *addButton = [[UIBarButtonItem alloc] initWithBarButtonSystem
  Item:UIBarButtonSystemItemAdd target:self action:@selector(insertNewObject:)];
  self.navigationItem.rightBarButtonItem = addButton;
}


- (void)didReceiveMemoryWarning
{
  [super didReceiveMemoryWarning];
}
- (void)insertNewObject:(id)sender
{
  if (!_objects) {
    _objects = [[NSMutableArray alloc] init];
  }
  [_objects insertObject:[NSDate date] atIndex:0];
  NSIndexPath *indexPath = [NSIndexPath indexPathForRow:0 inSection:0];
  [self.tableView insertRowsAtIndexPaths:@[indexPath] withRowAnimation:UITableV
  iewRowAnimationAutomatic];
}
```

MasterViewController.m

```
- (BOOL)tableView:(UITableView *)tableView canEditRowAtIndexPath:(NSIndexPath
*)indexPath
{
  return NO;
}

- (void)tableView:(UITableView *)tableView commitEditingStyle:(UITableViewCellE
ditingStyle)editingStyle forRowAtIndexPath:(NSIndexPath *)indexPath
{
  if (editingStyle == UITableViewCellEditingStyleDelete) {
    [_objects removeObjectAtIndex:indexPath.row];
    [tableView deleteRowsAtIndexPaths:@[indexPath] withRowAnimation:UITableViewR
owAnimationFade];
  } else if (editingStyle == UITableViewCellEditingStyleInsert) {

  }
}
```

MasterViewController.m

② **Add the code to work with the `AlbumDataController` in `MasterViewController.m`.**
Add the imports for the `AlbumDataController` and Album classes at the top of the file, declare
a property to hold our `AlbumDataController` and initialize the `AlbumDataController`
property in `awakeFromNib`.

```
#import "MasterViewController.h"
#import "DetailViewController.h"
#import "AlbumDataController.h"
#import "Album.h"


@interface MasterViewController ()
  @property (nonatomic, strong) AlbumDataController
*albumDataController;
@end
```

The reference to our AlbumDataController is a
strong property, which means it won't be wiped out
even if the view is unloaded.

MasterViewController.m

Exercise Solution

```
@implementation MasterViewController

- (void)awakeFromNib
{
    [super awakeFromNib];
    self.albumDataController = [[AlbumDataController alloc] init];
}
```

This is where you can do one time initialization when the view is first created. Note that it won't be visible on the screen yet.

MasterViewController.m

Go!!

SLOW

You're ready to get back in it!

Now the data and the logic to handle the data are in place. Get back in and let's make those table views work.

A table is a collection of cells

Now that we know how to get to the albums, we need to get them visible on the screen. To do that, we'll use our table view. Right now we only have a handful of albums set up, but if we were to put the whole inventory of the store in there we'd have hundreds or maybe thousands of albums to deal with. Rather than loading all of the albums and trying to jam them into the table at once, table views optimize memory usage by taking advantage of the fact that a user can't tell if a cell that would be off the screen has any data in it or not.

UITableViews only have to display enough data to fill an iPhone screen or the view in an iPad—it doesn't really matter how much data you might have in total. The UITableView does this super efficiently by reusing cells that scrolled off the screen.

When the table view has to scroll a new row onto the screen, it asks the datasource for a cell for that row.

The cells that are off the view go into a bucket until iOS needs memory or the table view can reuse them when the user scrolls.

As the user scrolls, some cells slide off the screen.

This is the active view with the table cells that are currently visible.

The datasource checks the cell bucket to see if there are any cells available to reuse. If so, it just replaces the row's contents and returns the row.

If there aren't any for reuse, the datasource creates a new one and sets its content.

The table view takes the new cell and scrolls it in.

OK, but how do we get the table view to actually show that data?

Table Cell Code Up Close

The table view methods are all inside the `MasterViewController` (which makes sense, since the master view is responsible for the table view). The template code comes with the required methods for the table views plus some optional code to rearrange cells, but that's commented out. This is a read-only application, so we won't need that code anyway.

```objc
#pragma mark - Table View


- (NSInteger)numberOfSectionsInTableView:(UITableView *)tableView
{
    return 1;
}


- (NSInteger)tableView:(UITableView *)tableView numberOfRowsInSection:(NSInteger)section
{
    return [self.albumDataController albumCount];
}


- (UITableViewCell *)tableView:(UITableView *)tableView cellForRowAtIndexPath:(NSIndexPath *)indexPath

{
    UITableViewCell *cell = [tableView dequeueReusableCellWithIdentifier: @"AlbumCell"
    forIndexPath:indexPath];

    Album *album = [self.albumDataController albumAtIndex:indexPath.row];
    NSDate *object = _objects[indexPath.row];
    cell.textLabel.text = album.title;
    return cell;
}
```

These methods tell the table view how many sections we have and how many rows are in each section.

Update the table view to get the number of rows from the albumDataController.

The indexPath contains a representation of the section and row number for the needed cell.

Here we're customizing the text in the cell with the information for the specific album we need to show.

MasterViewController.m

That AlbumCell identifier is what ties the cell to the code, and it needs a specific name. So it has to be changed here and in the storyboard.

This is the second part of naming
the table cells...

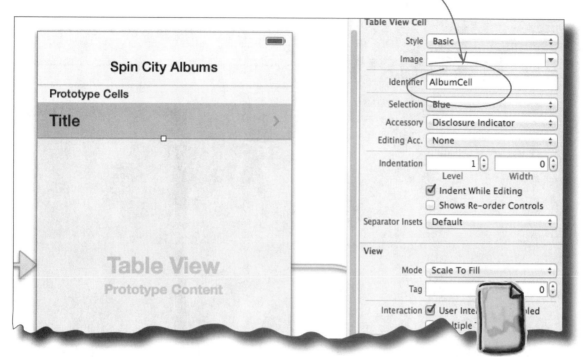

MainStoryboard.storyboard

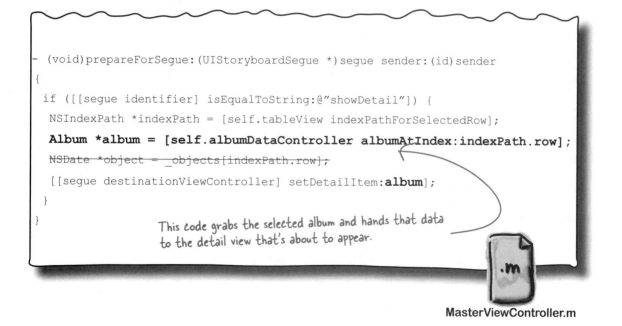

```
- (void)prepareForSegue:(UIStoryboardSegue *)segue sender:(id)sender
{
  if ([[segue identifier] isEqualToString:@"showDetail"]) {
    NSIndexPath *indexPath = [self.tableView indexPathForSelectedRow];
    Album *album = [self.albumDataController albumAtIndex:indexPath.row];
    NSDate *object = _objects[indexPath.row];
    [[segue destinationViewController] setDetailItem:album];
  }
}
```

This code grabs the selected album and hands that data
to the detail view that's about to appear.

MasterViewController.m

Test Drive

After tying the table view to the data, you should be able to fire up the app and see the albums you put in the DAO in the table view. Feel free to add more albums in the DAO too if you want!

Try it out—the list will scroll, too!

Carrier 🗢	3:56 PM	▬▬
	SpinCity Albums	
Infected Splinter		›
Hairy Eyeball		›
Squish		›
Acid Fog		›

there are no Dumb Questions

Q: **What were all those methods we removed from the MasterViewController for?**

A: The MasterViewController inherits from UITableViewController, which is a built-in class that works with table views. The tableview is set up to use our view controller as its datasource and delegate, meaning the table view will call methods on the view controller whenever things happen.

Out of the box, the template view controller has support for putting a + button in the app to add new items and for letting the user delete and rearrange items in the list. Our

app doesn't support that, so we removed those template methods. You can check out what delegate methods are available by looking at the UITableViewDelegate protocol in the iOS documentation.

Q: **What the heck is going on with that segue thing?**

A: Remember in the storyboard where we have the two scenes connected together with a push segue transition? The template code is set up so that when someone taps on a row, the app fires off that segue. The segue handles getting the next view ready, then calls back into the view controller to let it know things are about to transition (that's the prepareforSegue call we

filled in). In prepareForSegue, we can do just that, get ready for the next view to show up. Sometimes you want to close network connections or whatever you need to do to clean up for the view that's about to disappear. Other times, like in our case, we need to tell the new view that's about to appear what's going on. We simply grab the new view from the segue and tell it which album the user tapped on. The new view exposes that setDetailItem method (via a property). If you had other things on a view that's about to come in, you can use those here too. Notice that we check which segue is doing the transition in this method because it's possible that there might be multiple segues coming out of a view, all leading to different places.

Squish >

It looks like it'll work, but that's really not enough info for me in the table view...can we get more info in the cell?

Sure!

After talking it over with Rob, we figured out he needs a summary included in the table view cell, too. Like this:

Stuff I want on the first screen:

Album name
Summary

Price

Sharpen your pencil

Layout the new cell using the information that Rob wants shown in each table view cell on the main view of the app.

There aren't any wrong answers here...

Keep in mind that you can use more than one column...

Sharpen your pencil Solution

Here's how we laid out the cell to get some more information in there. This is a spot where pulling in a designer can help a lot. You want to balance showing enough information to be useful but not so much that the table becomes unusable.

We're going to make the album title the most prominent thing on the cell, and then the summary underneath..

Album Title

Price >

Summary

We need a disclosure indicator here to keep those folks at Apple happy...

Storyboards can layout custom table view cells too

So far we've used the default table view cell layout in our app. It works fine, but we want more. Tableview cells actually come with a couple different layout styles using properties like `detailTextLabel` and `imageView`. If those work for your application, then by all means you should use those. We're going to show how to build a custom cell, though, since it's not much more difficult and gives you the flexibility to do whatever you want with cells.

Since we're not going to be using a default table cell, we need to create a new class that inherits from the basic `UITableViewCell` and adds the custom properties we want to show.

Start here and try out the different cell types. None of the defaults work for us.

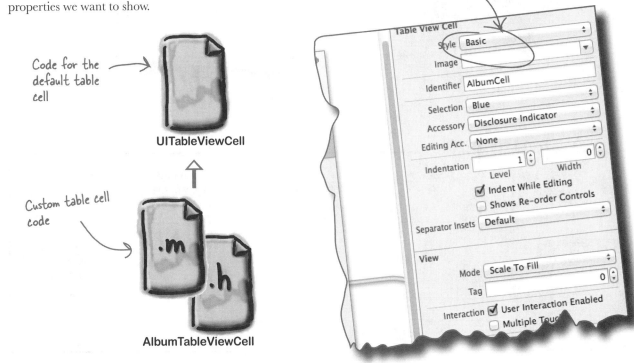

Code for the default table cell

UITableViewCell

Custom table cell code

AlbumTableViewCell

CUSTOM TABLE CELL CONSTRUCTION

To get into making the new table cells, we need to create a new class which subclasses the
basic **UITableViewCell**.

1 Create a new class that is an Objective-C class titled
AlbumTableViewCell that is a subclass of UITableViewCell
and make sure it's in the Spin City group and that the Spin City target
is checked.

2 Next you need to modify the storyboard to use your custom table view
cell instead of the basic one. Go back into *Main.storyboard* and click on
the default empty table view cell in the table view scene.

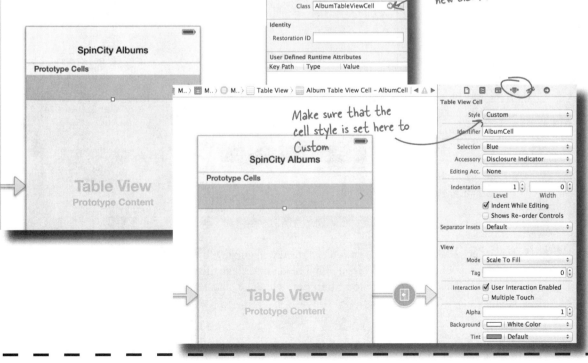

Select the empty cell and then change the class for the table view cell here to your new class, AlbumTableViewCell.

Make sure that the cell style is set here to Custom

CUSTOM TABLE CELL CONSTRUCTION (CONT.)

Now to layout the actual cell we need to work inside of the storyboard and drag elements into the cell just like we do for elements of a view.

3 Drag a label over to be the albumTitle. Align it to the top half of the cell, left guideline. Drag the width out to about half the cell. Change the default text to be albumTitle.

4 Grab a second label to be the albumSummary. Put it in the bottom half of the cell, left guideline drag it out to 3/4 of the cell. In the Attributes inspector, change the font size to 12, color to Light Gray Color. Change the default text to be albumSummary.

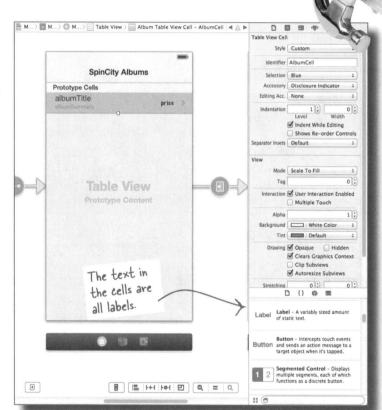

The text in the cells are all labels.

5 For the price label, put it in the middle vertically, aligned with the right guideline. Change the font to custom, Marker Felt Thin, 14pt. Make the text right aligned. Stretch the label left to bump up against the right edge of the summary label. Change the default text to be price.

Test Drive

Now that the cells are all laid out, all that's left is to wire the labels up with their outlets and actions. Do that and you're ready to see the new cells!

1 **Open up the assistant editor and show the AlbumTableViewCell.h.**
You should have the storyboard next to the assistant editor. Control-drag from the albumTitle label to in between @interface and @end in the AlbumTableViewCell.h. Make sure the pop up is for an Outlet. Set the name to be albumTitleLabel, type UILabel, and weak storage.

2 **Repeat the process for the albumSummaryLabel and priceLabel.**
When you're finished, there should be three filled in circles in the gutter next to the *AlbumTableViewCell.h* file.

3 **Go into MasterViewController.m.**
Add an import for the new *AlbumTableViewCell.h* file and then update cellforRowAtIndexPath to use the new custom cell type.

```
- (UITableViewCell *)tableView:(UITableView *)tableView cellForRowAtIndexPath:(NSIndexPath *)
indexPath
{
AlbumTableViewCell *cell = [tableView dequeueReusableCellWithIdentifier:@"AlbumCell"
forIndexPath:indexPath];
  Album *album = [self.albumDataController albumAtIndex: indexPath.row];
  cell.albumTitleLabel.text = album.title;
  cell.albumSummaryLabel.text = album.summary;
  cell.priceLabel.text = [NSString stringWithFormat:@"$%01.2f", album.price];
  return cell;
}
```

4 **Run it....**

TEST DRIVE

It works!

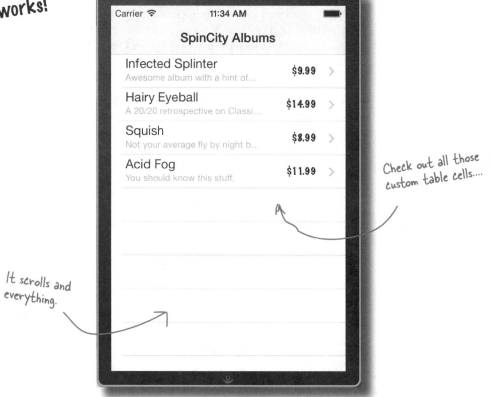

Check out all those custom table cells....

It scrolls and everything.

I like it, but when you tap a row there aren't any details!

We know...

Now that the app is working and all is well, it's time to dive into the details in the next chapter...

 # Table View Cross

Exercise the right half of your brain and make sure
you know your terms.

Across

1. _____ cells allow you to do your own layout.
2. You use a _____ method for use in just one class.
3. Use _____-drag to create code graphically.
5. _____ files are used to lay out and transition between
   views.
7. Table views with details are great for _____ data.
8. The DAO is the data _____ object.
9. MVC stands for _____-view-controller.

Down

1. A table is a collection of _____.
4. The _____ bar holds the buttons for navigating through
   views.
6. Data works best when it's in its own _____.
7. Apple uses the _____ to dictate interaction patterns.

Your View toolbox

You've got Chapter 3 under your belt and now you've added table views to your toolbox.

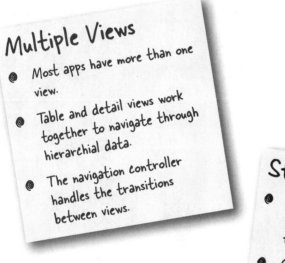

Multiple Views

- Most apps have more than one view.

- Table and detail views work together to navigate through hierarchial data.

- The navigation controller handles the transitions between views.

Storyboards

- Used to edit all the views for your application and the transitions between them.

- Custom table view cells can be editied here.

BULLET POINTS

- iOS applications work using touch—and they were the first to do so.

- MVC is the primary design pattern for iOS applications.

- Data Access Objects are used to hide low-level data access.

- Tableview cells are allocated based on which rows are visible and reused whenever possible.

 # Table View Cross Solution

Exercise the right half of your brain and make sure
you know your terms.

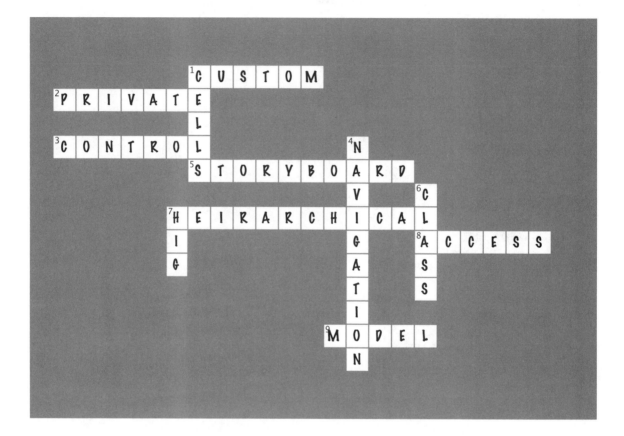

Across

1. _____ cells allow you to do your own layout. [CUSTOM]
2. You use a _____ method for use in just one class.
   [PRIVATE]
3. Use _____-drag to create code graphically. [CONTROL]
5. _____ files are used to lay out and transition between
   views. [STORYBOARD]
7. Table views with details are great for _____ data.
   [HEIRARCHICAL]
8. The DAO is the data _____ object. [ACCESS]
9. MVC stands for _____-view-controller. [MODEL]

Down

1. A table is a collection of _____. [CELLS]
4. The _____ bar holds the buttons for navigating through
   views. [NAVIGATION]
6. Data works best when it's in its own _____. [CLASS]
7. Apple uses the _____ to dictate interaction patterns. [HIG]

4 multiview applications

It's all about the details

It's important to pay attention to the details, like where the trees are...

Most iOS apps have more than one view.

We've gotten this app off to a quick start using built-in templates and doing some really nice updates to the table view. Now it's time to dive into the details, setting up the new view and working with the navigation between them. Because most of the widely used apps up on the store are giving you a good and easy way to work through a lot of data. Spin City is doing just that—giving users an easier way to get through the records than flipping through boxes!

An app with a view...

Spin City's app is up and running with a nice table view and the data in the app. Now that we have the overview of the data, it's time to get into some details. This is the detail view that we came up with earlier.

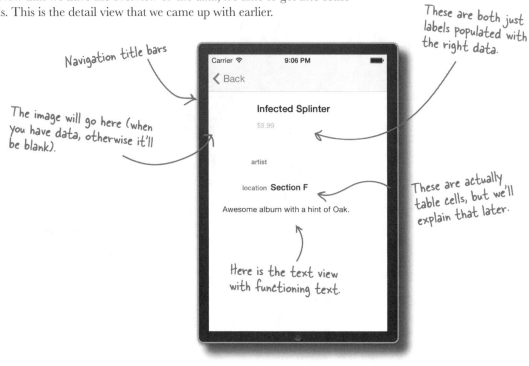

Navigation title bars

The image will go here (when you have data, otherwise it'll be blank).

These are both just labels populated with the right data.

These are actually table cells, but we'll explain that later.

Here is the text view with functioning text.

Detail views are everywhere

Lots of applications use detail views and anybody who's used them has a rough idea of what they're about. It's zooming in on data, which means for the most part it's the bottom of the hierarchical view stack and gives information down to the finest grain detail the app can provide.

They are also used to shift the user into a different mode of the application (think going into your wall in the Facebook app and leaving your news feed). Because applications have become more complicated, there can be extra types of interaction with an application and they are frequently accessed through completely different detail views.

Our application has a lot of information about the album in the table view, and that's good, but we need to be able to display more details so that the customers can learn as much as they want about Rob's fantastic artists.

> That's mostly a bunch of labels and text, right? How do we lay it out so that it looks good? What if the name for the album is really long?

Always look for built-in views whenever possible.

You can lay things out by hand and that'll work, but there's a better way, especially for so much text-based information.

Table views can be customized to make the layout a bit prettier, but you get to keep all the advantages of the table view. Since you're such a pro from working in the last chapter, setting that up shouldn't be too hard.

BRAIN POWER

Check out some apps on your iPhone or iPad. Can you tell which ones use table views for their details and which ones don't?

Table views don't always look like...tables

You've seen one table view already for our master view. If you think about it, as long as you can't select anything, tables are just a great way to lay things out and keep them neat—like using a table in a text document or using a spreadsheet.

If you work with the Apple Mail app or Contacts, when you dive into the detail views they don't really look like tables, but they are....

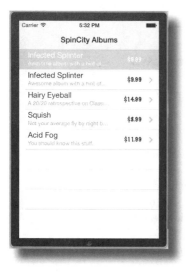

But tables don't have to look like this!

there are no Dumb Questions

Q: What do we gain by using a table view instead of laying out a detail view?

A: Easy layout and all those nice, built-in tools. The table view already comes with scrolling and the navigation is built right in; you can also hook in new views to the app later on without much trouble.

Q: How often do applications do this? What does Apple think?

A: All the time! We gave you some examples already, but just go using your apps and you'll see they're probably more common in productivity and business applications than custom views. Apple uses them in their own apps all the time...

Jim

Frank

Joe

Joe: OK, so we need to create a detail view. Where do we even start?

Frank: I think we should go back into the storyboard, right?

Jim: But then what? This thing needs to be a tableview now. The one that the template came with is just a plain `DetailViewController`.

Joe: We'll need to change that just like we did for the table cells, right? You think we can just use the UIKit table view controller?

Frank: The default table view was what we just changed to get the master view looking the way we wanted. It's going to be another new custom class.

Jim: Oh right, but we'll subclass the default table view controller and then we can use all of the built-in support plus tweak the layout, right?

Frank: Exactly. And we can build a custom storyboard to handle the actual layout.

Joe: What about actually displaying the data?

Jim: I have some ideas on how to make that work, when we get there.

Joe: If you say so. Into the storyboard file then...

Change your UIViewController to a UITableView Controller

Since the master detail template came with just a basic detail view, we need to change the class for that view to get all the table view goodness for free. Just like we did for the table cells, we need to use the attributes inspector.

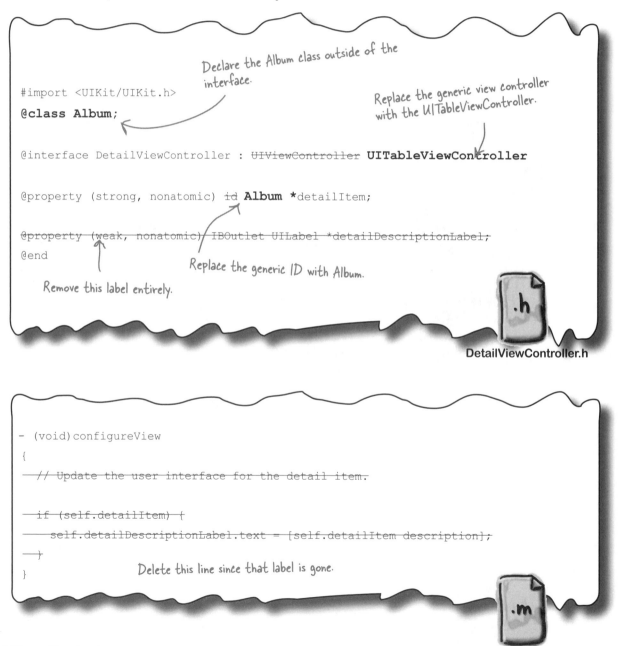

Declare the Album class outside of the interface.

```
#import <UIKit/UIKit.h>
@class Album;

@interface DetailViewController : UIViewController UITableViewController

@property (strong, nonatomic) id Album *detailItem;

@property (weak, nonatomic) IBOutlet UILabel *detailDescriptionLabel;
@end
```

Replace the generic view controller with the UITableViewController.

Replace the generic ID with Album.

Remove this label entirely.

DetailViewController.h

```
- (void)configureView
{
    // Update the user interface for the detail item.

    if (self.detailItem) {
        self.detailDescriptionLabel.text = [self.detailItem description];
    }
}
```

Delete this line since that label is gone.

DetailViewController.m

Match each controller to what it does.

Controller

What the controller does

UIViewController

Presents the navigation stack for transitioning between views; embeds the navigation bar in the top of the view as well.

UINavitgationController

This controller is good for apps with multiple paths that have equal importance so that the user can jump between views.

UITableViewController

This controller comes with the basic tools you need for a view.

UITabbarController

Gives you the system interface to edit video directly on the device.

UIPageViewController

This view embeds the table view in the view you're using. It can be used for a detail view or a more traditional table view.

UIVideoEditorController

You can use this controller just to handle passing between view controllers with the required transition.

Answers on page 162.

Layout for the new detail view

Based on our existing sketch and now that the app knows it's talking to a
`UITableViewController` and not a `UIViewController`, we can get the
view elements set up in the storyboard.

☐ The detail view needs to get changed into a
table view on the storyboard.

☐ We'll need to properly transition between the
new detail view and the table view.

☐ Then the view needs to get laid out the way we
designed it.

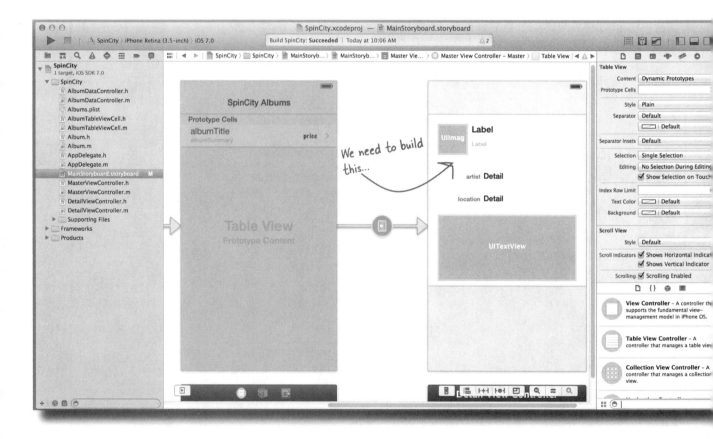

Layout your view within the storyboard

Because this process is a little involved, we're going to need to detail it out carefully. We're breaking away from the template here, so we need to get into some details about both the view and how we get to it. First off, to complete the work that we did in code earlier.

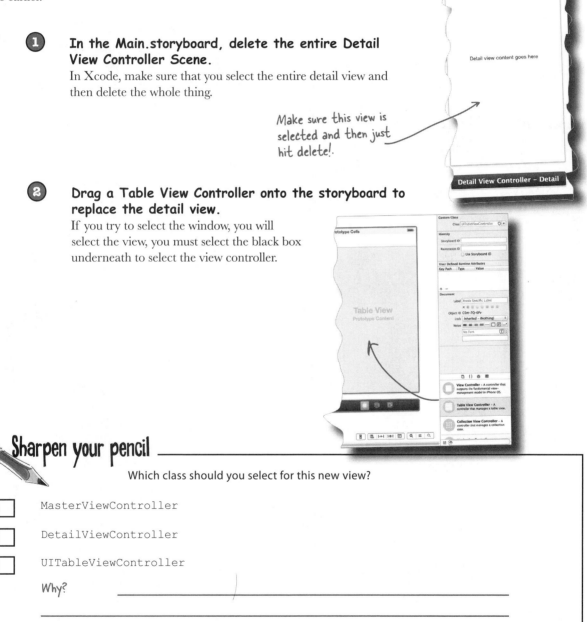

1 **In the Main.storyboard, delete the entire Detail View Controller Scene.**

In Xcode, make sure that you select the entire detail view and then delete the whole thing.

Make sure this view is selected and then just hit delete!

2 **Drag a Table View Controller onto the storyboard to replace the detail view.**

If you try to select the window, you will select the view, you must select the black box underneath to select the view controller.

Detail view content goes here

Detail View Controller – Detail

Table View
Prototype Content

Sharpen your pencil

Which class should you select for this new view?

☐ MasterViewController

☐ DetailViewController

☐ UITableViewController

Why? _____

_____

Sharpen your pencil

Which class should you select for this new view?

☐   `MasterViewController`

☑   `DetailViewController`

☐   `UITableViewController`

Why?   <u>You're selecting a detail view here that is both a detail view and a table view.</u>
<u>The class level needs to be a detail view first, table view second.</u>

Design the rest of the view dynamically

Now we need to layout the new table view. Unlike the last table view we used, where we didn't know how many rows we needed, in this one we know exactly what we want to show and are using the table view to help us with layout. In this case, we want to use a static table instead of a dynamic one.

Dynamic is the default for table views, and it's used when the table view layout changes based on the data. Since we have the same information coming in and want the view to be laid out consistently, it's static.

After selecting the table view, change the content to be "static cells."

It's in the inspector under Separator Insets.

Geek Bits

We're going to change the separator type here too. That's the biggie for faking the table view to look like a detail view. Normally there is a single line separating the cells, but once you remove that, the user won't be able to see any difference.

Select the top table view cells; either drag or use the inspector so that it's 100 pt high.

Drag an ImageView into the left side of the table cell and use the guidelines to make it 60pts wide and 60 pts high along the left edge.

g a label into the cell use the guidelines ut it near the right e of the Image view stretch the right e of the label to right edge of the l. Align the cell with e top guideline. In the tributes Inspector, ange the font to be ystem Bold.

Drag another label into the cell and use the guidelines to put it near the right edge of the image view, right below the label we just added, and stretch the label to the right guideline of the table view. Change thev font color to the Light Gray Color. Change the font to System 12.0.

ct the second and d table cells. In the ributes Inspector ge the style to t Detail.

Make sure the Cell type is custom. Drag the cell to be 150 pts high.

Double click on the 'Title' label and change it to 'artist' and 'location'

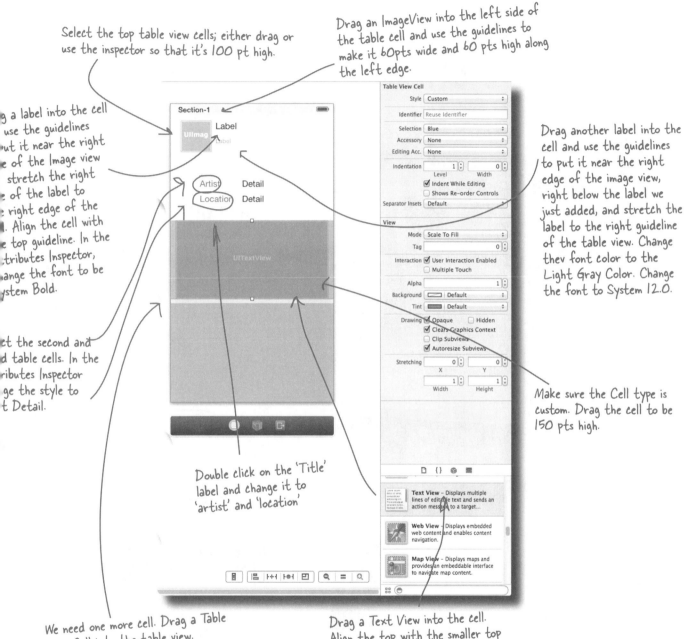

We need one more cell. Drag a Table View Cell into the table view.

Drag a Text View into the cell. Align the top with the smaller top guideline in the cell. Align the bottom, left and right with the normal cell guidelines.

Let's run it!

Test Drive

Nothing!

Are you kidding? All that work and we can't even get to it? Is it because the data isn't hooked up?

You have to segue from your master view to your detail view.

When we deleted the view, we also deleted the transition into the view as well. The storyboard can support more than just editing the views, it also supports adding a transition to that view.

Segues connect view controllers

These appear as scenes in your storyboard.

A **segue** is how the transition between views is represented on the storyboard. They are relatively new (they appeared in iOS 6), and give a lot of options for configuring these transitions. We have talked about the transition between views, but in the storyboard editor there is also a concept called a **scene**. On iPhone, a scene is always a view, but for iPad you can have multiple scenes (think about views where you have a fixed pane and one that changes, like mail). A segue serves as the way to get from scene to scene, not view to view.

There are a number of standard segues (which we'll use for Spin City), but you can also write custom segues. iOS creates segues for you when one is triggered by your app. First, the destination scene is created, then the segue object gets created; the source view calls `prepareForSegue:sender:`. Finally, the segue's `perform` method is called and the transition is complete.

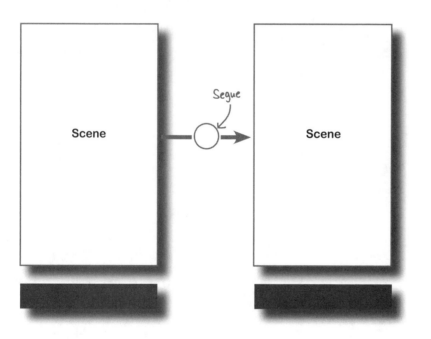

Segue

Scene

Scene

Segues transition from scene to scene, not necessarily view to view.

Now let's make it work...

Connect your scenes in your storyboard

Back in Spin City, we have two scenes that aren't connected, so we can't get to that newly laid-out detail view. We're going to work in the storyboard editor so that we can add the new transition.

Right-click on the Table View cell to bring up the segues and outlets and then control drag to the second view.

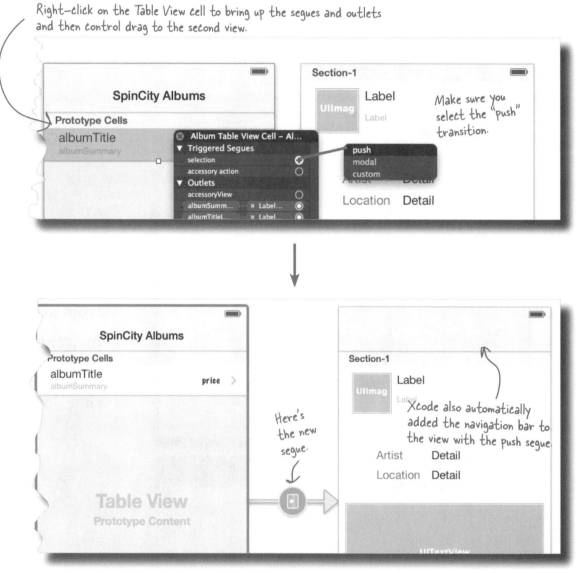

Make sure you select the "push" transition.

Here's the new segue.

Xcode also automatically added the navigation bar to the view with the push segue.

Select the segue and change the identifier to ShowAlbumDetails.

Q: Why are scenes important? It seems like one more thing...

A: Because that's the level of granularity you have with control for the transitions. If you want to dictate how things move between one view and the next, you can do that! Transitioning between views is such a core part of most applications that support

for it is built into the framework.

Q: What do segues get us besides linking scenes?

A: The segue pattern wraps up and eliminates a bunch of boilerplate code in applications. Segues give you a clean way to pass data to an incoming view, they provide hooks for cleaning up before a vew is about to leave, and provide a nice clean place to

configure how views should transition in and out visually.

Q: Why did including the segue add the navigation control bar at the top of the detail view?

A: We picked a push transition, which will be realized through a Navigation Controller. Xcode will set up the space needed for the Navigation Bar for us.

TEST DRIVE

Run it!

It works, but...

OK, that's cool,
but where's the
album info?

We just need to populate it like we did before!

The detail view is there, but we haven't added the actions and outlets and attached the fields to the data. Just like we did for Marco Pollo in his app, we need to get the data into the view.

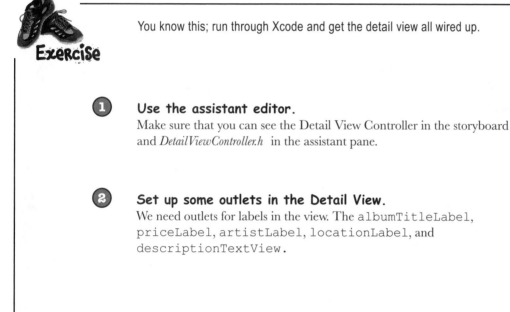

You know this; run through Xcode and get the detail view all wired up.

Exercise

① **Use the assistant editor.**
Make sure that you can see the Detail View Controller in the storyboard and *DetailViewController.h* in the assistant pane.

② **Set up some outlets in the Detail View.**
We need outlets for labels in the view. The albumTitleLabel, priceLabel, artistLabel, locationLabel, and descriptionTextView.

Exercise Solution

Here's how you should've gotten your views set up.

1 **Use the assistant editor.**

Make sure that you can see the Detail View Controller in the storyboard and *DetailViewController.h* in the assistant pane.

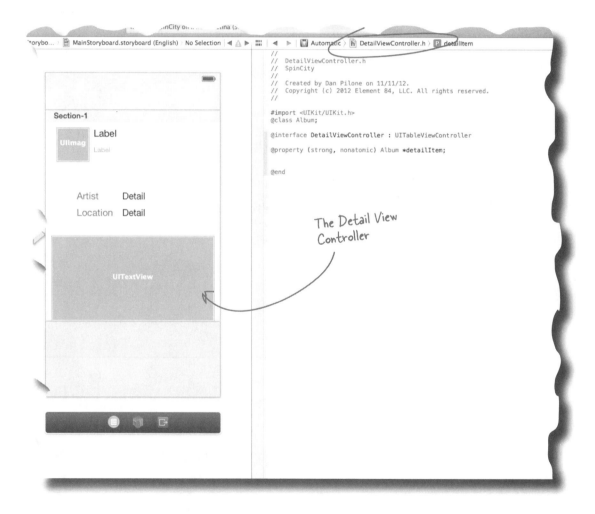

The Detail View Controller

2 **Set up some outlets in the Detail View.**

We need outlets for labels in the view. The `albumTitleLabel`, `priceLabel`, `artistLabel`, `locationLabel`, and `descriptionTextView`.

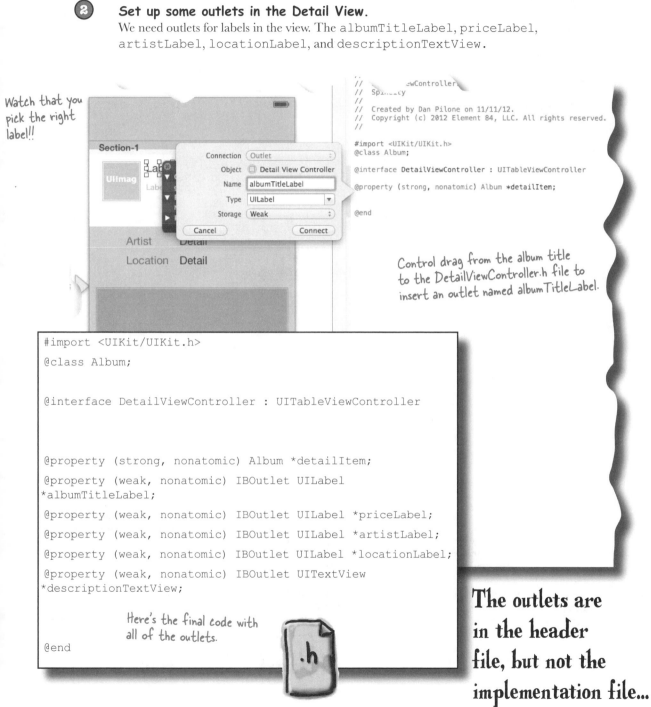

Watch that you pick the right label!!

Control drag from the album title to the DetailViewController.h file to insert an outlet named albumTitleLabel.

```objc
#import <UIKit/UIKit.h>
@class Album;


@interface DetailViewController : UITableViewController



@property (strong, nonatomic) Album *detailItem;
@property (weak, nonatomic) IBOutlet UILabel
*albumTitleLabel;
@property (weak, nonatomic) IBOutlet UILabel *priceLabel;
@property (weak, nonatomic) IBOutlet UILabel *artistLabel;
@property (weak, nonatomic) IBOutlet UILabel *locationLabel;
@property (weak, nonatomic) IBOutlet UITextView
*descriptionTextView;

@end
```

Here's the final code with all of the outlets.

DetailViewController.h

The outlets are in the header file, but not the implementation file...

iOS Magnets

Here's the code to access the properties of an album in the
DetailViewController.m file.

```objc
- (void)configureView
{
    // Update the user interface for the detail item.

    if (self.detailItem) {
        self._____.text = self.detailItem.title;
        self._____.text = [NSString
stringWithFormat:@"$%01.2f", self.detailItem.price];
        self._____.text = self.detailItem.artist;
        self._____.text = self.detailItem.
locationInStore;
        self._____.text = self.detailItem.summary;
    }
}
```

DetailViewController.m

priceLabel

summary

descriptionTextView

albumTitleLabel

self

title

location.Label

NSString

album

artistLabel

there are no
Dumb Questions

Q: **Why did we call the field "summary" on the album but use** `descriptionTextView`**. Why not call the field description on the Album?**

A: "description" is actually a method on NSObject already that is supposed to return a text overview of the NSObject itself. By default it returns the class name at the hex address of the object. You can override that method to return something else, a meaningful overview of the object, but it really isn't the same as an album summary like you might find on the back of a CD. We didn't want to hijack the "description" method so we named it summary.

BRAIN
BARBELL

Why won't this work yet? The view still isn't quite ready to populate. Any thoughts on that? Hint: it's something that we've already talked about in this chapter...

iOS Magnets Solution

Fill in the code necessary to link up the data with the detail view.

```objc
#import "Album.h"
```

```objc
- (void)configureView
{
    // Update the user interface for the detail item.

    if (self.detailItem) {
        self.albumTitleLabel.text = self.detailItem.title;
        self.priceLabel.text = [NSString
stringWithFormat:@"$%01.2f", self.detailItem.price];
        self.artistLabel.text = self.detailItem.artist;
        self.locationLabel.text = self.detailItem.locationInStore;
        self.descriptionTextView.text = self.detailItem.summary;
    }
}
```

DetailViewController.m

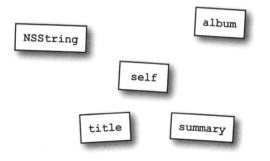

NSString   album   self   title   summary

The missing link is that segue again!

Segues let you prepare for a new scene

Segues contain more than just how to perform the transition between scenes; they also include the data that needs to be passed between scenes. In our case, we need to pass the information that was in the table cell that is selected by the user and pass that information into the detail view. From there, the detail view can make sure it's accessing the right record and displaying the correct data.

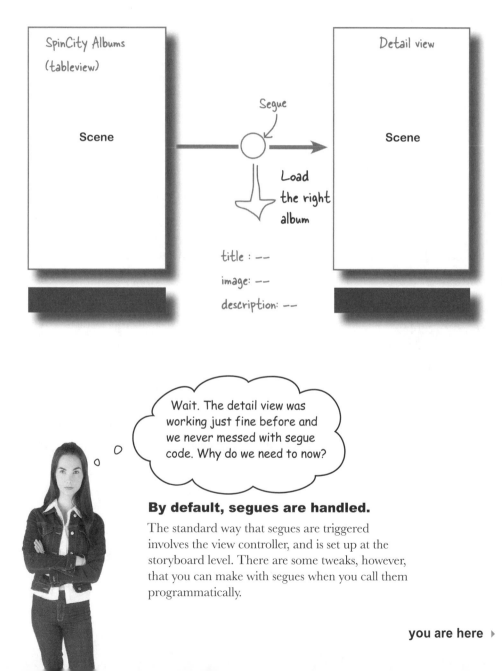

Wait. The detail view was working just fine before and we never messed with segue code. Why do we need to now?

By default, segues are handled.

The standard way that segues are triggered involves the view controller, and is set up at the storyboard level. There are some tweaks, however, that you can make with segues when you call them programmatically.

Update your prepareforSegue callback

prepareforSegue and performSegueWithIdentifier are two methods that iOS uses to let you work programmatically with segues. While the view controller handles it normally, sometimes you have flow within the app that needs to be clarified (more than one transition can get you to a view, for example). If there's some awesome custom transition that you worked up, it can be used instead too.

performSegueWithIdentifier allows you to get to any segue in code by referencing the string identifier that you set up in the storyboard. prepareForSegue is already in our code, by default it will be overridden by the view controller at run time but in our case we want to specify which view controllers are involved and what data we need.

```
- (void)prepareForSegue:(UIStoryboardSegue *)segue sender:(id)
sender
{
  if ([[segue identifier] isEqualToString:@"showAlbumDetails"])
{
    NSIndexPath *indexPath = [self.tableView
indexPathForSelectedRow];
    Album *album = [self.albumDataController
albumAtIndex:indexPath.row];
    [[segue destinationViewController] setDetailItem:album];
  }
}
```

This is the only spot that needs changing.

You can use this method in any segue call to specify which segue gets used when.

MasterViewController.m

Test Drive

At this point, your code should all be compiling and acting nice. Go ahead and run it. When you select a cell in the main view...

I love the scene!

Get it?

Carrier 📶   5:02 PM

‹ Back

Acid Fog

$11.99

artist **Josh and Chuck**

location **Section 9 3/4**

You should know this stuff

BULLET POINTS

- Segues provide a way to control the transitions between scenes.

- By default, segues are handled by editing the storyboard file.

- Segues can be customized and called manually in code.

- On iPhone, a single scene is a single view. On iPad, there can be multiple views in one scene.

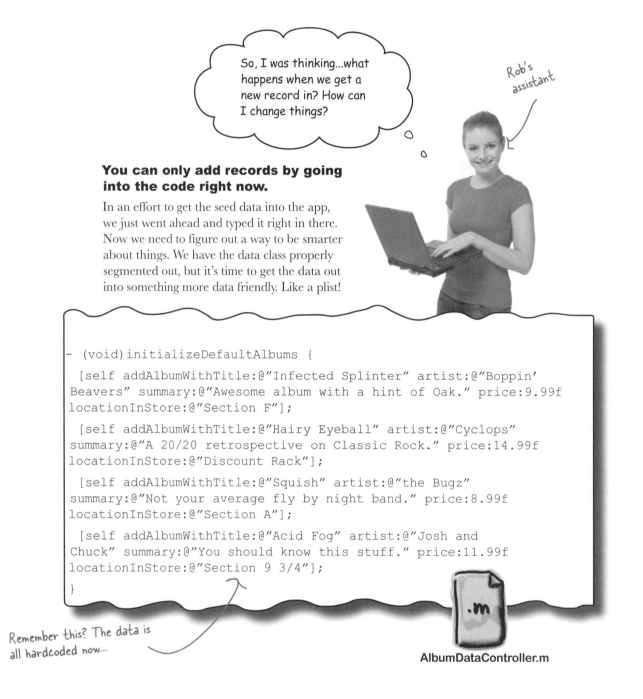

So, I was thinking...what happens when we get a new record in? How can I change things?

Rob's assistant

You can only add records by going into the code right now.

In an effort to get the seed data into the app, we just went ahead and typed it right in there. Now we need to figure out a way to be smarter about things. We have the data class properly segmented out, but it's time to get the data out into something more data friendly. Like a plist!

```objc
- (void)initializeDefaultAlbums {

  [self addAlbumWithTitle:@"Infected Splinter" artist:@"Boppin'
Beavers" summary:@"Awesome album with a hint of Oak." price:9.99f
locationInStore:@"Section F"];

  [self addAlbumWithTitle:@"Hairy Eyeball" artist:@"Cyclops"
summary:@"A 20/20 retrospective on Classic Rock." price:14.99f
locationInStore:@"Discount Rack"];

  [self addAlbumWithTitle:@"Squish" artist:@"the Bugz"
summary:@"Not your average fly by night band." price:8.99f
locationInStore:@"Section A"];

  [self addAlbumWithTitle:@"Acid Fog" artist:@"Josh and
Chuck" summary:@"You should know this stuff." price:11.99f
locationInStore:@"Section 9 3/4"];

}
```

Remember this? The data is all hardcoded now...

AlbumDataController.m

There's ~~an app~~ a list for that

Plist stands for "property list" and has been around for quite a while with OS X. In fact, there are a number of plists already in use in your application. We've already worked with the most important plist, the *Info.plist* for our app. This is created by Xcode when you first create your project, and besides the app icons, it stores things like the main storyboard file to load when the application starts, the application version, and more. Xcode can create and edit these plists like any other file. Click on *SpinCity-Info.plist* to take a look at what's inside.

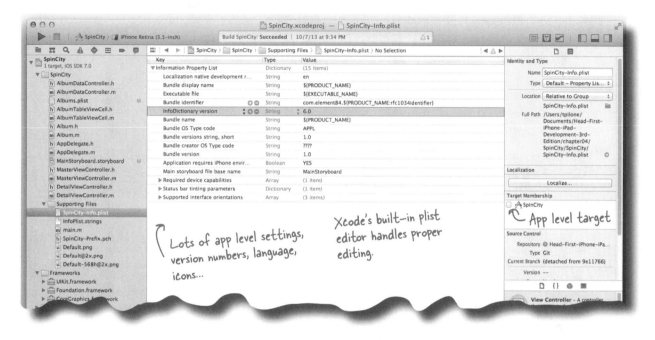

Lots of app level settings, version numbers, language, icons...

Xcode's built-in plist editor handles proper editing.

App level target

there are no Dumb Questions

Q: What does plist stand for?

A: Property list and it's specific to Mac and iOS programming, although it comes from NeXTSTEP and GNUstep frameworks. They can organize data based on Core Foundation types: CFString, CFNumber, CFBoolean, CFDate, CFData, and CFDictionary. From there, the editor can convert them to XML or a binary format.

Q: Are we going to be dealing with XML in our app?

A: No, we're going to use the iOS frameworks to load the plist (and parse it, etc.). Once loaded, we'll just see an array of dictionaries that make it really easy to work with our album data.

Create a new property list

All of the built-in types we've been using, like NSArray and NSString, can be loaded or saved from plists automatically. They do this through the NSCoding protocol. We can take advantage of this and move our album list out of our source code and into a plist.

Create the empty plist.
Go back into Xcode and expand the **Supporting Files** folder. Right-click on **Supporting Files** and select **New file→Mac OS X Resource**, and **Property List**. Call the new list *AlbumArray.plist*.

Plists are used in Mac development as well as iOS development, but they're listed here.

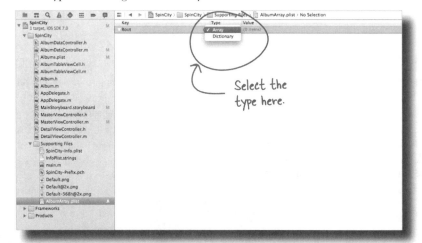

Change the plist to an array.
Go back into Xcode and open up the new *AlbumArray.plist* file. In the editor, select the type and change it to an array.

Select the type here.

Put your data into the plist.

Since we're going to be pulling all the album information from the plist, we need to move the information that is resident in code into the *AlbumArray.plist* file.

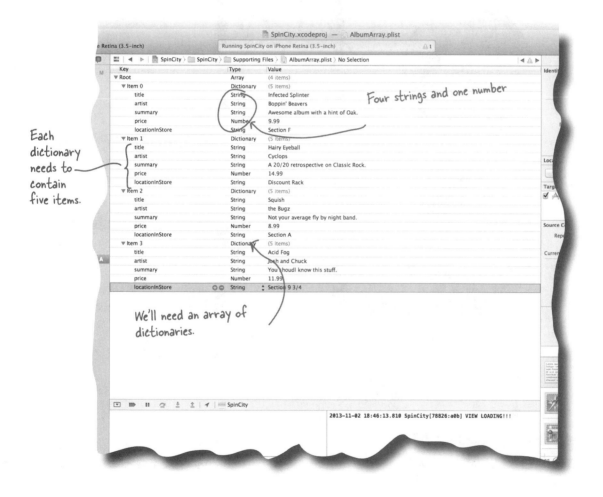

Each dictionary needs to contain five items.

Four strings and one number

We'll need an array of dictionaries.

You need to load each album from the plist

When we implemented all the code in the AlbumDataController we used the initializeDefaultAlbums method to generate an array called _albumList. Now we're going to have it generate an array from the new plist. It's going to be an array of dictionaries...

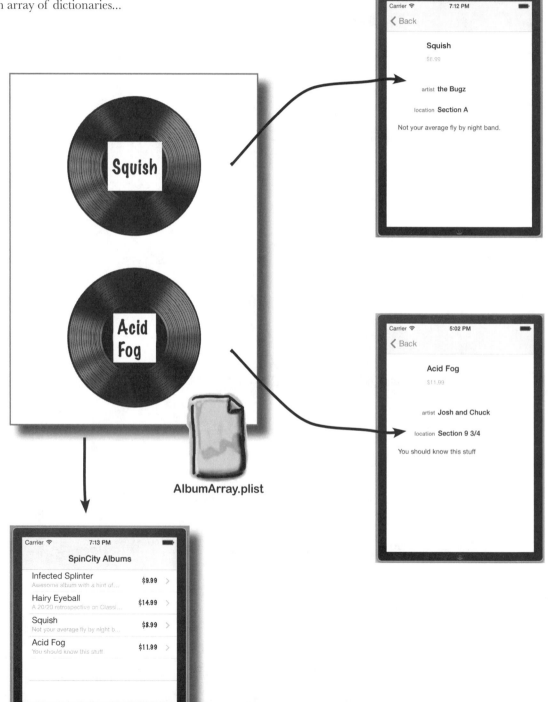

AlbumArray.plist

Convert your data to plists in one easy step

Since everything is set up to go through the `initializeDefaultAlbums` method in
AlbumDetailController.m, we just need to change that method to match the one below.

```
- (void)initializeDefaultAlbums {
        NSString *pathToAlbumsPlist = [[NSBundle mainBundle]
pathForResource:@"AlbumArray" ofType:@"plist"];
        NSArray *defaultAlbumPlist = [NSArray arrayWithContentsOfFile:
pathToAlbumsPlist];
for (NSDictionary *albumInfo in defaultAlbumPlist) {
        [self addAlbumWithTitle:albumInfo[@"title"]
artist:albumInfo[@"artist"] summary:albumInfo[@"summary"]
price:[albumInfo[@"price"] floatValue] locationInStore:albumInfo[@
"locationInStore"]];
        }
}
```

AlbumDataController.m

TEST DRIVE

Go ahead and see if it works...

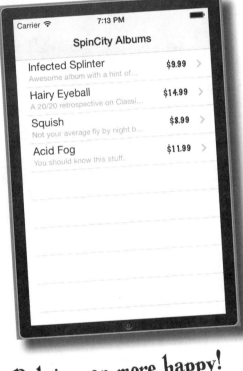

Rob is even more happy!

View Cross

Let's make sure that you have all the lingo under your belt.

Across

2. Signals that the compiler will retain the object.
3. This is sent between objects
5. In Objective-C, a _____ is made up of a .h and a .m file.
8. Automatic methods
10. Arguments can have an _____ and external name.
11. Objective-C tries to match your message to an existing

_____.

Down

1. This incorporates another file
2. You send messages to _____.
4. Unique names for methods after Objective-C translation are

_____.

6. This property creates a setter for the basic types.
7. This tells the compiler to skip mutexes.
9. _____ management is important for iPhone apps.

Sharpen your pencil

Which reasons below are true facts about plists and why you should use them?

☐   It's one of the easier data storage options to use when you're getting started.

☐   Plists can't support more complex types of data, only strings.

☐   It's a database structure.

☐   Plists are an XML format.

View Cross Solution

Let's make sure that you have all the lingo under your belt.

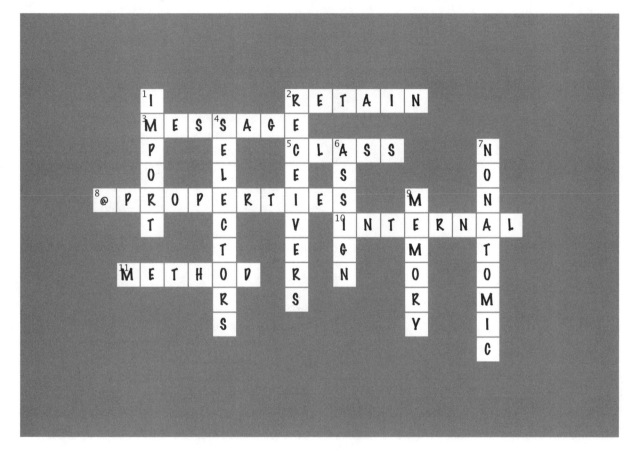

Across

2. Signals that the compiler will retain the object. [RETAIN]
3. This is sent between objects [MESSAGE]
5. In Objective-C, a _____ is made up of a .h and a .m file. [CLASS]
8. Automatic methods [@PROPERTIES]
10. Arguments can have an _____ and external name. [INTERNAL]
11. Objective-C tries to match your message to an existing _____. [METHOD]

Down

1. This incorporates another file [IMPORT]
2. You send messages to _____. [RECEIVERS]
4. Unique names for methods after Objective-C translation are _____. [SELECTORS]
6. This property creates a setter for the basic types. [ASSIGN]
7. This tells the compiler to skip mutexes. [NONATOMIC]
9. _____ management is important for iPhone apps. [MEMORY]

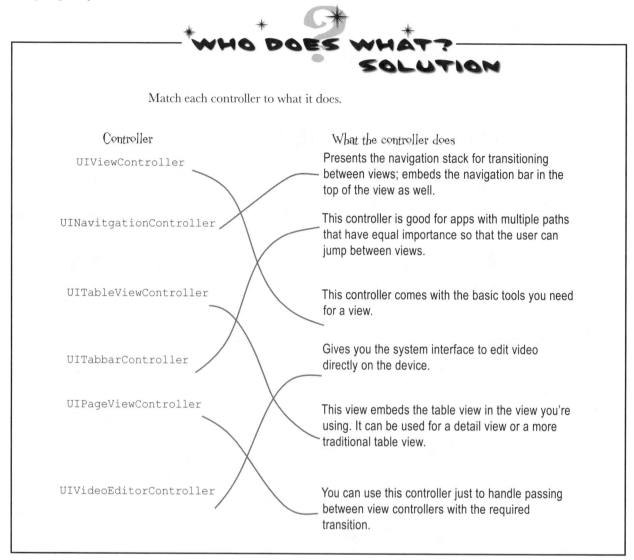

WHO DOES WHAT? SOLUTION

Match each controller to what it does.

Controller	What the controller does

UIViewController — Presents the navigation stack for transitioning between views; embeds the navigation bar in the top of the view as well.

UINavitgationController — This controller is good for apps with multiple paths that have equal importance so that the user can jump between views.

UITableViewController — This controller comes with the basic tools you need for a view.

UITabbarController — Gives you the system interface to edit video directly on the device.

UIPageViewController — This view embeds the table view in the view you're using. It can be used for a detail view or a more traditional table view.

UIVideoEditorController — You can use this controller just to handle passing between view controllers with the required transition.

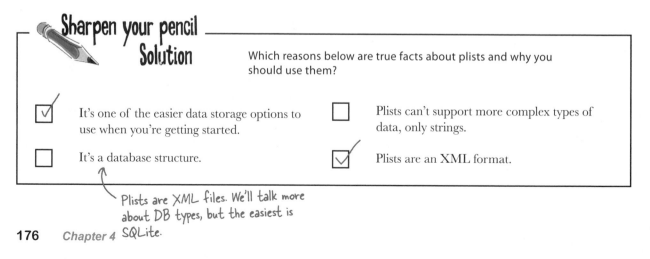

Sharpen your pencil Solution

Which reasons below are true facts about plists and why you should use them?

☑ It's one of the easier data storage options to use when you're getting started.

☐ It's a database structure.

☐ Plists can't support more complex types of data, only strings.

☑ Plists are an XML format.

Plists are XML files. We'll talk more about DB types, but the easiest is SQLite.

Your View toolbox

You've got Chapter 4 under your belt and now you've added mulitview applications to your toolbox.

Segues

@ Transition from scene to scene.

@ iPad apps usually have two scenes per view.

@ Can be customized in code.

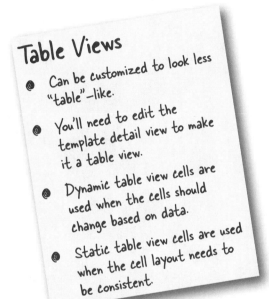

Table Views

@ Can be customized to look less "table"-like.

@ You'll need to edit the template detail view to make it a table view.

@ Dynamic table view cells are used when the cells should change based on data.

@ Static table view cells are used when the cell layout needs to be consistent.

Plists

@ Can easily represent arrays and dictionaries of numbers and strings.

@ Can only store strings and numbers.

BULLET POINTS

- Segues provide a way to control the transitions between scenes.

- By default, segues are handled by editing the storyboard file.

- Segues can be customized and called manually in code.

- On iPhone, a single scene is a single view. On iPad, there can be multiple views in one scene.

5 The review process, design, and devices

How to live with Apple

Momma says if I don't have an Apple a day, I'll be rejected by everyone I know and love. I'll take mine sliced up and skinless!

iOS development comes with some strings.

Everybody has heard the war stories. The Apple review process is famous for being painful and having tons of rules you'll have to follow. Yes, there are some hoops to jump through, but once you know what you're doing, it's not nearly so bad. And besides, once you've gotten your app approved, the massively popular App Store is waiting for you... full of eager device owners with a few bucks to burn. So what's not to love?

Fire up Xcode. Pull a project from Git. Drag around a few controls, write a bit of Objective-C...it all sounds so easy. It really sounds kinda easy...

Yes, writing apps can be simple when you know what you're doing. But there's a little more work involved to actually sell your app in the App Store.

The App Store could just as well be named the Apple store. It *is* Apple's world you're playing in, and they take their ownership of the store (and your device's hardware and software) pretty seriously.

If you spend much time developing iOS apps, you'll start to hear the war stories. Some beautiful app got rejected three or four times by Apple's review process, while the Facebook and Apple Trailers app released four new versions. Or what seems like the smallest detail—a URL in a description or a bad naming choice—got an app shot down.

Yes, you have to get your app approved by Apple for sale. And yes, there are lots of reasons your app might get rejected. But...most rejections are for minor things that can be fairly easily fixed. And if you know what you're doing, you can avoid long hang-ups and costly app rewrites pretty easily.

It's <u>Apple's</u> world...you're just living in it

There's a big difference between developing for iOS and developing for Android (as well as most other platforms): Apple's App Store is a curated, gated community. That means Apple retains **exclusive rights** to approve or deny apps on their store based on certain criteria. It ensures consistency and some degree of quality. Apple censors applications, so violent or vulgar apps just won't get approved.

Love it or hate it, Apple holds the keys. Whether you think that results in a better, more secure device or a Big Brother situation, you've got to live by Apple's rules in the iOS world.

So, you might as well **accept that this process is part of your life** if you want to play in the iOS space. Parts of your schedule are going to be beyond your control and sometimes hard to predict, like when a new version of iOS comes out, and what it'll mean for your app. iOS 7 made some major changes to the designs of applications and suddenly "new UI" got run up to the top of everyone's to-do list. Review times vary from a week to a month, and a rejection usually means you start the review "clock" over on re-submission.

You also are going to have to learn from a few documents that take you beyond writing code specific to your app. You need to get familiar with...

The App Store... if you understand how Apple sells apps, you'll be ahead of the game.

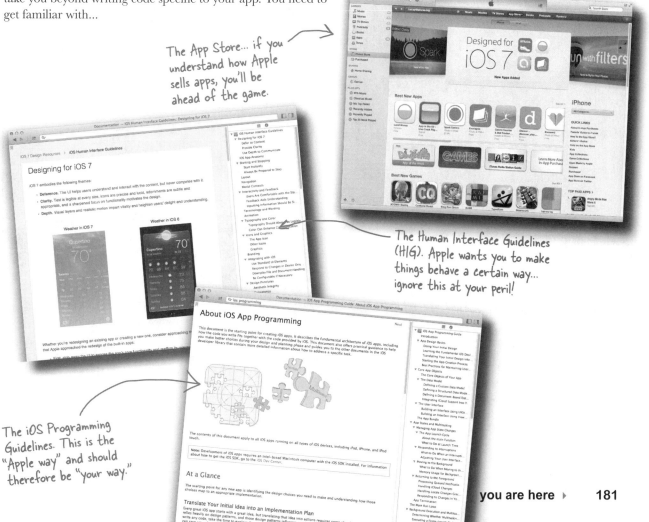

The Human Interface Guidelines (HIG). Apple wants you to make things behave a certain way... ignore this at your peril!

The iOS Programming Guidelines. This is the "Apple way" and should therefore be "your way."

These aren't actual rejections...
Apple doesn't allow that. But
they're <u>typical</u>... the types of
rejections that are really common.

Apple Rejections... Up Close

Wondering about what a typical rejection looks like? Here are some representative examples. Read each rejection carefully... in most cases, you'll quickly see that you can avoid these rejections with a little forethought.

To: Dean "the Machine" Developer

From: Apple Review Folks

Subject: App rejection

We've reviewed your app and determined that you are in violation of the guidelines.

"Apps that link to external mechanisms for purchases or subscriptions to be used in the app, such as a "buy" button that goes to a website to purchase a digital book, will be rejected."

Apple is extremely particular about your app linking to external websites. If those sites sell anything digital—books, music, movies, whatever—then your app is going to get rejected.

And don't think Apple is too busy to check each link out. They're notorious for making sure you don't sell digital content except through the App Store's In App Purchase mechanism.

In this day and age, most apps have to function on both the iPhone and iPad. If that's your case, you need several resolutions of your icons to get approved. You've got to support the various device resolutions, as well as what's shown on iTunes and the App Store.

Fortunately, the <u>iOS Human Interface Guidelines</u> (more on those later) are very clear about what you need. You just have to read those guidelines and make sure you include the right resolutions. Easy!

To: Moe Ney Coming

From: Apple Review Folks

Subject: App rejection

"We've reviewed your app and determined that your application icons need additional resolutions."

Apple Rejections... Up Close

To: Slo Mo Apper

From: Apple Review Folks

Subject: App rejection

"We've reviewed your app and determined that your app doesn't pass the performance testing. Your application fails on iOS 4.0."

Those older phones don't really matter anymore, right? <u>Wrong!</u> Apple allows you to indicate which versions of iOS you support, but whatever you say you'll support, Apple makes sure you <u>DO</u> support.

What does this mean for you? Testing on every device you want to have your app work on... no exceptions!

Even with giant 64GB phones and iPads, Apple is serious about your app being a good (and unselfish) device citizen. While there aren't any written rules here, you should try to only use the space you really need.

User-generated content is generally acceptable, too, but if your app downloads lots of stuff when it launches—especially without user intervention—watch out. This rejection might be coming your way...

To: Upfront Development

From: Apple Review Folks

Subject: App rejection

"We've reviewed your app and determined that your app downloads too much initial content. Applications are limited in the resources that they can consume on initial download."

Exercise

OK, so that's only a few rejections, but you should already be getting an idea of the basic reasons that Apple might reject an app. Use what you've just learned, put on your Apple hat, and see if you can figure out why the app shown below is sure to get rejected.

In fact, if you're feeling really mean, come up not with just one, but three reasons this app is sure to get red-carded from Apple.

Carrier 🛜   8:54 AM   ▭

InstaTwit for Iphone

Notes: [   ]

I'm...   ...and feeling...

networking	awesome
coding	confident
tweeting	smart

...about it.

[Tweet]

www.instatwit.com

Tap here to purchase a montly subscription!

<h1 style="text-align:center">there are no
Dumb Questions</h1>

Q: Foul! Unfair! What a ripoff!

A: Yeah, it can seem that way sometimes. But this whole process is what you have to go through for the very cool right to see your app on an iOS device. It's simply the only way to get there. Of course, the prize is really significant: the App Store far out-earns its competitors, and that makes it the best place to sell your app!

Q: How can I be sure my app won't get rejected *before* I submit?

A: Well, you can't know, at least not 100%. The best you *can* do is to carefully review the App Store review guidelines before you really get into coding. (Yes, *before* coding!) If there's any functionality in your app that you think may be questionable, spending some time combing through the App Store and try to find other apps that are tackling similar issues. If those apps got approved, they probably have a handle on any land mines you might need to avoid.

At the end of the day, though, you really won't know for sure until you submit your app. Practically, that means you should *plan for at least one rejection and re-submission*! That way, if something hangs you up, your marketing and business schedules aren't totally trashed!

Q: They rejected my app! How do I resubmit?

A: It depends on why your app got rejected. If it's a metadata problem, sometimes you can jump right back in at the head of the line. That's your best case.

Unfortunately, most rejections require code-level changes, beyond just your app's metadata. That means you need to resubmit the entire app...and that means you have to start the whole process over again.

Q: Can you appeal a rejection?

A: Sure! When your app gets rejected, appealing is always an option. But the appeal process isn't quick, so be sure that if you want to appeal, you're **really** sure that you have a good case. Otherwise, you'll burn time on an appeal *and* another re-submission, too.

Q: How in the world can you plan for all this? What a mess...

A: Yup, from a scheduling perspective, this isn't easy. But it's not something you can choose to opt out of. Seriously, experienced app developers often plan at least a month for the submission (and re-submisson) process.

Q: But some of this is nuts! I really can't even link to external sites? What about my own website?

A: Well, not all external links are forbidden... but many are. What gets tricky with external links is that if there is any navigation path from the external site to any kind of payment mechanism, Apple's probably going to reject you. Even if it's not intentional, Apple sees this as an app trying to get around Apple's payment processes (In App Purchase or IAP), and they're very serious about shutting that kind of thing down.

Even worse, external links can negatively affect your app's rating. Your kid-friendly game that's going to be a hit in middle school could get slapped with an adult rating because of content three pages away from a page you link to. Yeah, it's happened...in general, you should be very, very careful using external links.

Exercise Solution

Rejection... such an ugly word. Hopefully, you figured out a couple of reasons that the app below would get rejected. Make sure you understand what's wrong from Apple's perspective. The better you are at seeing things from their point of view, the less you'll see of their rejection emails.

Think Apple takes their trademarks seriously? You bet they do. Don't even try to get away with an app that doesn't get iPhone or iPad spelled and capitalized right.

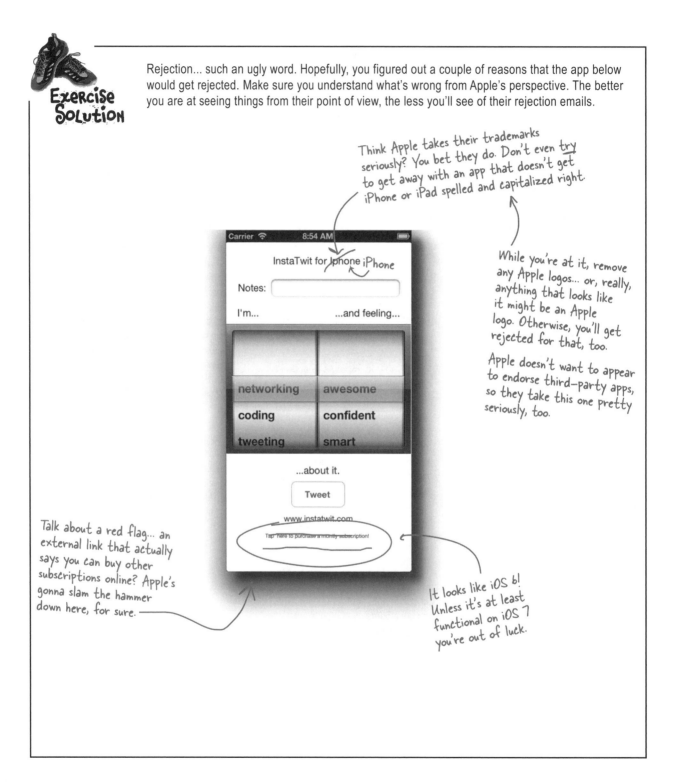

While you're at it, remove any Apple logos... or, really, anything that looks like it might be an Apple logo. Otherwise, you'll get rejected for that, too.

Apple doesn't want to appear to endorse third-party apps, so they take this one pretty seriously, too.

Talk about a red flag... an external link that actually says you can buy other subscriptions online? Apple's gonna slam the hammer down here, for sure.

It looks like iOS 6! Unless it's at least functional on iOS 7 you're out of luck.

Device checking... it's not optional

The first iPod came out back in 2001, and the first iPhone in 2007. That's something like 32,000 years in tech terms. And even though Apple is good about pushing out OS updates, these older devices simply can't be updated past a certain point. That means you've got to explicitly decide which OS versions you'll support... and therefore which devices you'll support.

Even more importantly, what does that mean for devices that are too old to update to the version of iOS you support? These older devices may or may not have cameras, the ability to capture video, internal speakers, and GPS... just for starters!

The technical term for handling these situations responsibly and gracefully is **device checking**. That's the process you'll have to use to ensure that devices that can run your app all behave, even if they don't support the hardware and software that your app can take advantage of.

"Handle gracefully" is a nice way of saying, "doesn't brick your iPad."

Your app may support all of these devices...

...but none of these. That's something you're responsible for!

iPods as late as third generation still don't have camera support.

First generation iPads had no camera... a pretty big deal. And iOS 7 doesn't go back to the early devices, or even some relatively recent iPod Touches.

So how does device checking actually work?

Device checking case study: the camera

How does device checking actually work? Let's say your application needs a camera supported on devices. As soon as your app needs something in a device's hardware, you've got some pretty specific additional requirements to consider.

Any application written for the iPhone also **must** be able to run on an iPod Touch *and* on an iPad. That means that when you use a feature like the camera that's only on some of the supported devices, you've got to check for that feature... and handle the case where it's not present.

Yes, you can specify "iPad only," but for the most part, you've got to support every device (iPad, iPod, iTouch, iSomethingNewIn2015) that runs the iOS your app targets.

So take the camera: the `UIImagePickerController` has a method to check for the camera.

```
[UIImagePickerController
    isSourceTypeAvailable:UIImagePickerControllerSourceTypeCamera]
```

The camera is a source, so this code makes sure that source is available... before using that source.

iOS handles the heavy lifting

iOS is smart enough to know which features a specific device has. So if you ask the `UIImagePickerController` which source types are available, you can decide which options to show the user.

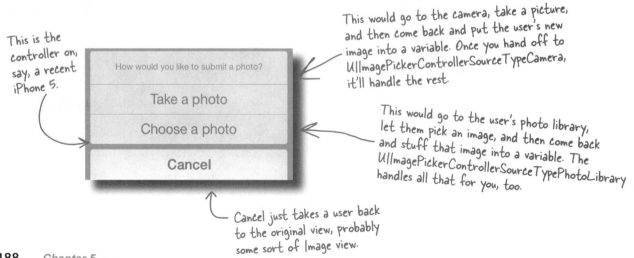

This is the controller on, say, a recent iPhone 5.

This would go to the camera, take a picture, and then come back and put the user's new image into a variable. Once you hand off to UIImagePickerControllerSourceTypeCamera, it'll handle the rest.

How would you like to submit a photo?

Take a photo

Choose a photo

Cancel

This would go to the user's photo library, let them pick an image, and then come back and stuff that image into a variable. The UIImagePickerControllerSourceTypePhotoLibrary handles all that for you, too.

Cancel just takes a user back to the original view, probably some sort of Image view.

Hmmm... supported device, missing feature

OK, so checking for a source like the camera is a must. But just because you *check* for a source doesn't mean the device actually *has* that source. Remember those third-generation iPods?

This is a pretty recent iPod, probably something you'll need to support... but there's no camera.

In a case like this, you have to figure out what should happen without that feature. You may need to disable an entire section of your application. Of course, that's a pretty nuclear option, so it's better to try to figure out if there's some subset of things that those devices can still take advantage of.

So taking a new photo on many iPods and older iPads definitely can't be an option...

...but choosing an existing photo is still something your app—and the user's older device—can support.

With images there's almost always another good option: the photo library. If there's no camera, a user still can get images from their existing photos. So think about whether most of your app still works, and you can just disable certain buttons (and if possible, hide the controls that don't make sense for that device).

If your application can't work at all without a camera (or net access or accelerometer, etc.), you can specify device capabilities for your application so users without those capabilities can't even install your application on their device.

So Apple makes sure my app works on their devices. At least they're not making me design my app some certain way to look "uniform."

Well... they kinda do that, too. Welcome to the <u>Human Interface Guidelines</u>.

By now you've probably noticed that all the apps on iOS devices (except for games), have pretty consistent designs and interaction patterns. It makes for a "feel" for iOS apps, and that means things are generally easier for the user. It's called having a minimum accessibility standard: you can count on it being relatively easy to use almost any app because you've used other apps, and they function and look similar.

All those interactions are described and detailed in the **Human Interface Guidelines**. It's another document up on the Developer Portal that gives you details on interaction patterns.

iOS 7 meant a major overhaul to app look and feel. The new HIG helps you look like an iOS 7 app and feel like an iOS 7 app.

Chafing a bit at Apple's design restrictions? It's OK... lots of people do until they think things through a bit more.

The HIG helps, rather than hurting you

The HIG is full of rules that help you. It's a long document, but one that's worth going through so that you only have to refer to it from time to time for a refresher. Everything from app design tips to rules about icon use is covered. You'll learn how to design apps that "feel" like standard Mac apps, like Apple Mail...

You've already used the navigation bar in your own iPhone apps... here it is in a split view iPad controller.

Wanna know how high these bars should be? Look in the HIG.

What should be in the top status bar? Check the HIG.

Even the icons that should be on toolbars are covered, along with placement and size.

The placeholder text for text and search boxes is in the HIG... with lots of specifics.

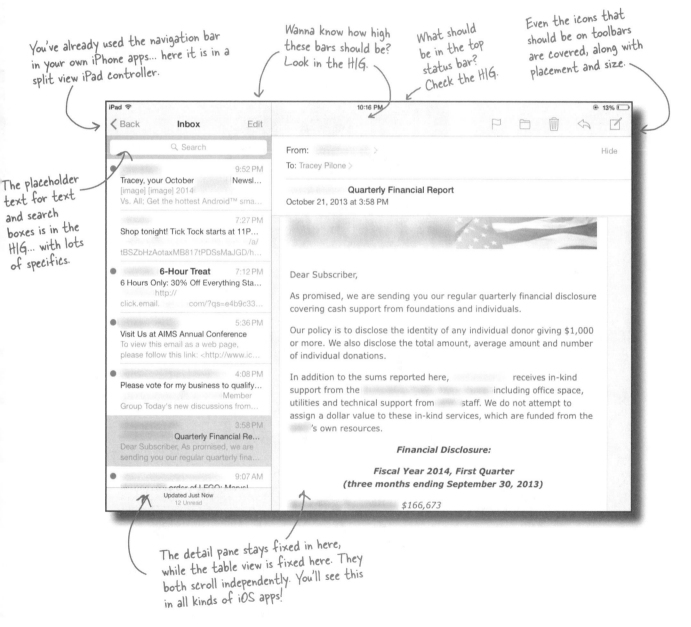

The detail pane stays fixed in here, while the table view is fixed here. They both scroll independently. You'll see this in all kinds of iOS apps!

You've already gotten used to the HIG...

You may be starting to feel like the HIG is just documenting the kinds of things you're already used to... and you'd be right! You may not have realized it, but every time you used an app like Mail, you were really teaching your eyes (and fingers) to work with a HIG-designed app.

Take iTunes as another example...

This is a segmented control... and the HIG helps you make yours look and feel like other apps' controls.

The HIG has information about what controls you can put in a top toolbar and how to use them... and suddenly your apps just start to feel "familiar" to your users. That's a good thing!

The HIG has lots of information about how to use tab bars, and navigation, and icons... it's a massive bootstrap for your own app design.

Tab bar controller is another standard control. And "standard" means it behaves the same way almost all the time... this isn't a place where you want your app to be unique.

there are no Dumb Questions

Q: OK, I get it... but surely there are some apps that don't need the HIG, right?

A: Actually, that's not true. There are some apps that need a lot less of the HIG... like games that are immersive and completely graphical. But even then, the HIG helps you design interactions that feel natural and "iOS-like." That's really important...

So this is all just about keeping up the Apple and iOS 7, right? The "new iPhone look?"

No. The HIG involves the design of your app, but it isn't only about your visual design.

Information architecture is an important consideration in designing your app for real people to interact with it. And iOS7 did significantly change the look and feel of iOS but it also moved functionality around. iOS now has a control center that comes up from the bottom of the device at any time and holds cross-device functionality for any app to use, and there are other goodies as well.

Things like Bluetooth, AirPlay, messaging via various networks— things that lots of apps want to use.

Design = look + feel

...and some other stuff, too.

The more precise fonts and increased resolution of screens as the iOS ecosystem has matured mean that the new iOS has started to leverage the extra space for extra detail.

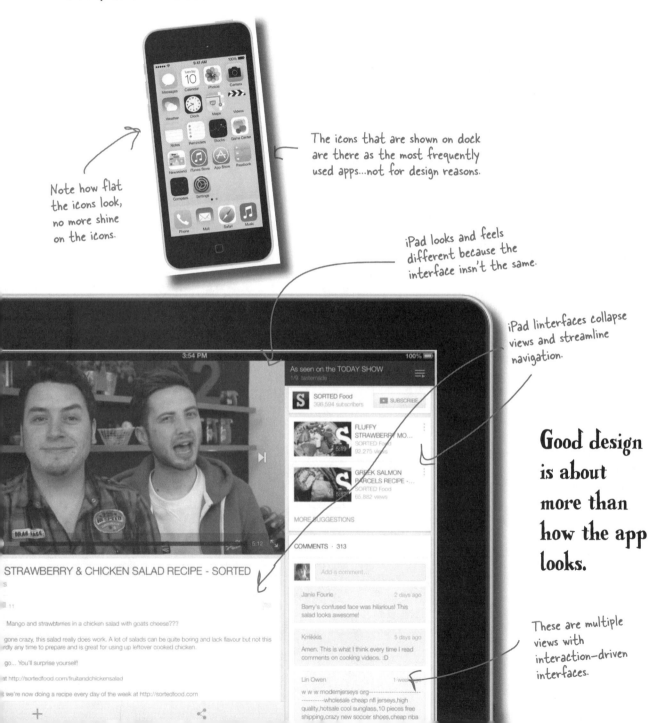

Note how flat the icons look, no more shine on the icons.

The icons that are shown on dock are there as the most frequently used apps....not for design reasons.

iPad looks and feels different because the interface insn't the same.

iPad linterfaces collapse views and streamline navigation.

Good design is about more than how the app looks.

These are multiple views with interaction-driven interfaces.

iOS 7 Top 5

 Flat design is in.
The design trends all over the web and on iOS are toward flat design. Gone are the drop shadows and blue underlined links of the old Internet. Now the devices and web are shadowless with no depth.

 Skeumorphism is out. In a big way.
Up through iOS 6, Apple was encouranging developers to mimic real-world interfaces to leverage people's knowledge of how to use a menu or a calendar into using an iOS device. With iOS 7, apps are much more similar across devices because they are embracing their digital nature.

 More unified interactions across devices.
iPad and iPhone are different, and we're going to get into how to effectively use what each piece of hardware has to offer in the coming pages. But with iOS 7, Apple has made a full-court press to unified interaction patterns between iPhone and iPad.

 Strategic use of color.
Apps on iOS have a tint color that indicates interactivity (rather than all of those drop shadows and buttons), so gone are old school underlined links. Instead, the text you can interact with is tinted.

People who are color blind may have trouble with certain colors, so do some research.

 iOS provides a sense of depth.
Parallax is used by iOS 7 with the springboard of the device that gives the illusion of depth behind the app icons. In addition, the use of translucency within apps means that you can see views slipping under navigtion elements in the app and show a sense of layers.

More to think about: your iPad is <u>not</u> your iPhone

So far, you've not really had to think much about whether your app will run on an iPhone or an iPad. The code's been the same for both. But there *are* differences: besides screen size, iPad always supports multiple orientations, whereas many iPhone apps are portrait only. Interaction time is a key difference between the two devices as well. iPhone apps are designed for quick, easy access to information. iPad users are expecting to interact with the device and the app for longer periods of time and expect a more involved experience.

All these differences mean you've got to start thinking about devices...differently.

You can't just make images and fonts bigger for iPad, either. Not only will it look lousy, Apple might reject your app.

Device Differences...
Up Close

Take a look at how Calendar looks on each device. Take some time studying the decisions Apple made... you'll need to make similar choices in your own apps!

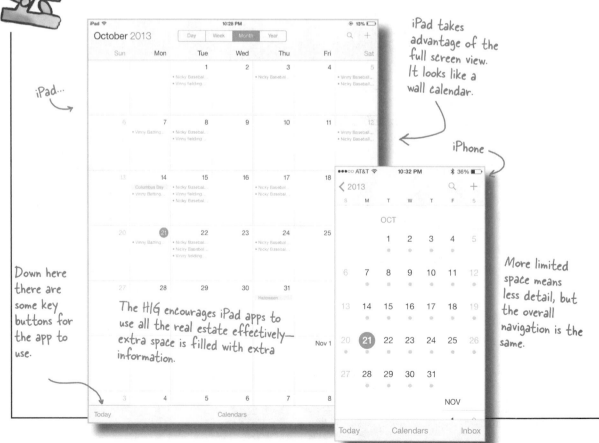

iPad...

iPad takes advantage of the full screen view. It looks like a wall calendar.

iPhone

Down here there are some key buttons for the app to use.

The HIG encourages iPad apps to use all the real estate effectively— extra space is filled with extra information.

More limited space means less detail, but the overall navigation is the same.

Device Differences...
Up Close

Safari between the iPhone and iPad is very similar. You'll see that some options are on the top or the bottom of the different interactions but otherwise the same. There's one different interaction pattern though...

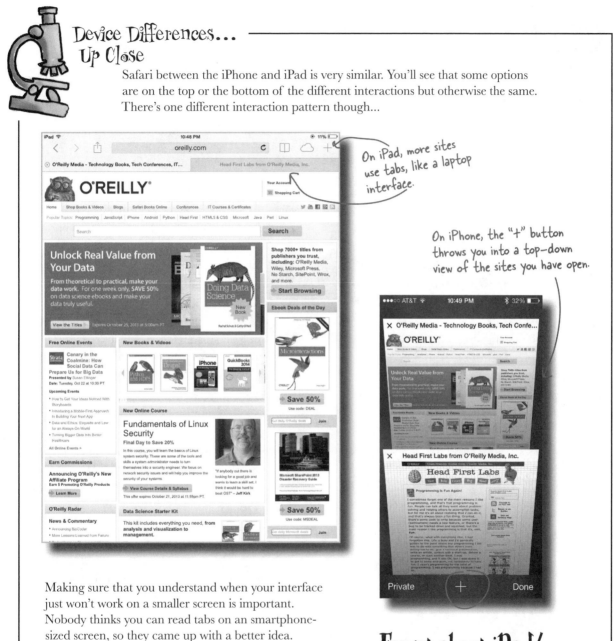

On iPad, more sites use tabs, like a laptop interface.

On iPhone, the "+" button throws you into a top-down view of the sites you have open.

Making sure that you understand when your interface just won't work on a smaller screen is important. Nobody thinks you can read tabs on an smartphone-sized screen, so they came up with a better idea.

Forget about iPad/ iPhone... How is iOS different from Android?

Fireside Chats

Tonight's talk: **What's it like developing apps for other devices?**

Apple Developer:

Hi there. Now that we've gotten the gist of what it's like to live in my world with Apple, it'll be nice to get a fresh perspective.

Yeah, there's definitely a programming guide. It gives you lots of information about the latest and greatest with Objective-C, interaction and software patterns you should follow, that sort of thing. What language do you all use for apps?

What do you mean, you don't have to? Don't your apps need to be approved to go up on the App Store?

So... you can just make your apps however you want? I've heard users complain about a lot of weird Android apps that behave oddly...

Wait, you're actually changing basic device behavior? Who's making sure that code works on all those Android phones and tablets out there?

Android Developer:

It sounds like there are an awful lot of rules for iOS developers to follow. The HIG, the approval process, and isn't there a programming guide, too?

Android apps are all written in Java. And we have lots of reference tools, too—free for us to use, but we don't *have* to use all that stuff if we don't want!

Which app store? We have lots, not just one like on iOS. There's Google Play, the Amazon Appstore, and probably more by now, too. We don't have to get approval, either. Our apps just go right up on the store. Sweet, huh?

Well, sure, but that's just because some developer made bad choices. My choices are always awesome, especially when it's nothing anyone's ever done before. Besides, you wouldn't believe the new code tricks I'm figuring out to make devices do things the hardware designers *never* thought about...

Well, nobody... but it works on my phone and my two tablets!

Apple Developer:

Yeah, but there are like... a zillion Android devices!

Uhhh... yeah. So you can write apps that only work on *your* phone, and *your* tablet? Maybe the Apple approval process isn't looking so dumb when my app doesn't brick my user's devices...

Sure. That's awesome. So you can push out your new broken app really fast, right? That must be a real benefit.

How could I? They're all the same, so I can actually make sure that what works for me works for everyone else, Android boy.

Anarchist!

See ya... all I'm doing today is checking my sales on the App Store...

Android Developer:

Isn't it great? So many options! You only have, what, three sizes? We have a ton more than that! And we can use each device however we want. Designing my app is wide open!

Well, yeah, it happens, but so what? I just release an update. And no waiting around for some stupid team to approve anything!

Android is all about flexibility. Don't get your Lightning connector all in a wad, ok?

Lemming!

Whatever. You're just... oh, gotta run, just got another crash report. Gotta push version 324...

BULLET POINTS

- The Human Interface Guidelines (HIG) are important to follow if you want to have a good app.

- You give up some flexibility in design to ensure that users get a consistent experience with their apps.

- Plan for approvals to take time, but also plan for less buggy apps to get released as a result.

- Apple exerts more control over their apps. Love it or hate it, that's the iOS way, for good or (and!) bad.

there are no
Dumb Questions

Q: How has the HIG changed over time?

A: Apple has become more flexible with the HIG as time has gone on. As more and more applications go up on the App Store, new innovations add interaction patterns to apps, and Apple has let those innovations through and made them acceptable.

For example, there are lots of apps that are using a control that slides in from the side of the app and partially covers the main screen (Facebook is using this heavily). That control isn't anywhere in the HIG, but it's becoming fairly standard for iOS apps.

Q: Will following the HIG just make my app look generic?

A: Yes and no. The goal is to make your app interactions like other apps, which is easier for users. But creativity is great, and new UIs are a cool way to differentiate from a competing app. You can be original in your design without totally ditching the HIG and standard interaction patterns.

Q: What if I'm writing a game? What are the rules then?

A: As soon as you start straying from standard controls, you start straying from the HIG. Once you spend some time doing iOS development you'll get a feel for when you're going to need to care about the HIG (like putting settings in the settings bundle), and when you can really go all-out custom.

Q: What about natural user interfaces? Is that still a thing?

A: It used to be a *big* thing. Apple initially made a pretty big push, especially with iPad, to have you mimic a real-world interface in your apps whenever possible. The calendar app is a great example of that—the torn pages and familiar wall calendar design look like "real" objects. As the iOS platform has matured, though, apps seem to be moving away from that look.

Q: So Android developers really don't have to get approval on their apps?

A: Nope. Android is an open source platform, and that community is based on the idea that there isn't a "gatekeeper" adding an approval layer to apps.

Don't think that means that it's a free-for-all, though. Most of the Android apps that do well are those that follow the voluntary app guidelines. Android has similar programming and interaction guides to those that we're using on the Apple side... they're just not mandatory.

Q: Is device fragmentation a problem for iOS too?

A: It is definitely something to keep in mind when you're designing a UI. There are now three sizes to deal with: the original iPhone/iPod touch screen, the new iPhone 5 screen, and the iPad screen. There are also multiple resolutions for each of these devices. You're going to have to use more and more relative positioning with your views, which will ultimately make designing for these different devices easier.

You can be original in your design without ignoring the HIG and standard iOS interaction patterns.

Pŏŏl Puzzle

Your **job** is to take items from the pool and place them into the list for iPhone, iPad, or iPod Touch. You may use the same item more than once. Your **goal** is to make a complete list of functionality for the iPhone, iPad, and iPod Touch. If the device has it, add the functionality; if not, leave it in the pool!

iPod Touch   **iPhone**   **iPad**

Note: Each feature from the pool can be used more than once!

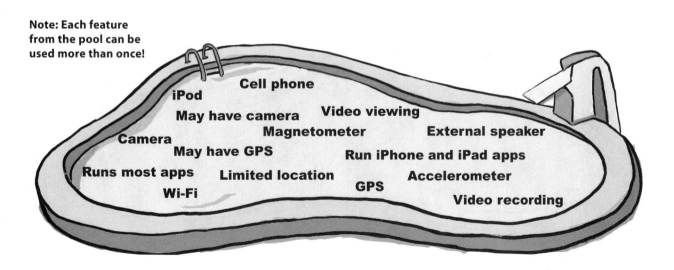

iPod
Cell phone
May have camera
Video viewing
Magnetometer
External speaker
Camera
May have GPS
Run iPhone and iPad apps
Runs most apps
Limited location
Accelerometer
Wi-Fi
GPS
Video recording

Pool Puzzle Solution

Your **job** was to take items from the pool and place them into the list for iPhone, iPad, or iPod Touch. You could use each item more than once. Your **goal** was to make a complete list of functionality for the iPhone, iPad, and iPod Touch.

Watch it!

This list will change.

Apple is always coming out with new devices and updating capabilities. You need to check for yourself!

iPod Touch

iPod

Runs most apps

Video viewing

Limited location

Accelerometer

Wi-Fi

May have Camera

You can get some info about location from Wi-Fi on iPod.

iPhone

iPod

Runs most apps

Video viewing

GPS

Accelerometer

Wi-Fi

Cell phone

Camera

External speaker

Video recording

Magnetometer

This one can be an issue.

You may have noticed some random stuff on this list— who would've thought about the speaker?

Only on the 3GS and newer...

iPad

iPod

Runs iPhone and iPad apps

Video viewing

May have limited location

Accelerometer

Wi-Fi

May have GPS

May have Camera

External speaker

Video recording

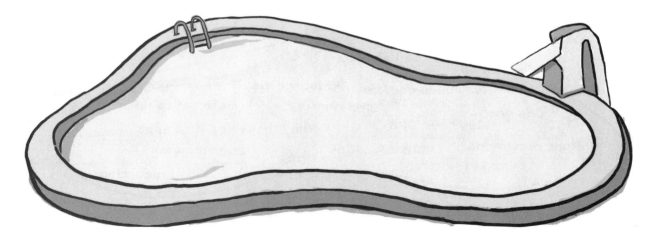

Apple World Cross

You've spent some serious time in the Apple universe in this chapter. Make sure you know all the lingo!

Across

1. Device _____ in code prevents failures when hardware is missing.
7. The name of the process Apple uses to review apps
8. You can _____ if your app is rejected.
10. _____ is used to implement purchases from within iOS apps.

Down

2. _____ linking can be problematic.
3. The _____ Interface Guidelines have design and interaction guidance.
4. iOS _____ support is developer-configured and Apple tested.
5. Hardware that can be missing
6. ____ isn't available on an iPod touch.
9. That other smartphone operating system
11. The ____ Library is used to hold pictures.

Apple World Cross Solution

You've spent some serious time in the Apple universe
in this chapter. Make sure you know all the lingo!

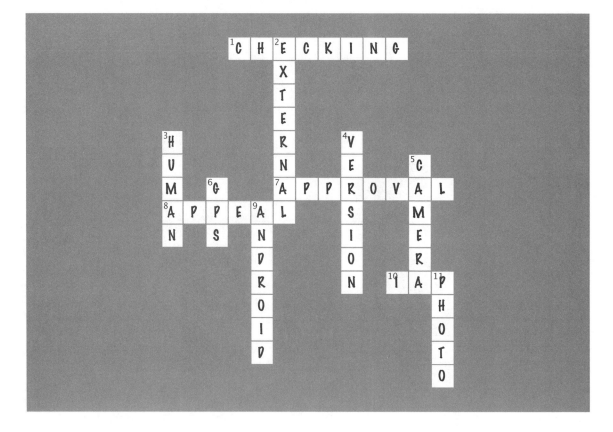

Across

1. Device _____ in code prevents failures when hardware
   is missing. [CHECKING]
7. The name of the process Apple uses to review apps
   [APPROVAL]
8. You can _____ if your app is rejected. [APPEAL]
10. _____ is used to implement purchases from within iOS
    apps. [IAP]

Down

2. _____ linking can be problematic. [EXTERNAL]
3. The _____ Interface Guidelines have design and
   interaction guidance. [HUMAN]
4. iOS _____ support is developer-configured and Apple
   tested. [VERSION]
5. Hardware that can be missing [CAMERA]
6. ____ isn't available on an iPod touch. [GPS]
9. That other smartphone operating system [ANDROID]
11. The ____ Library is used to hold pictures. [PHOTO]

Your Apple toolbox

Now you've added some tools from the Apple ecosystem to your toolbox.

The Review Process

- If you want an app up on the App Store, you'll have to take that app through the review process.

- Planning for the review process by leaving time for re-submission.

- You'll need to check and support different devices and different capabilities on each device.

Don't...

...try to get around in-app purchasing.

...mis-spell any Apple products, or use those products in advertising.

...take up a ton of storage space, especially for things that don't include user-created content.

BULLET POINTS

- The Human Interface Guidelines (HIG) are important to follow if you want to have a good app.

- You give up some flexibility in design to ensure that users get a consistent experience with their apps.

- Plan for approvals to take time, but also plan for less buggy apps to get released as a result.

- Apple exerts more control over their apps. Love it or hate it, that's the iOS way, for good or (and!) bad.

6 basic core data and table view cells

Reruns are hard to find

I'm playing Gilligan's Island. I wish we could watch it on TV sometime!

Just sit right back and you'll hear a tale, a tale of a fateful trip.

A challenge faced today is how to work with big data and make it presentable in a more appropriate format for mobile. There are lots of ways to do that, including manipulating the data and presenting it to the users in an easy to navigate and interpret way. TV presents one of those challenges because there are so many showings on the air. What's a *Gilligan* fan to do?

This is your application

Gaming and reading apps aside, most applications on mobile are used to allow a user to sift efficiently through data on the go. Calorie tracking apps, calendar apps, mail, news readers, weather apps—they're all some variation on that theme. Until now, we've worked with very basic storage, arrays, and plists.

Plists are great for just storing local data that is mostly numbers and strings. You want to get into storing photos or videos? Images? Plists are not a great solution. Performance starts to suffer and communicating data off the device is inefficient. Plists are XML files: they have to be loaded and saved in their entirety. Plists don't support partial random access like a DB store.

Just text and strings here, remember?

This is your application on data

Most applications are driven by some more extensive use of data. There are
limits to the relationships and size of data that can exist in a plist. To have
more data manipulation capabilities, we need to move into a more complex
data management structure.

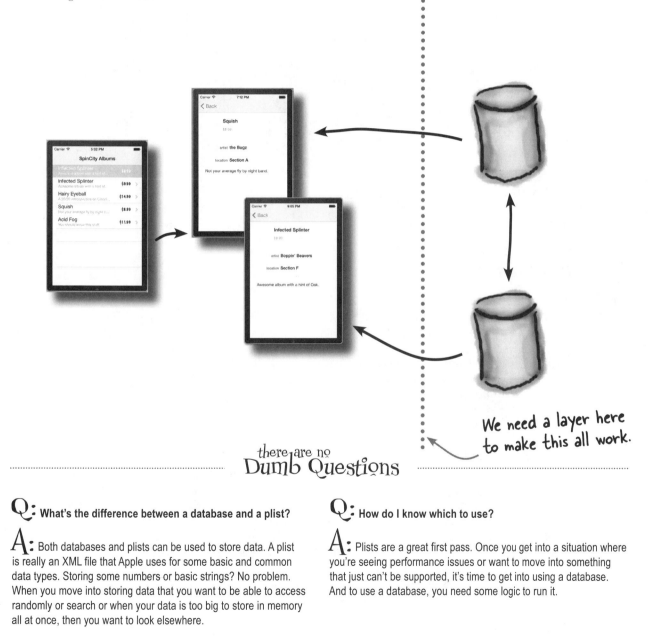

We need a layer here
to make this all work.

there are no
Dumb Questions

Q: What's the difference between a database and a plist?

A: Both databases and plists can be used to store data. A plist
is really an XML file that Apple uses for some basic and common
data types. Storing some numbers or basic strings? No problem.
When you move into storing data that you want to be able to access
randomly or search or when your data is too big to store in memory
all at once, then you want to look elsewhere.

Q: How do I know which to use?

A: Plists are a great first pass. Once you get into a situation where
you're seeing performance issues or want to move into something
that just can't be supported, it's time to get into using a database.
And to use a database, you need some logic to run it.

Introducing Core Data

Loading and saving data, particularly lots of data, is a major part of most applications. But what if you wanted to sort that data in a bunch of different ways? Writing code to handle that kind of persistence gets really old, really quickly. Enter Core Data...

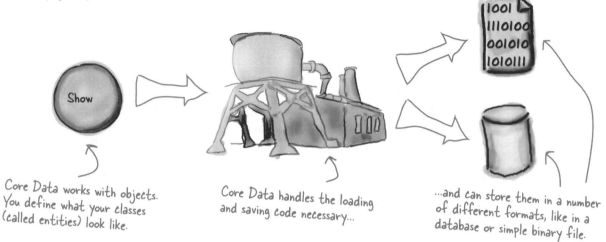

Core Data works with objects. You define what your classes (called entities) look like.

Core Data handles the loading and saving code necessary...

...and can store them in a number of different formats, like in a database or simple binary file.

But wait, there's more!

Core Data makes loading and saving your data a snap, but it doesn't stop there. It's a mature framework that Apple brought over from Mac OS X to iOS in version 3.0 and gives you:

 The ability to load and save your objects
Core Data automatically loads and saves your objects based on entity descriptions. It can even handle relationships between objects, migrating between versions of your data, required and optional fields, and field validation.

 Different ways to store your data
Core Data hides how your data is actually stored from your application. You could read and write to a SQLite database or a custom binary file by simply telling Core Data how you want it to save your stuff.

 Memory management with undo and redo
Core Data can be extremely efficient about managing objects in memory and tracking changes to objects. You can use it for undo and redo, paging through huge databases of information, and more.

...and speaking of data

Head First Network has a great idea for a new app. But they're
running into some trouble.

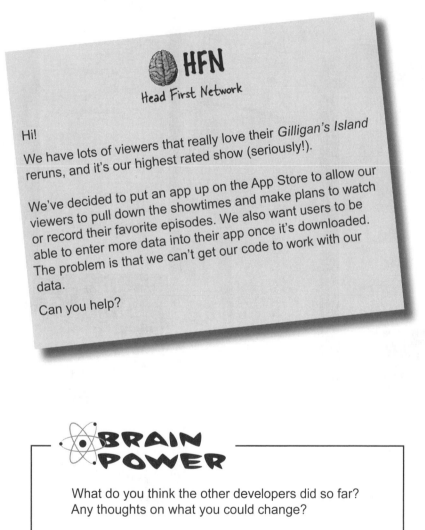

🧠 **HFN**

Head First Network

Hi!

We have lots of viewers that really love their *Gilligan's Island*
reruns, and it's our highest rated show (seriously!).

We've decided to put an app up on the App Store to allow our
viewers to pull down the showtimes and make plans to watch
or record their favorite episodes. We also want users to be
able to enter more data into their app once it's downloaded.
The problem is that we can't get our code to work with our
data.

Can you help?

⚛️ **BRAIN POWER**

What do you think the other developers did so far?
Any thoughts on what you could change?

The Gilligizer app

The other developers have already gotten the views up and running, they just need some help with the data management. The basics of setting up the views are going fine, but they can't get anything to display. It's right where we got Spin City before the app was showing anything.

To get an entry so you can see the detail view, hit the plus button.

Here's the detail view all laid out for us to use.

This is mostly the basic split view template.

This is the initial file structure for Gilligizer. It's pretty close to the basic template up here.

Down here you'll see some new frameworks. The CoreData framework gets added if you check that "use Core Data" box when you create the app.

Exercise

Get and build Gilligizer. Just like before, this app is up on GitHub for you to download and get started.

 Check out the existing code from GitHub.
Just like we did in Chapter 1, instead of creating a new project you need to check it out from a repository. From the "Welcome to Xcode" screen, select Checkout an Existing Project, then select the "Repository" option. You should have *https://github.com/dpilone/Head-First-iPhone-iPad-Development-3rd-Edition.git* from earlier in the book.

 Select the right branch.
The starting code for each chapter is listed under that chapter's branch. Go ahead and select the Chapter 6 branch and hit next. Finally, you need to select a saving location and name for the chapter (we'd suggest chapter 6 or Gilligizer) and select the "Checkout" button.

 Test.
Now that you have the project on your machine, go ahead and build and run what's there. It should be working with the basics!

Now that you've got everything set up, let's move on to the data!

Core Data starts with...data

Like most data management, we first need to build the data model to incorporate into the application. Since the detail view is already fleshed out, we can use that to figure out what data needs to be included. For now, the easiest way to enter data into the application is manually by the user. Don't worry, we'll get to a bigger database of shows to add to the application later.

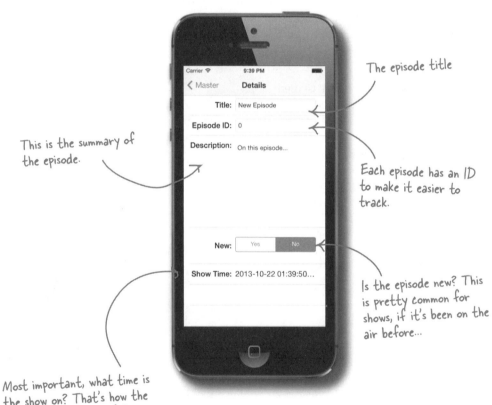

The episode title

This is the summary of the episode.

Each episode has an ID to make it easier to track.

Is the episode new? This is pretty common for shows, if it's been on the air before...

Most important, what time is the show on? That's how the users can figure out if they are going to be able to see the show.

Data Magnets

Use what you learned from Spin City to fill in the blanks for our show data. For now, we just want an idea of the fields we'll need.

Show

_____

_____

_____

_____

_____

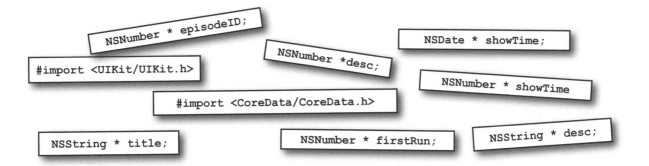

```
NSNumber * episodeID;
```

```
NSDate * showTime;
```

```
#import <UIKit/UIKit.h>
```

```
NSNumber *desc;
```

```
NSNumber * showTime
```

```
#import <CoreData/CoreData.h>
```

```
NSString * title;
```

```
NSNumber * firstRun;
```

```
NSString * desc;
```

Data Magnets Solution

Here's what we came up with for the data for this app.

Show

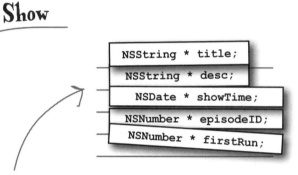

```
NSString * title;
NSString * desc;
NSDate * showTime;
NSNumber * episodeID;
NSNumber * firstRun;
```

iOS calls this an entity.

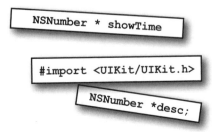

```
NSNumber * showTime
```

```
#import <UIKit/UIKit.h>
```

```
NSNumber *desc;
```

there are no Dumb Questions

Q: Why is the episode ID an NSNumber, not an integer?

A: If you jump on Wikipedia (not that we have done this!), the episode numbers are actually formatted with the season.episode number. It's pretty typical actually, so it's not an integer.

Core Data works with entities

Now that we know what the data needs to look like, we have to figure out how to map that to the way Core Data wants to talk about it. Core Data has some very specific terminology that it uses to describe the different parts of the data process. An **entity** is a representation of something you want to store in the database. In our case, entities are showings of *Gilligan's Island* and they will be made up of attributes (title, description, etc.) and in the case of more complex data, relationships between entities.

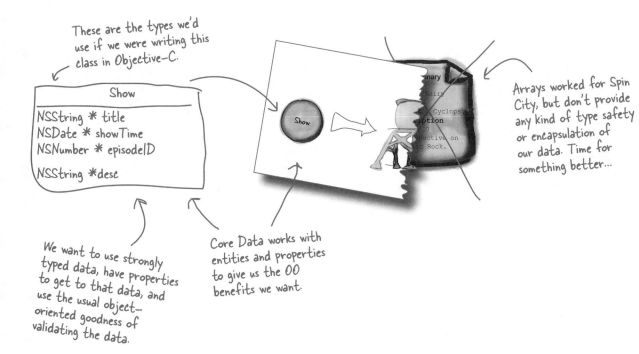

These are the types we'd use if we were writing this class in Objective-C.

Show

NSString * title
NSDate * showTime
NSNumber * episodeID

NSString *desc

We want to use strongly typed data, have properties to get to that data, and use the usual object-oriented goodness of validating the data.

Core Data works with entities and properties to give us the OO benefits we want.

Arrays worked for Spin City, but don't provide any kind of type safety or encapsulation of our data. Time for something better...

We need to define the entity for Core Data

Entities are abstract, so they need to be represented in code so the application can interact with them (we'll get to that in a bit); but first off they need to be represented in a way that Core Data can work with.

Not only can Core Data give us the OO-based view of our data that we want, it can even define our data graphically. There's one snag though—out of the box, Core Data supports a specific set of data types, so as we define our entity it must be done using the types Core Data offers...

Core Data describes entities with a Managed Object Model

Entities controlled by Core Data are called **Managed Objects**. The way you capture your entity descriptions (properties, relationships, type information, etc.) for Core Data is through a Managed Object Model. Core Data looks at that Managed Object Model at runtime to figure out how to load and save data from its persistence store (e.g., a database). The Xcode split-view template using Core Data we used comes with an empty Managed Object Model to get us started.

The Managed Object Model describes the objects we're going to ask for or try to save.

It also contains all of the information Core Data needs to read and write this data from storage.

Our template comes with an empty Managed Object Model in the Shared group called Gilligizer. xcdatamodeld. Click on that to get this view.

The template is set up so that Core Data will try to load all of the Managed Object Models defined in your application at startup. We'll only need this one.

By default, our object model comes with an Event entity; we'll need to delete it and define the Show entity.

Technically you can create a Managed Object Model in code or by hand, but the Xcode tools make it much, much easier.

Let's go ahead and create our Show entity...

Build your Show entity

We need to create a Show entity in our Managed Object Model. Since our Show doesn't have any relationships to other classes, we just need to add properties. Open up *Gilligizer.xcdatamodeld* to create the Show data type.

1 Delete the Entity that the code ships with, the "Event" entity by clicking on it and hitting delete.

2 To add the Show entity, click the "plus" button here, and change the **name** to "Show".

3 Once the entity exists, you can add attributes to the data model, using a plus button again.

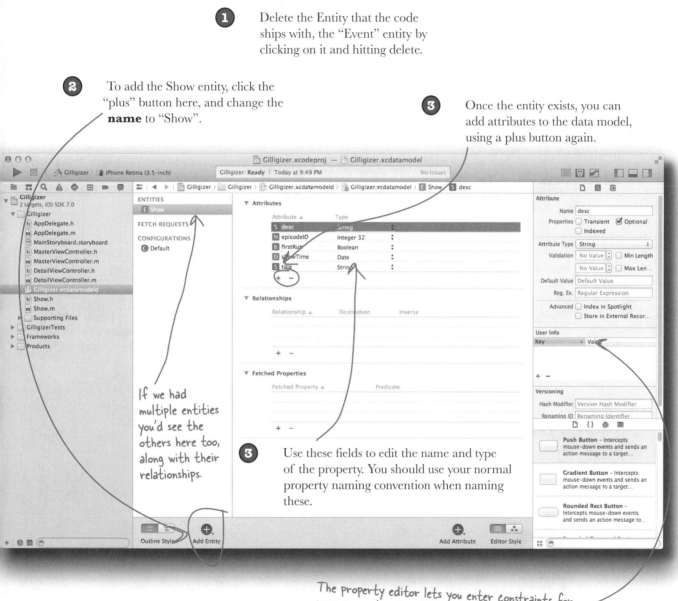

If we had multiple entities you'd see the others here too, along with their relationships.

3 Use these fields to edit the name and type of the property. You should use your normal property naming convention when naming these.

The property editor lets you enter constraints for your properties too (min, max, whether it's required, etc.). We're not going to use these just yet...

there are no
Dumb Questions

Q: What are the transient and indexed checkboxes for in Xcode when you create properties?

A: The transient checkbox indicates that Core Data doesn't need to load or save that property. Transient properties are typically used to hold values that you only want to calculate once for performance or convenience reasons, but can be calculated based on the other data you save in the entity. If you use transient properties, you typically implement a method named `awakeFromFetch:` that is called right after Core Data loads your entity. In that method, you can calculate the values of your transient properties and set them.

The indexed checkbox tells Core Data it should try to create an index on that property. Core Data can use indexes to speed up searching for items, so if you have a property that you use to look up your entities (customer IDs, account numbers, etc.), you can ask Core Data to index them for faster searching. Indexes take up space and can slow down inserting new data into the store, so only use them when they can actually improve search performance.

Q: I've seen constants declared with k's in front of them. Are they different somehow?

A: Nope. It's just a naming convention. C and C++ programmers tend to use all caps, while Apple tends to use the lowercase "k" instead.

Q: What if I need to use a type that Core Data doesn't support?

A: The easiest way is obviously to try and make your data work with one of the built-in types. If that doesn't work, you create custom types and implement methods to help Core Data load and save those values. Finally, you could stick your data into a binary type (binary data or BLOB) and write some code to encode and decode it at runtime.

Q: What other types of persistence does Core Data support?

A: Core Data supports three types of persistence stores on iOS: binary files, SQLite DBs, and in-memory. The SQLite store is the most useful and what we're using for Gilligizer. It's also the default. Binary files are nice because they're atomic, meaning either everything is successfully stored at once or nothing is. The problem with them is that in order to be atomic, the iPhone has to read and write the whole file whenever something changes. They're not used too often in iOS. The in-memory persistence store is a type of store that isn't actually ever saved on disk, but lets you use all of the searching, sorting, and undo-redo capabilities that Core Data offers with data you keep in-memory.

Q: What SQL datatypes/table structures does Core Data use when it writes to a SQLite database?

A: The short answer is you don't need to know. Even though it's writing to a SQLite database, the format, types, and structures are not part of the public API and could potentially be changed by Apple. You're supposed to treat the SQLite database as a blackbox and only access it through Core Data.

Q: So this comes with lots of default code, but I don't see what this gets us over an array yet. It seems like a lot of work.

A: We had to tell Core Data what kind of information we're working with. Now that we've done that, we can start putting it to work.

Watch it!

Make sure your object model matches ours exactly!

When you're writing your own apps, there are lots of ways to set up your data model, but since we're going to give you a database for Gilligizer, your model must match ours exactly!

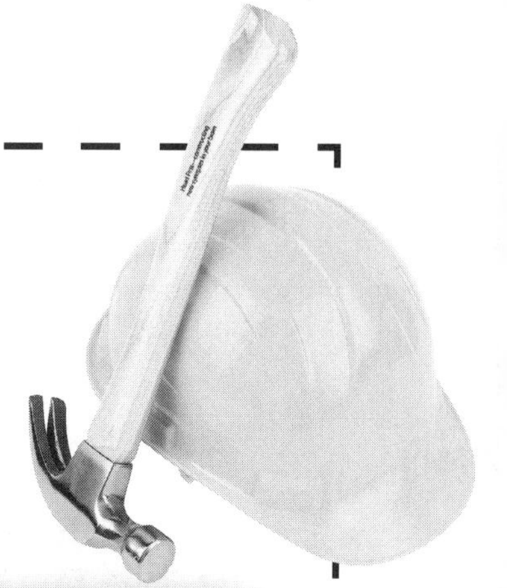

MANAGED OBJECT MODEL CONSTRUCTION

Finish building the Show entity in the Managed Object Model based on the
episode information we want to store. Remember, Core Data types won't match our
Objective-C types exactly. Make sure you name your properties the same as we have
in the Show diagram shown below.

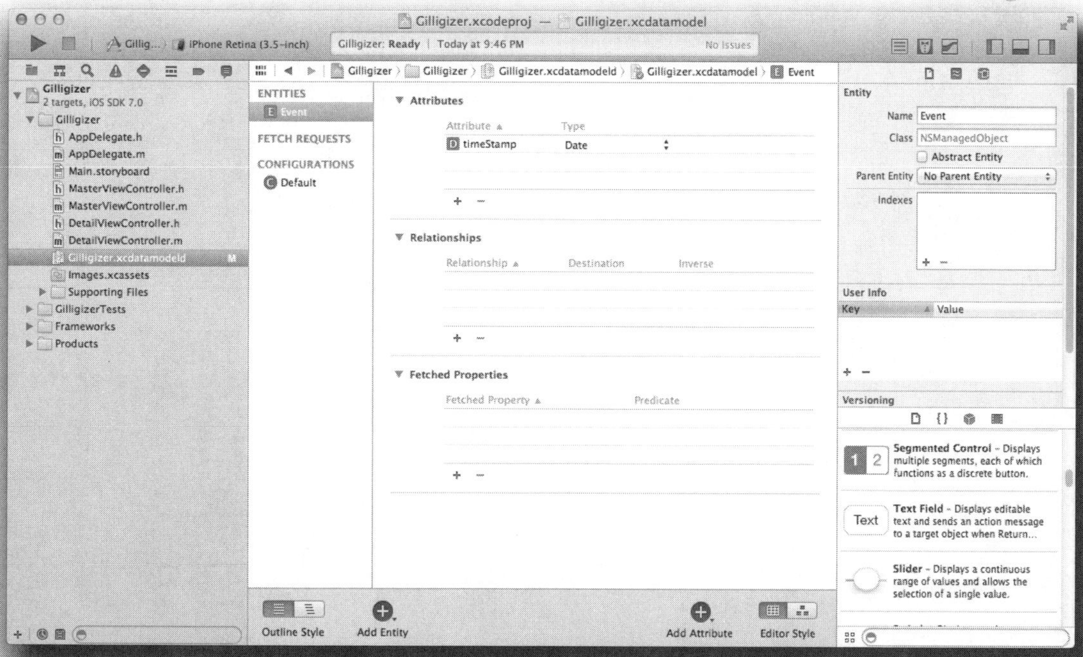

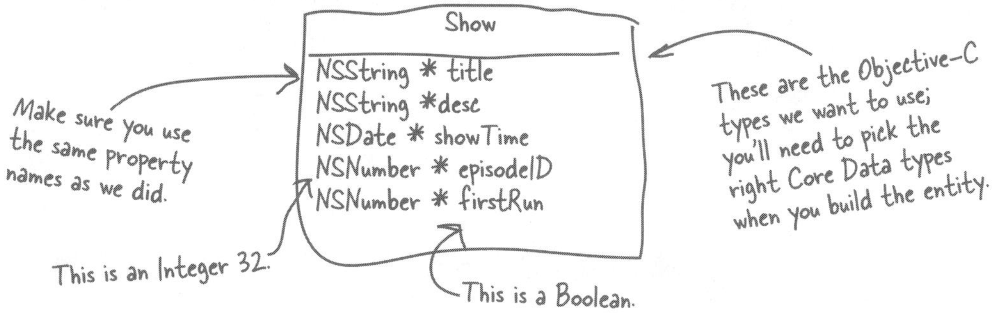

Show

NSString * title
NSString *desc
NSDate * showTime
NSNumber * episodeID
NSNumber * firstRun

Make sure you use the same property names as we did.

This is an Integer 32.

This is a Boolean.

These are the Objective-C types we want to use; you'll need to pick the right Core Data types when you build the entity.

MANAGED OBJECT MODEL CONSTRUCTION SOLUTION

We finished building the Show entity in the Managed Object Model based on the Show information we want to store. Remember, Core Data Types won't match our Objective-C types exactly.

Make sure that the "optional" box is unchecked for all of the properties.

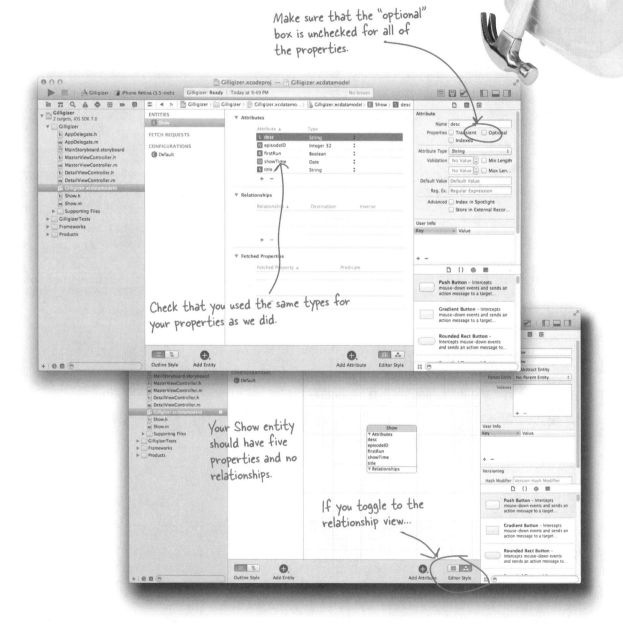

Check that you used the same types for your properties as we did.

Your Show entity should have five properties and no relationships.

If you toggle to the relationship view...

Core Data Up Close

Core Data is about managing objects

So far we've talked about how to describe our objects to Core Data, but not how we're actually going to do anything with them. In order to do that, we need to take a quick look inside Core Data.

Inside of Core Data is a stack of three critical pieces: the **Managed Object Context**, the **Persistent Store Coordinator**, and the **Persistent Object Store**.

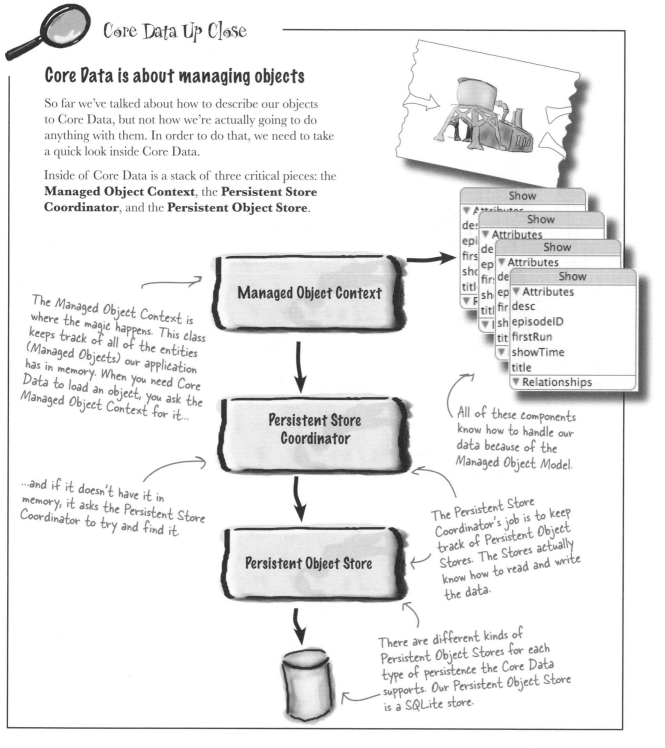

The Managed Object Context is where the magic happens. This class keeps track of all of the entities (Managed Objects) our application has in memory. When you need Core Data to load an object, you ask the Managed Object Context for it...

Managed Object Context

All of these components know how to handle our data because of the Managed Object Model.

...and if it doesn't have it in memory, it asks the Persistent Store Coordinator to try and find it.

Persistent Store Coordinator

The Persistent Store Coordinator's job is to keep track of Persistent Object Stores. The Stores actually know how to read and write the data.

Persistent Object Store

There are different kinds of Persistent Object Stores for each type of persistence the Core Data supports. Our Persistent Object Store is a SQLite store.

Great, so now we can load and save using this Managed Object Context?

You can call it MOC for short.

Exactly!

The Managed Object Context is what interacts with your database to get out the data. That's all set. What you need now is a class that can talk to the MOC and translate that into something usable for the application. We need a Show class....

But you need code. Core Data can do that for you.

Sharpen your pencil

Xcode can create a Show class from our Managed Object Model that we can use like any other class.

 Select the Gilligizer.xcdatamodel and click on the Show entity.
You need to have a Core Data entity selected before you ask Xcode to generate a class for you.

 Create a new Managed Object Class...
Select Editor→Create NSManagedObject Subclass... You will be prompted to select where the file should be saved. Because there is only one entity type in the file, you won't be prompted to choose which type to save.

 And generate the .h and .m.
Click Create and you should have a *Show.h* and a *Show.m* added to your project. Go ahead and drag these up to the */Gilligizer* group if they aren't there already.

Sharpen your pencil
                    Solution

Here's how Xcode can create a Show class from our Managed Object Model that we can use like any other class.

1 **Select the Gilligizer.xcdatamodel and click on the Show entity.**
You need to have a Core Data entity selected before you ask Xcode to generate a class for you.

2 **Create a new Managed Object Class...**
Select **Editor** → **Create NSManagedObject Subclass...** You will be prompted to select where the file should be saved. Since there is only one entity type in the file you won't be prompted to choose which type to save.

3 **And generate the .h and .m**
Click Create and you should have a Show.h and a Show.m added to your project. Go ahead and drag these up to the **/Gilligizer** group if they aren't there already.

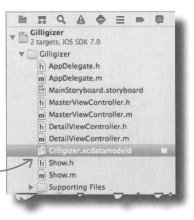

Our generated Show class matches our Managed Object Model

Xcode created two new files from our Show entity: a *Show.h* header file and a *Show.m* implementation file. Open up both files and let's take a look at what was created.

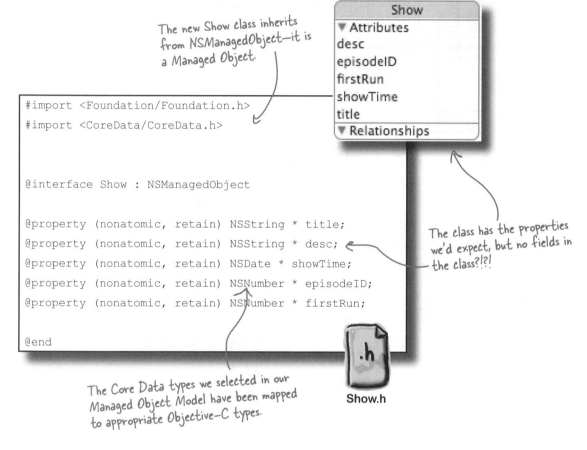

The new Show class inherits from NSManagedObject—it is a Managed Object.

```objc
#import <Foundation/Foundation.h>
#import <CoreData/CoreData.h>


@interface Show : NSManagedObject

@property (nonatomic, retain) NSString * title;
@property (nonatomic, retain) NSString * desc;
@property (nonatomic, retain) NSDate * showTime;
@property (nonatomic, retain) NSNumber * episodeID;
@property (nonatomic, retain) NSNumber * firstRun;


@end
```

Show
▼ **Attributes**
desc
episodeID
firstRun
showTime
title
▼ **Relationships**

The class has the properties we'd expect, but no fields in the class?!?!

The Core Data types we selected in our Managed Object Model have been mapped to appropriate Objective-C types.

Show.h

---

there are no Dumb Questions

Q: I don't understand where those types came from. Why is the `NSNumber` for both the `episodeID` and `firstRun`?

A: When we defined our attributes in our Managed Object Model, we used basic types (e.g., Integer32, Boolean) as the type. This works well for the data model, but when Core Data turns an entity into a Managed Object, we have to use objects to define data types. Since Objective-C supports both basic types and objects, Core Data wraps some basic types in the `NSNumber` class.

There's no code in there either... but I'm guessing that I'm not going to need to worry about that?

Right! The Core Data framework takes care of it.

The Show.m class is nearly empty, and instead of synthesizing the properties, they're declared with a new directive, @dynamic.

The implementation of the Show class is almost completely empty!

```
#import "Show.h"
@implementation Show

@dynamic title;
@dynamic desc;
@dynamic showTime;
@dynamic episodeID;
@dynamic firstRun;

@end
```

Show.m

there are no
Dumb Questions

Q: Hey, wait: if I have to regenerate the class, anything I customize gets rewritten. What do I do about that?

A: That's true right now. If you have custom code you're worrried about, you can do a couple of things. You can create a category on the Managed Object or you can subclass it.

NSManagedObject also implements the properties

The new @dynamic directive tells the compiler not to worry about the getter and setter methods necessary for the properties. They need to come from somewhere, though, or else code is going to crash at runtime when someone tries to access those properties. This is where NSManagedObject steps in again. Because NSManagedObject handles the memory for the fields backing the properties, it also provides runtime implementations for the getter and setter methods. By having NSManagedObject implement those methods, you get a number of other neat benefits:

 The NSManagedObject knows when properties are changed, can validate new data, and can notify other classes when changes happen.

You get all of this without writing a line of code!

 NSManagedObject can be lazy about fetching property information until someone asks for it. For example, it does this with relationships to other objects.

 NSManagedObject can keep track of changes to properties and provide undo-redo support.

Now it's just a matter of asking Core Data to load a Show...

Ready Bake Code

We snuck some extra code into your GitHub project to help along this part. If you download it directly, you'll see we've commented the code to help you along. Since you've already populated a detail view once, we figured we'd give you this code.

```objc
- (void)configureView
{
    // Update the user interface for the detail item.
    if (self.detailItem) {
        self.titleField.text = [self.detailItem valueForKey:@"title"];
        self.episodeIDField.text = [NSString stringWithFormat:@"%d",
[[self.detailItem valueForKey:@"episodeID"] integerValue]];
        self.descriptionView.text = [self.detailItem
valueForKey:@"desc"];
        self.firstRunSegmentedControl.selectedSegmentIndex = [[self.
detailItem valueForKey:@"firstRun"] boolValue];
        self.showTimeLabel.text = [[self.detailItem
valueForKey:@"showTime"] description];
    }
}
```

We're just filling out the UI with the data from our Show object.

We use 'boolValue' or 'integerValue' when our property is an instance of NSNumber, but we know (from our entity description) that we really want a basic type.

DetailViewController.m

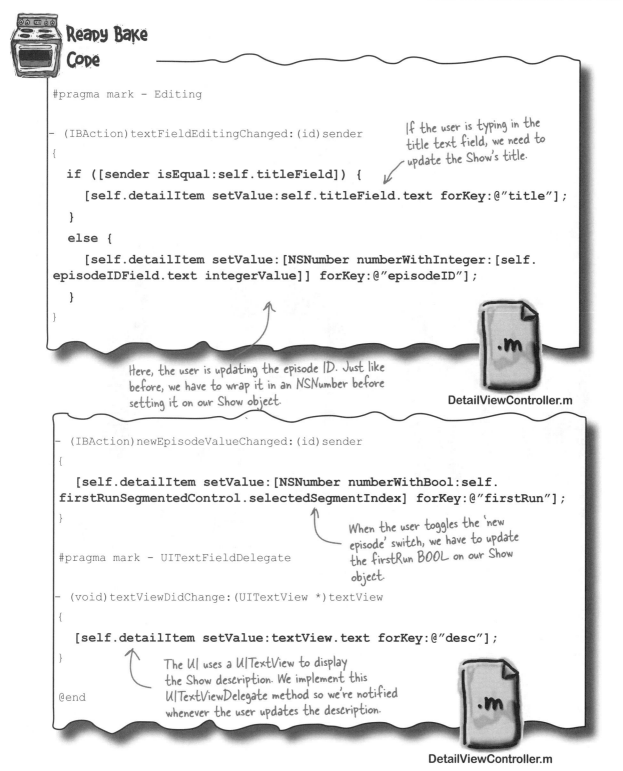

Ready Bake
Code

```
#pragma mark - Editing

- (IBAction)textFieldEditingChanged:(id)sender
{

  if ([sender isEqual:self.titleField]) {

    [self.detailItem setValue:self.titleField.text forKey:@"title"];

  }
  else {

    [self.detailItem setValue:[NSNumber numberWithInteger:[self.
episodeIDField.text integerValue]] forKey:@"episodeID"];

  }

}
```

If the user is typing in the title text field, we need to update the Show's title.

Here, the user is updating the episode ID. Just like before, we have to wrap it in an NSNumber before setting it on our Show object.

DetailViewController.m

```
- (IBAction)newEpisodeValueChanged:(id)sender
{

  [self.detailItem setValue:[NSNumber numberWithBool:self.
firstRunSegmentedControl.selectedSegmentIndex] forKey:@"firstRun"];

}

#pragma mark - UITextFieldDelegate

- (void)textViewDidChange:(UITextView *)textView
{

  [self.detailItem setValue:textView.text forKey:@"desc"];

}

@end
```

When the user toggles the 'new episode' switch, we have to update the firstRun BOOL on our Show object.

The UI uses a UITextView to display the Show description. We implement this UITextViewDelegate method so we're notified whenever the user updates the description.

DetailViewController.m

Jim: Head First Network is getting anxious...

Frank: Well, we've got the model now...

Joe: ...and the view from GitHub.

Jim: There's an Add button right? They want users to be able to add showings and look at them.

Jim

Joe

Frank

This button here, remember?

Frank: So what does that button do?

Jim: Just look in the code!

Joe: What about the insert new object method? I saw that in the *MasterViewController.m* file when we were adding that other code in.

```
- (void)insertNewObject:(id)sender
{
    NSManagedObjectContext *context = [self.fetchedResultsController
managedObjectContext];

    // Insert a new Show entity.
    Show *show = [NSEntityDescription insertNewObjectForEntityForName:@"Show"
inManagedObjectContext:context];
    show.desc = @"On this episode...";
    show.title = @"New Episode";
    show.firstRun = [NSNumber numberWithBool:FALSE];

    NSInteger count = [[self.fetchedResultsController sections][0]
numberOfObjects];
    show.episodeID = [NSNumber numberWithInteger:count];
    show.showTime = [NSDate dateWithTimeIntervalSinceNow:(86400 * count)];

    // Save the context.
    NSError *error = nil;
    if (![context save:&error]) {
        // Replace this implementation with code to handle the error
appropriately.
        // abort() causes the application to generate a crash log and
terminate. You should not use this function in a shipping application,
although it may be useful during development.
        NSLog(@"Unresolved error %@, %@", error, [error userInfo]);
        abort();
    }
}
```

NSEntityDescription is Core Data's way of looking up an entity from your Managed Object Model and inserting a new Managed Object into your MOC.

Since we made sure each of our attributes was non-optional we have to set some default values.

Here we tell our MOC to save, persisting our new Show object to the database. If the Show object was invalid, this save would fail.

MasterViewController.m

You have an <u>object</u>...now <u>present</u> it.

We have everything we need to create a new Show object and add it to the database. But that doesn't mean that anybody can see it! Now we need code to fetch that object back out and present it in the table view.

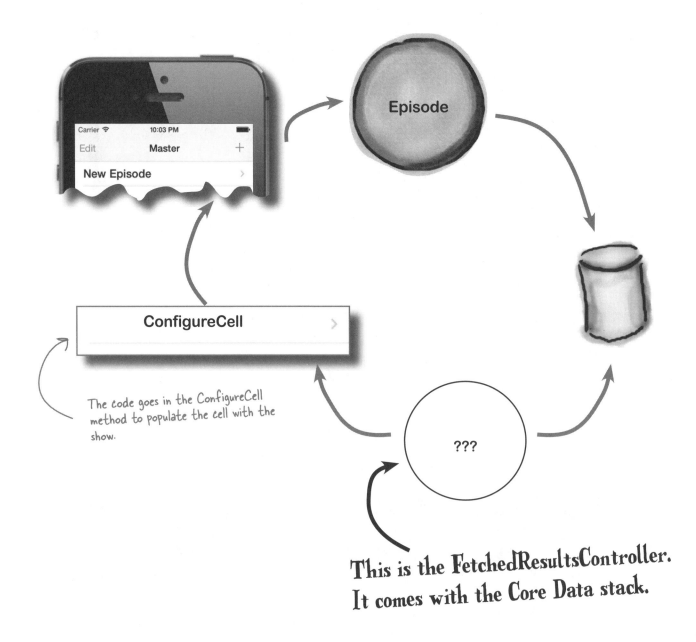

The code goes in the ConfigureCell method to populate the cell with the show.

This is the FetchedResultsController. It comes with the Core Data stack.

Present each entity in Gilligizer

In order to display a Show, we need to grab the right Show and pull the information we want to display. Our table view will let us know which Show we need by looking at the indexPath for the row in question. We can get the show from the FetchedResultsController and configure the cell based on Show properties.

We get the Show object for this table row from our FetchedRestultsController. Once we have the show, all we need to do is tell our cell to display the show's title.

```
- (void)configureCell:(UITableViewCell *)cell atIndexPath:(NSIndexPath *)
indexPath
{
    NSManagedObject *object = [self.fetchedResultsController
objectAtIndexPath:indexPath];
    cell.textLabel.text = [[object valueForKey:@"title"] description];
}
```

MasterViewController.m

there are no
Dumb Questions

Q: How is this data getting into the DB?

A: Through the + button that you're creating. Once the user hits that, we create a new instance of our Show entity and then save the updated ManagedObjectContext. For now, the user (and that's you when you're testing) is going to need to add shows manually. We'll get into adding a database of shows to work with soon.

Q: How does Core Data know which object to create in our 'insertNewObject:' method?

A: Remember how we talked about the differences between Entity and NSManagedObject? When we want to create a new Show object, we ask the class NSEntityDescription to insert a new object with the name "Show". This class will look at our Managed Object Model for an entity named "Show". When it finds one, it'll handle initializing an instance of our NSManagedObject subclass that maps to the Show entity.

We create entities in the DB... and we display objects from the DB. But how do we get those objects out?

No problem! The app needs to fetch results from the DB.

The Core Data stack comes with lots of the code that you already need to use to fetch data out of the database. If you dig into the code you can find it...

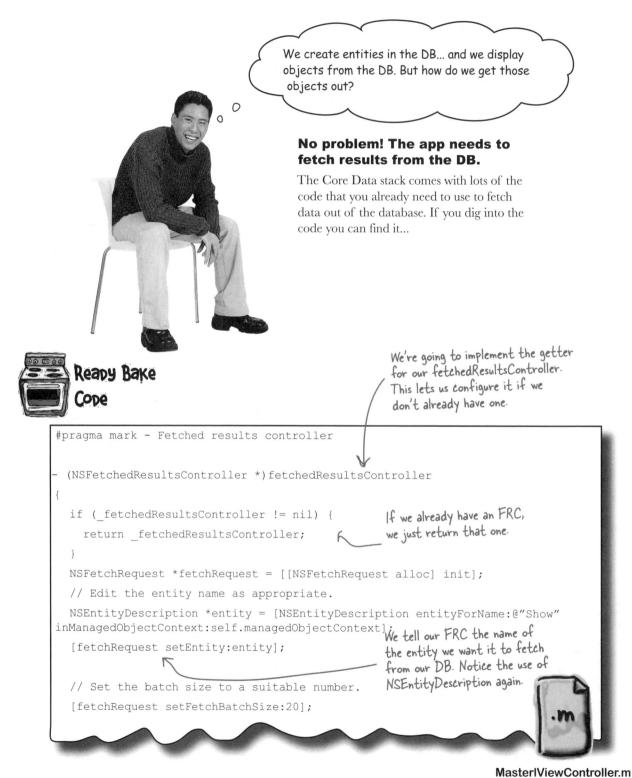

Ready Bake Code

We're going to implement the getter for our fetchedResultsController. This lets us configure it if we don't already have one.

```objc
#pragma mark - Fetched results controller

- (NSFetchedResultsController *)fetchedResultsController
{
    if (_fetchedResultsController != nil) {
        return _fetchedResultsController;
    }
    NSFetchRequest *fetchRequest = [[NSFetchRequest alloc] init];
    // Edit the entity name as appropriate.
    NSEntityDescription *entity = [NSEntityDescription entityForName:@"Show"
inManagedObjectContext:self.managedObjectContext];
    [fetchRequest setEntity:entity];

    // Set the batch size to a suitable number.
    [fetchRequest setFetchBatchSize:20];
```

If we already have an FRC, we just return that one.

We tell our FRC the name of the entity we want it to fetch from our DB. Notice the use of NSEntityDescription again.

.m

MasterViewController.m

Ready Bake
Code

```objc
// Edit the sort key as appropriate.
  NSSortDescriptor *sortDescriptor = [[NSSortDescriptor alloc]
initWithKey:@"showTime" ascending:YES];
  NSArray *sortDescriptors = @[sortDescriptor];

  [fetchRequest setSortDescriptors:sortDescriptors];


  // Edit the section name key path and cache name if appropriate.
  // nil for section name key path means "no sections".
  NSFetchedResultsController *aFetchedResultsController =
[[NSFetchedResultsController alloc] initWithFetchRequest: fetchRequest
managedObjectContext:self.managedObjectContext sectionNameKeyPath:nil
cacheName:@"Master"];

  aFetchedResultsController.delegate = self;
  self.fetchedResultsController = aFetchedResultsController;

      NSError *error = nil;
      if (![self.fetchedResultsController performFetch:&error]) {
        NSLog(@"Unresolved error %@, %@", error, [error userInfo]);
        abort();
      }

  return _fetchedResultsController;
}
```

A sort descriptor ensures that our data comes back from the DB in a predefined order. Useful for displaying the data in a table!

.m

MasterViewController.m

We initialize an instance of NSFetchedResultsController and tell it to performFetch. This call will use the fetch request we set up a few lines above to fetch and sort data from the DB.

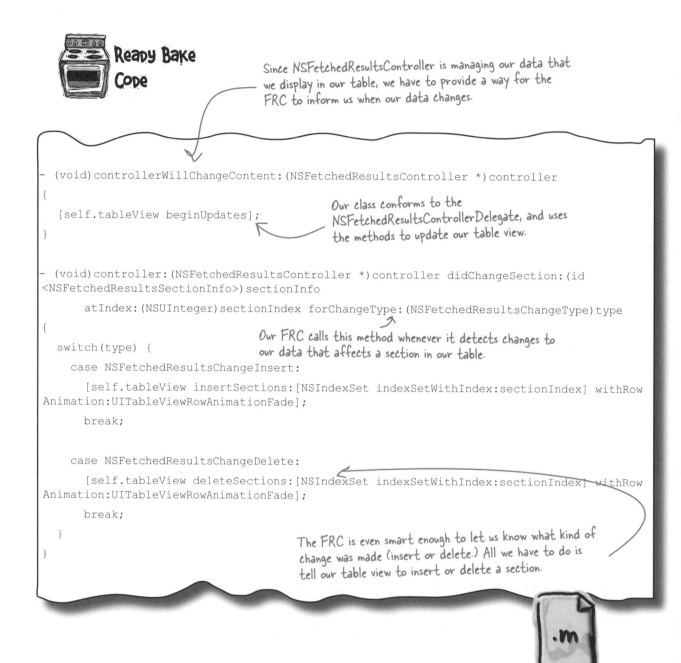

Ready Bake Code

Since NSFetchedResultsController is managing our data that we display in our table, we have to provide a way for the FRC to inform us when our data changes.

```objc
- (void)controllerWillChangeContent:(NSFetchedResultsController *)controller
{
    [self.tableView beginUpdates];
}
```

Our class conforms to the NSFetchedResultsControllerDelegate, and uses the methods to update our table view.

```objc
- (void)controller:(NSFetchedResultsController *)controller didChangeSection:(id
<NSFetchedResultsSectionInfo>)sectionInfo
    atIndex:(NSUInteger)sectionIndex forChangeType:(NSFetchedResultsChangeType)type
{
    switch(type) {
    case NSFetchedResultsChangeInsert:
        [self.tableView insertSections:[NSIndexSet indexSetWithIndex:sectionIndex] withRow
Animation:UITableViewRowAnimationFade];
        break;

    case NSFetchedResultsChangeDelete:
        [self.tableView deleteSections:[NSIndexSet indexSetWithIndex:sectionIndex] withRow
Animation:UITableViewRowAnimationFade];
        break;
    }
}
```

Our FRC calls this method whenever it detects changes to our data that affects a section in our table.

The FRC is even smart enough to let us know what kind of change was made (insert or delete.) All we have to do is tell our table view to insert or delete a section.

.m

MasterIViewController.m

```
- (void)controller:(NSFetchedResultsController *)controller didChangeObject:(id)anObject
    atIndexPath:(NSIndexPath *)indexPath forChangeType:(NSFetchedResultsChangeType)type
  newIndexPath:(NSIndexPath *)newIndexPath
{
  UITableView *tableView = self.tableView;

  switch(type) {
    case NSFetchedResultsChangeInsert:
      [tableView insertRowsAtIndexPaths:@[newIndexPath] withRowAnimation:UITableViewRowA
nimationFade];
      break;

    case NSFetchedResultsChangeDelete:
      [tableView deleteRowsAtIndexPaths:@[indexPath] withRowAnimation:UITableViewRowAnim
ationFade];
      break;


    case NSFetchedResultsChangeUpdate:
      [self configureCell:[tableView cellForRowAtIndexPath:indexPath]
atIndexPath:indexPath];
      break;


    case NSFetchedResultsChangeMove:
      [tableView deleteRowsAtIndexPaths:@[indexPath] withRowAnimation:UITableViewRowAnim
ationFade];
      [tableView insertRowsAtIndexPaths:@[newIndexPath] withRowAnimation:UITableViewRowA
nimationFade];
      break;
  }
}
- (void)controllerDidChangeContent:(NSFetchedResultsController *)controller
{
  [self.tableView endUpdates];
}
```

This method is where most of the magic happens. It's called whenever there is a change to one of the objects our FRC is managing.

Just like with sections, the FRC will let us know what kind of change was made to our object. And just like with sections, all we need to do is update our table view so it correctly reflects the data it's presenting.

Called when the controller is done informing us a change has taken place. This is where we tell our table view that we're all done with updates.

MasterViewController.m

Test Drive

Go ahead and take it for a spin. Just to be on the safe side, make sure you uninstall the app from the simulator and also clean the build in Xcode (Shift+Command+K).

By clicking the add button, you can get into the detail view and add text.

Once you add the text in here, if you back out then you'll see it in the master view.

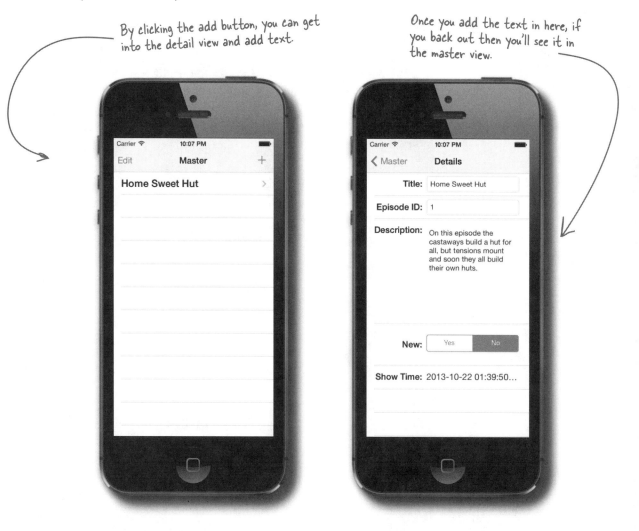

This is ridiculous! First, we generated the model. Now there's all this results controller stuff. What's going on?

Fetch results is not trivial. But it's coming...we'll explain more soon!

Core Data Cross

We've got some Core Data under our belts and some
multiple views work. There's a lot of terminology
here. Check it out!

Across

3. When you need Core Data to load an object, the Managed Object _____ is asked.

5. You can _____ a class from your entity.

6. The _____ Store Coordinator keeps track of object stores.

9. Template code written in Objective-C to help handle data.

10. Core Data supports three kids of persistence, including _____ DB's.

11. The _____ Results Controller gets the code from the database.

Down

1. The Managed Object Context is ___ for short.

2. This is where the code to populate your view lives.

4. The file you edit to work with the data model has an _____ extension.

7. Each conceptual piece of data is an _____.

8. Objects are described using the Managed Object _____.

Your Core Data toolbox

You've got Chapter 6 under your belt and now you've added some Core Data and table view cells to your toolbox.

Core Data

- Loads and saves objects.
- Options to store data include SQLite and custom binary files.
- Helps with memory management and undo and redo.
- Works using the concept of entities.
- An entity is an abstract representation of the data.

Core Data Stack

- The Managed Object Model is used to describe an entity in Core Data.
- Includes the Managed Object Context, the persistent store coordinator, and the persistent object store.

Fetching Data

- configureCell is where the data is loaded into the view.
- The Fetched Results Controller is code that comes with Core Data to help get results from the database.

Core Data Cross Solution

We've got some Core Data under our belts and some multiple views work. There's a lot of terminology here. Check it out!

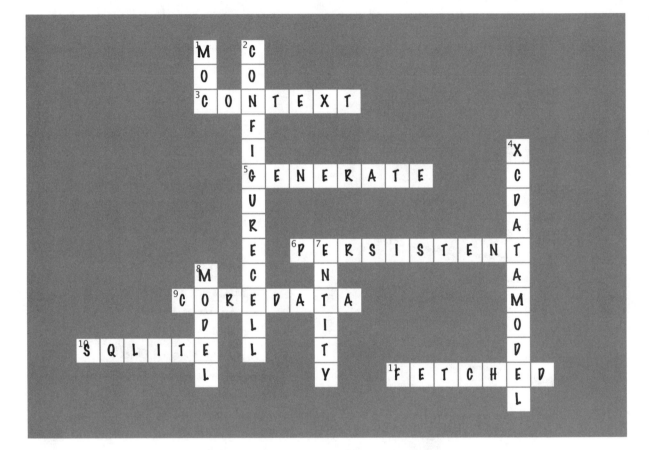

Across

3. When you need Core Data to load an object, the Managed Object _____ is asked. [CONTEXT]
5. You can _____ a class from your entity. [GENERATE]
6. The _____ Store Coordinator keeps track of object stores. [PERSISTENT]
9. Template code written in Objective-C to help handle data. [COREDATA]
10. Core Data supports three kids of persistence, including _____ DB's. [SQLITE]
11. The _____ Results Controller gets the code from the database. [FETCHED]

Down

1. The Managed Object Context is ___ for short. [MOC]
2. This is where the code to populate your view lives. [CONFIGURECELL]
4. The file you edit to work with the data model has an _____ extension. [XCDATAMODEL]
7. Each conceptual piece of data is an _____. [ENTITY]
8. Objects are described using the Managed Object _____. [MODEL]

7 implementing search with core data

✳ Looking for info ✳

There's got to be a better way to find that show we're looking for...

It's not enough to just be able to see data anymore.

The era of big data is here and just being able to look at it doesn't get you very far anymore. Now you probably won't have a couple of petabytes on your phone (famous last words), but you will most likely have enough data that you'll need to be able to sort and filter it to make it useful for your users. Core Data comes with some built-in functionality to slice through stacks of data and we're going to show you how to use it!

The app is working, but it's limited...

The first beta went over to HFN but it doesn't have all the functionality they want. You've gotten the app to the point where it can hold and display episodes, and users can add their own. But once you get a big chunk of data in there, there's a usability issue.

Imagine a giant list of TV shows and you're trying to find just one....

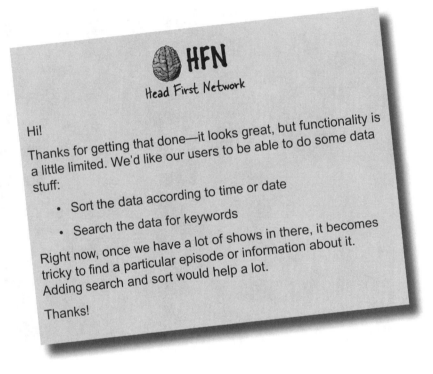

🧠 **HFN**

Head First Network

Hi!

Thanks for getting that done—it looks great, but functionality is a little limited. We'd like our users to be able to do some data stuff:

- Sort the data according to time or date
- Search the data for keywords

Right now, once we have a lot of shows in there, it becomes tricky to find a particular episode or information about it. Adding search and sort would help a lot.

Thanks!

We're going to get to explaining the FetchedResultsController

We know we implemented a lot of ready-baked FetchedResults code at the end of the last chapter. We're getting there, promise!

Jim

Joe

Frank

Jim: We're going to need some kind of UI so that the user can get to that functionality.

Frank: That sounds like a good idea to me. What do we need to sort by?

Joe: Time and date.

Frank: So, only two options? How about a segmented control, that makes sense.

Jim: OK, what if we use one part of the segment for sorting by time and the other by date?

Frank: Based on each segment, you'll need to create a new sort descriptor for the FetchedResultsController, too. One for date and one for time.

Joe: And then we can edit the fetch request on the FetchedResultsController and tell it to fetch again and reload the table.

Frank: Sounds good to me...

Exercise

Let's jump into Xcode and get a segmented control in there and get it sorting. It's actually pretty easy....

 Go ahead and create the segmented control that Jim, Frank, and Joe were talking about.
In the main storyboard file, you'll need to add the segmented control and update the titles to read "Show Time" and "Title". Add an Action and an Outlet in *MasterViewController.m* for the segmented control.

Segmented controller here.

 Update the FetchedResultsController and implement the segmentControlValueChanged method in MainViewController.m.
The FetchedResultsController sort key needs to update based on the selection of the segmented control and then the table will refresh.

Exercise Solution

Go ahead and get that segmented control in there and sorting. Once you get into it, the `NSFetchedResultsController` is really great at this sort of thing.

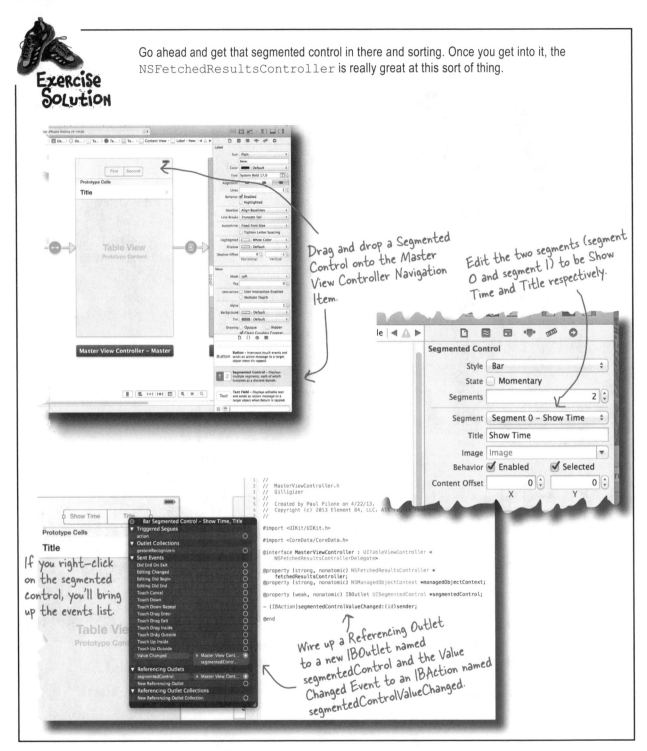

Drag and drop a Segmented Control onto the Master View Controller Navigation Item.

Edit the two segments (segment 0 and segment 1) to be Show Time and Title respectively.

If you right-click on the segmented control, you'll bring up the events list.

Wire up a Referencing Outlet to a new IBOutlet named segmentedControl and the Value Changed Event to an IBAction named segmentedControlValueChanged.

EXERCISE
SOLUTION

```
- (NSFetchedResultsController *)fetchedResultsController
{
  ...
  // Edit the sort key as appropriate.
  NSString *sortKey = [self.segmentedControl selectedSegmentIndex] == 0 ?
@"showTime" : @"title";
  NSSortDescriptor *sortDescriptor = [[NSSortDescriptor alloc]
initWithKey:sortKey ascending:YES];
  NSArray *sortDescriptors = @[sortDescriptor];

  [fetchRequest setSortDescriptors:sortDescriptors];
  ...
}
```

Change the sort key creation in the fetchedResultsController code to use either the showTime or title attributes of our Core Data entities based on the segemented controller.

.m

MasterlViewController.m

Implement the segmented control action to simply drop our old FetchedResultsController and force the table to reload. This will cause us to create a new FetchedResultsController with the appropriate sort key.

```
- (IBAction)segmentedControlValueChanged:(id)sender
{
  self.fetchedResultsController = nil;
  [self.tableView reloadData];
}
```

.m

MasterlViewController.m

Wait a second. You promised to explain all this fetching stuff to me...

That's true, we did.

Honestly, we've probably built it up more than we should. It's not very complicated.

The table gets populated like every other table we've used. Our `cellForRowAtIndexPath` method will be called looking for a `UITableViewCell`. We grab one and start configuring it. That's where we use our `FetchedResultsController`. The `NSFetchedResultsController` is designed to support UITableViews. All we need to do is tell it how to find the data it needs...

Use an NSFetchRequest to describe your search

In order to tell the `NSFetchedResultsController` what we're looking for, we need to create an `NSFetchRequest`. The `NSFetchRequest` describes what kind of objects we want to fetch, any conditions we want when it fetches them (like shows before 10 a.m.), and how Core Data should sort the results when it gives them back. Yeah, it does all that for us.

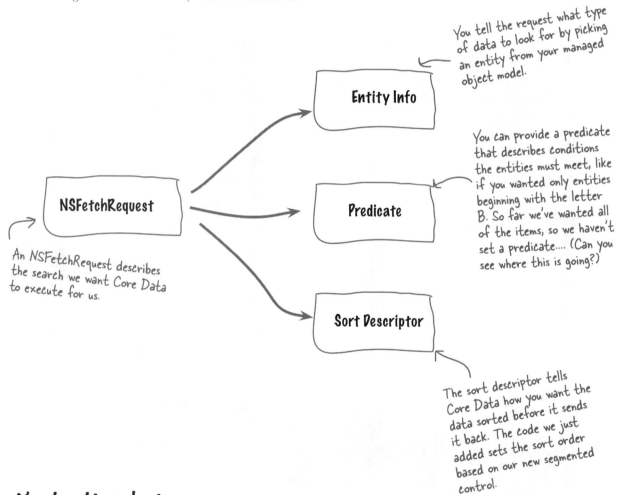

You tell the request what type of data to look for by picking an entity from your managed object model.

Entity Info

You can provide a predicate that describes conditions the entities must meet, like if you wanted only entities beginning with the letter B. So far we've wanted all of the items, so we haven't set a predicate.... (Can you see where this is going?)

Predicate

NSFetchRequest

An NSFetchRequest describes the search we want Core Data to execute for us.

Sort Descriptor

The sort descriptor tells Core Data how you want the data sorted before it sends it back. The code we just added sets the sort order based on our new segmented control.

Let's give it a shot...

TEST DRIVE

It works! Run the app and enter a few episodes. Tapping "Show Time" or "Title" changes the sort descriptor and the table updates accordingly. Nice work!

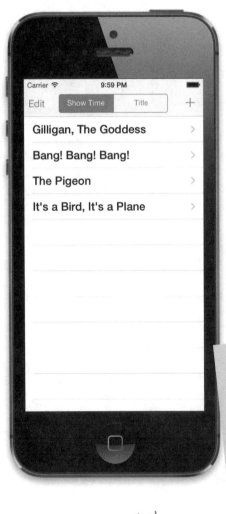

That letter from Head First Network...

HFN
Head First Network

Hi!
Thanks for getting that done—it looks great, but functionality is a little limited. We'd like our users to be able to do some data stuff:

- Sort the data according to time or date
- Search the data for keywords.

Right now, once we have a lot of shows in there, it becomes tricky to find a particular episode or information about it. Adding search and sort would help a lot.

Thanks!

Can we use different search predicates just like we used different sort descriptors?

Exactly!

The search control comes with its own table view so we'll give it its own FetchedResultsController but this time we'll manipulate the predicate as the user types.

iOS 7 has Core Data and UIKit support for searching

Searching data used by an application is such a common use case that iOS 7 and Core Data provide just about everything we need to make it happen. Like nearly everything else we've done, we can split the visual presentation of the information (UIKit) from the actual searching of the data (Core Data). We'll start with the UIKit part.

SearchDisplayController handles just about everything

iOS 7 includes a `SearchBar` and `SearchDisplayController` that provides us with all of the `UIComponent` classes we need. We can simply add the controller to our storyboard and that gets us our search bar, and a controller which gives us a modal table view that is filled with results. All we need to do is wire it up very much like our normal table views.

> So does this search controller magically search our data too?

No, but our results controller can!

The results controller supports more than just the sort descriptor. We can use Core Data's advanced searching and filtering capabilities with an `NSFetchedResultsController` to limit what data we get back. And that's exactly what the `UISearchDisplayController` does.

Use predicates for filtering data

In database languages all over the world, **predicates** are used to scope (or limit) a search to only find data that matches certain criteria. Remember the NSFetchRequest we talked about earlier in the chapter? For that we used the Entity Information and Sort Descriptor, but we haven't needed the predicate support...until now.

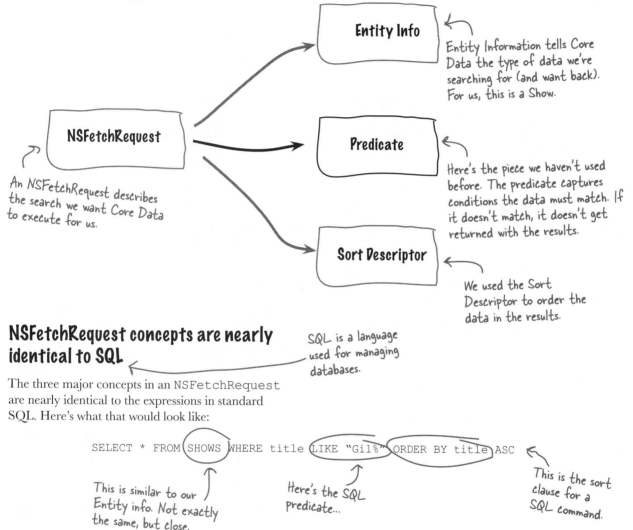

Entity Info

Entity Information tells Core Data the type of data we're searching for (and want back). For us, this is a Show.

NSFetchRequest

An NSFetchRequest describes the search we want Core Data to execute for us.

Predicate

Here's the piece we haven't used before. The predicate captures conditions the data must match. If it doesn't match, it doesn't get returned with the results.

Sort Descriptor

We used the Sort Descriptor to order the data in the results.

NSFetchRequest concepts are nearly identical to SQL

SQL is a language used for managing databases.

The three major concepts in an NSFetchRequest are nearly identical to the expressions in standard SQL. Here's what that would look like:

```
SELECT * FROM SHOWS WHERE title LIKE "Gil%" ORDER BY title ASC
```

This is similar to our Entity info. Not exactly the same, but close.

Here's the SQL predicate...

This is the sort clause for a SQL command.

You wrap up the search constraints in an NSPredicate and give that to the NSFetchRequest. Let's talk a little more about the predicate before we wire it all up.

The NSFetchRequest predicate controls what data is returned

NSPredicate is a deceptively simple class that lets us express logical constraints on our NSFetchRequest. You use entity and attribute names along with comparison operators to express your constraint information. You can create a basic NSPredicate with a string format syntax similar to NSString, like this:

```
fetchRequest.predicate = [NSPredicate predicateWithFormat:@"title
contains[cd] %@", searchText];
```

But NSPredicates don't stop with simple attribute comparisons. Apple provides several subclasses like NSComparisonPredicate, NSCompoundPredicate, and NSExpression, as well as a complex grammar for wildcard matching, object graph traversal, and more. You can even build complex fetch requests graphically in Xcode. There's a whole predicate authoring guide available in Apple's iOS documentation for all your searching needs.

The Search Bar lets you know what's happening through a delegate

Once we add the searchDisplayController to the storyboard, Xcode will automatically hook up our controller to a SearchDisplayController property. Like almost all other iOS controls, the Search Display can be given a delegate and lets that delegate know what's going on.

We need to react when the search bar changes. The search controller will ask us what it should do by invoking shouldReloadTableForSearchString when the search text changes. If we return YES from this, the search controller will refresh its results. The question is, how does it actually do the search?

Sharpen your pencil

What do you think we need to do next? Give it your best shot. What do we need so that the SearchDisplayController can actually execute searches against our Show database?

....

....

....

⟶ Answers on page 244

Drop a Search Bar and `SearchDisplayController` into our storyboard

In our MasterView scene in the storyboard you should add the "Search Bar and Search Display Controller. "Add this right above the Prototype Cells section header. This will anchor a Search Bar at the top of our table view and add a display controller to the list of controllers at the bottom of the scene.

Do this!

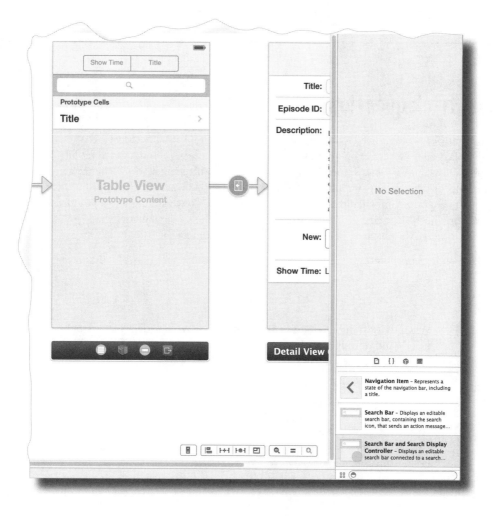

Sharpen your pencil
Solution

Here's what we came up with for some next steps so that the `SearchDisplayController` can actually execute searches.

We can use an NSFetchedResultsController to execute the appropriate search based on the text in the Search Bar. It just can't be the same NSFetchedResultsController!

It was a trick question...

The Search Controller doesn't need to actually execute the search for us! The Search Bar and searchDisplayController wrap up a nice text field we can use for searching and a modal controller that shows a table view. Remember how our current table view works? Whenever the table view needs to fill in rows with data, it asks for a cell for that row. We grab a cell, populate it with the correct information, and give it back. Where do we get the information for the row? From our `NSFetchedResultsController`. The table view itself has nothing to do with how we get the data or which data we're looking at.

We can use the same pattern here:

 When the search bar changes, the SearchDisplayController will ask us if it should refresh its table view. We can respond with a YES, ensuring that it reloads the data in the table.

 When it tries to refresh the table, its table view will start clamoring for rows. We can use a custom `NSFetchedResultsController` to grab results that match the current search bar contents.

BRAIN
BARBELL

Now that you have an idea of what to do, go through the list below. Pick what we need to do to wire up the SearchDisplayController. There are multiple answers, so pick a bunch!

☐ Conform to the UISearchDisplayDelegate protocol.

☐ Implement the `- (BOOL) searchDisplayController:(UISearchDisplayController *)controller shouldReloadTableForSearchString:(NSString *)searchString` method to tell the search controller is should always refresh the table.

☐ Add a new `NSFetchedResultsController` that is configured based on the search terms.

☐ Add a new `tableview` to show the results.

☐ Create a new entity to store Search Matches.

☐ Keep track of which `tableview` is visible so we know what to do in other methods

☐ Create a new detail view controller to show details of selecting a search result item.

☐ Create a property for the search results `tableview`.

☐ Create a property for a new `searchResultsFetchedController`.

BRAIN BARBELL Solution

Now that you have an idea of what to do, go through the list below. Pick what we need to do to wire up the Search Display Controller. There are multiple answers so pick a bunch!

 Conform to the UISearchDisplayDelegate protocol. *This is so we get notified when the search text changes.*

☑ Implement the - (BOOL)searchDisplayController:(UISea rchDisplayController *)controller shouldReloadTa bleForSearchString:(NSString *)searchString method to tell the search controller is should always refresh the table.

This way we can reconfigure the FetchedResultsController when the search text changes. We'll need to wipe out the old search controller so we'll use the new one when the table reloads.

☑ Add a new NSFetchedResultsController that is configured based on the search terms.

This will be cached in a property we'll need to create (see below) and will have a predicate set on it based on the search text.

☐ Add a new tableview to show the results. *This is handled by the SearchDisplayController.*

☐ Create a new entity to store Search Matches. *We're loading shows here just like the main tableview.*

 Keep track of which tableview is visible so we know what to do in other methods *We need to know whether the main tableview is visible or the search results table view is visible so we know which search results controller to use among other things*

☐ Create a new detail view controller to show details of selecting a search result item.

We'll need to tweak the prepareForSegue so that we grab the right row from the right tableview depending on which is visible, but we're just using shows and our current detail view controller can handle those.

BRAIN BARBELL   Solution

☐ Create a property for the search results tableview.

The SearchDisplayController handles that and we can get the tableview from there.

☑ Create a property for a new `searchResultsFetchedController`.

We'll want to cache this and only re-create it (and redo the search) if the search text changes.

What about the old methods with the FetchedResultsController? Don't they need updating?

Yes! Great catch!

You'll need to go through the various methods in our *MasterViewController.m* that deal with updating the table views to make sure you're updating the right table view and that we're using the right `NSFetchedResultsController`.

Wouldn't it be dreamy if I didn't have to type up all that code in all those little places? But I know it's just a fantasy...

It's not! Go grab the end of chapter code from the Git repo. You know what to do...

Do this!

To get the end of chapter code, go back and check out the master branch instead of the Chapter 7 code—you'll get the finished project.

Test Drive

Go ahead and check out the last of the code for the chapter. Once you
have it in Xcode, take it for a spin!

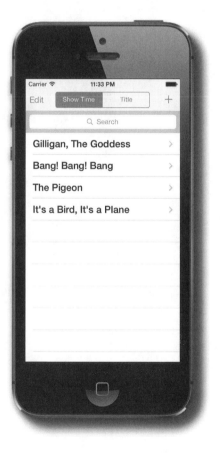

Look at that! The search bar is in there and works too.

Head First Network

To: Rock star developer

Awesome! We're really psyched about this app. Now anybody who needs a *Gilligan* fix can get one quick.

Thanks!

Search Cross

Ha! It's not a word find... use the new words you
learned here to solve the puzzle.

Across

1. The SearchDisplayController uses a _____ view that
   shows a table with search results.

6. The SearchDisplayController uses a _____ field to use for
   searching.

7. The _____ describes the conditions that the entities
   must meet to be fetched.

8. The _____ descriptor tells Core Data how you want the
   data sorted before it's sent back.

Down

2. The search bar lets you know what's happening through a
   _____.

3. The FetchedResultsController can be used to implement
   _____.

4. You can split the _____ presentation of the information from
   a search result from the searching of the data.

5. The FetchedResultsController uses NSFetchRequest to
   describe the _____ that we want to fetch.

8. NSFetchRequest concepts are very similar to _____.

Search Cross Solution

Ha! It's not a word find... use the new words you
learned here to solve the puzzle.

Across

1. The SearchDisplayController uses a _____ view that
   shows a table with search results. [MODAL]
6. The SearchDisplayController uses a _____ field to use for
   searching. [TEXT]
7. The _____ describes the conditions that the entities
   must meet to be fetched. [PREDICATE]
8. The _____ descriptor tells Core Data how you want the
   data sorted before it's sent back. [SORT]

Down

2. The search bar lets you know what's happening through a
   _____. [DELEGATE]
3. The FetchedResultsController can be used to implement
   _____. [SORTING]
4. You can split the _____ presentation of the information from
   a search result from the searching of the data. [VISUAL]
5. The FetchedResultsController uses NSFetchRequest to
   describe the _____ that we want to fetch. [OBJECTS]
8. NSFetchRequest concepts are very similar to _____. [SQL]

Your searching toolbox

You've got Chapter 7 under your belt and now you've added search and fetched results to your toolbox.

Fetching

- You use the fetched results controller to sort data.

- To perform a fetch, you need to issue a request describing the objects that we want to find.

- Use predicates to describe the conditions to be fetched.

Search

- Core Data and UIKit support search and maintain MVC.

- The search controller can't search data; the results controller can.

- The SearchDisplayController uses a text field and a modal view for searching.

NSFetchRequest

- Concepts are almost idential to SQL.

8 core data, map kit, and core location

Finding a phone booth

This is all I can use til I can get a fancy iPhone!

Now it's time to get to some goodies.

These devices come with so much in the way of built-in capabilities. iPhones and iPads are part computer, part library, part still and video camera, and part GPS device. The field of location-based computing is in its infancy, but it's very powerful. Fortunately, tapping into those hardware functions is something that iOS makes fairly easy.

Everything old is ^{cool} ~~new~~ again

Go Retro Unlimited

We need your help!

Here at Go Retro Unlimited, we value what's old... what's cool... and what's forgotten.

Before Goonies made it to the iTunes Store, we were the ones still laughing at a certain broken statue on our old VHS tape. Before most people had their mixtapes anywhere but in a shoe box, we turned ours into iTunes playlists.

But now there's a new casualty of culture: the phone booth! As people have been snatching up the newest, coolest iPhone, the phone booths you knew, loved, and never had enough quarters for are being bulldozed and removed! But we can preserve these phone booths forever!

We want phone booth photos to put on our iPads and iPhones... lots and lots of phone booths! We want 'em from San Francisco, from Sydney, from Darfur. We want pictures, and we want locations. And that's where you come in... we want an app that anyone with an iPhone or iPad can pull up anytime they see a phone booth. Snap a picture, send it to us, and best of all, geotag it. Just think... before long, you and your friends can all be sharing your phone booth photos on your fifth-generation iPhone. It's so very... meta!

We've gotten started, but now we need your help. Head out to GitHub now, and see what we've got. It's not much... that's why we need your help! So get coding, and we'll get to looking for the nearest phone booth.

Anybody got a quarter?

Jimi Vain
CEO,

There really are phone booths in Darfur! And who wouldn't want a picture of that?

  **BRAIN BARBELL**

After you download the app from GitHub, go ahead and check out what's done so far. Then you can move into the work!

Remember to check out the Chapter 8 branch and then pick the RetroPhoneHunter project.

An app, an iPad, and a phone booth

The app from GitHub really does need some work. Each phone booth needs to have a picture and several details: the city in which the phone booth was located, the zip code, and a place for the photographer to jot down a few notes... looks like there's plenty to add to the app already.

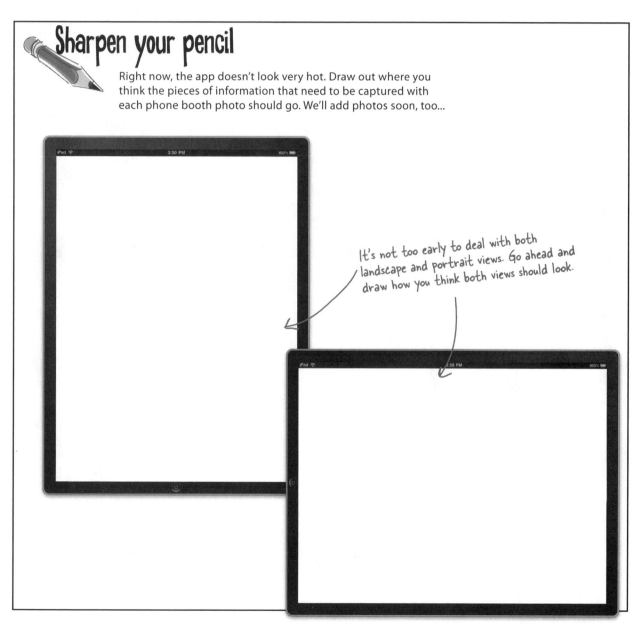

Sharpen your pencil

Right now, the app doesn't look very hot. Draw out where you think the pieces of information that need to be captured with each phone booth photo should go. We'll add photos soon, too...

It's not too early to deal with both landscape and portrait views. Go ahead and draw how you think both views should look.

Sharpen your pencil
Solution

How'd you do? Here's what we came up with. Remember, you can design your own app however you want. Just make sure you understand why you made the choices you did.

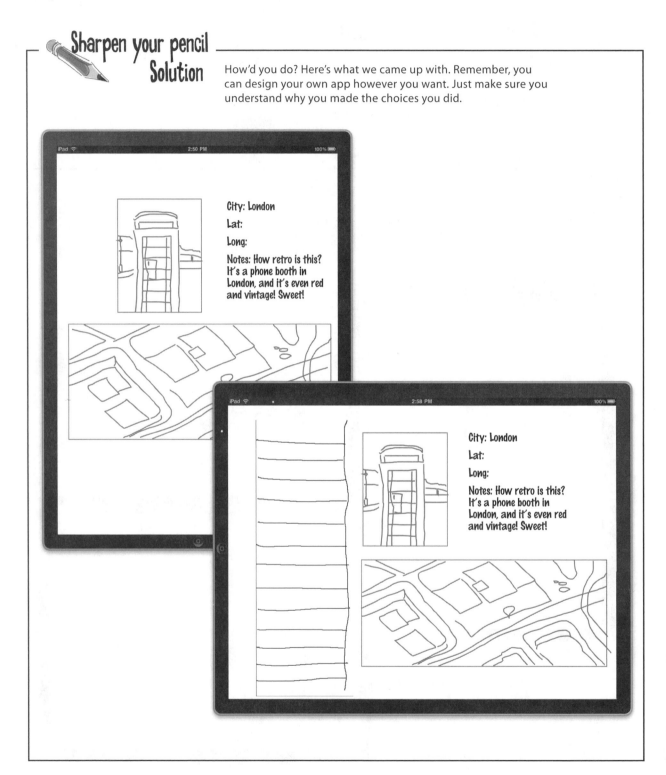

Long Exercise

First up is the photos. Go Retro Unlimited isn't going to be very impressed with your design drawings—or even a working app—if the app doesn't show real pictures of phone booths. So put down those no. 2 pencils and get your favorite code editor up. You need to...

1 **Connect your app to a database to pull those phone booth descriptions.**
This is going to be similar to what we did for Spin City. The app that came from GitHub is just template code, so you'll need to tweak that to work with our app.

2 **Generate the PhoneBooth class.**
Like we did for Gilligizer, create an NSManagedObject subclass: go to "Editor" then "Create NSManagedObject Subclass." Select PhoneBooth entity, confirm saving the entity in the project, then click Create.

For now, don't sweat actually taking the picture. You'll add that ability soon...

3 **Fix the template to use the new PhoneBooth entity instead of the default Event entity in MasterViewController.m.**
Edit the file to change references to "timestamp" to "name", import the *Phonebooth.h* file, change the NSManagedObject in the didSelectRowAtIndexPath, change the NSManagedObject to a Phonebooth, and instead of using setValue for a data, change it to @"NewPhoneBooth".

4 **Layout the detail view and add the supporting code to make it work.**
First, we'll need to add the required elements to the storyboard file, a UIImageView, a **Name** label and text field, a **City** label and text field, a **Notes** label and a text view for the description.

Long Exercise Solution

This shouldn't have been too hard, even though it might have taken a pretty fair bit of coding. Make sure you've got a working, buildable app. If you got stuck, you can walk through each step and see what we did.

1 **Connect your app to a database to pull those phone booth descriptions.**

This is going to be similar to what we did for Spin City. The app that came from GitHub is just template code, so you'll need to tweak that to work with our app.

Delete the default "event" entity. The easiest way is is to highlight it and click "delete."

Here's the final model we're building.

2 **Generate the PhoneBooth class.**

Like we did for Gilligizer, create an NSManagedObject subclass: go to "Editor" then "Create NSManagedObject Subclass." Select PhoneBooth entity, confirm saving the entity in the project, then click Create.

③ **Fix the template to use the new PhoneBooth entity instead of the default Event entity in MasterViewController.m.**

Edit the file to change references to "timestamp" to "name", import the *Phonebooth.h* file, change the NSManagedObject in the didSelectRowAtIndexPath, change the NSManagedObject to a Phonebooth, and instead of using setValue for a data, change it to @"NewPhoneBooth".

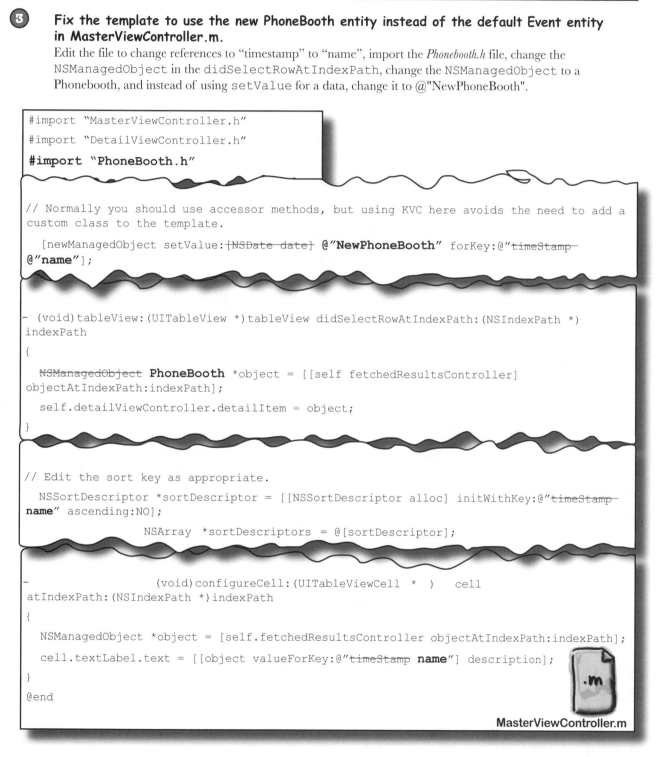

```objc
#import "MasterViewController.h"
#import "DetailViewController.h"
#import "PhoneBooth.h"
```

```objc
// Normally you should use accessor methods, but using KVC here avoids the need to add a
custom class to the template.
   [newManagedObject setValue:[NSDate date] @"NewPhoneBooth" forKey:@"timeStamp
@"name"];
```

```objc
- (void)tableView:(UITableView *)tableView didSelectRowAtIndexPath:(NSIndexPath *)
indexPath
{
   NSManagedObject PhoneBooth *object = [[self fetchedResultsController]
objectAtIndexPath:indexPath];
   self.detailViewController.detailItem = object;
}
```

```objc
// Edit the sort key as appropriate.
   NSSortDescriptor *sortDescriptor = [[NSSortDescriptor alloc] initWithKey:@"timeStamp
name" ascending:NO];
                NSArray *sortDescriptors = @[sortDescriptor];
```

```objc
-                (void)configureCell:(UITableViewCell *  )   cell
atIndexPath:(NSIndexPath *)indexPath
{
   NSManagedObject *object = [self.fetchedResultsController objectAtIndexPath:indexPath];
   cell.textLabel.text = [[object valueForKey:@"timeStamp name"] description];
}
@end
```

MasterViewController.m

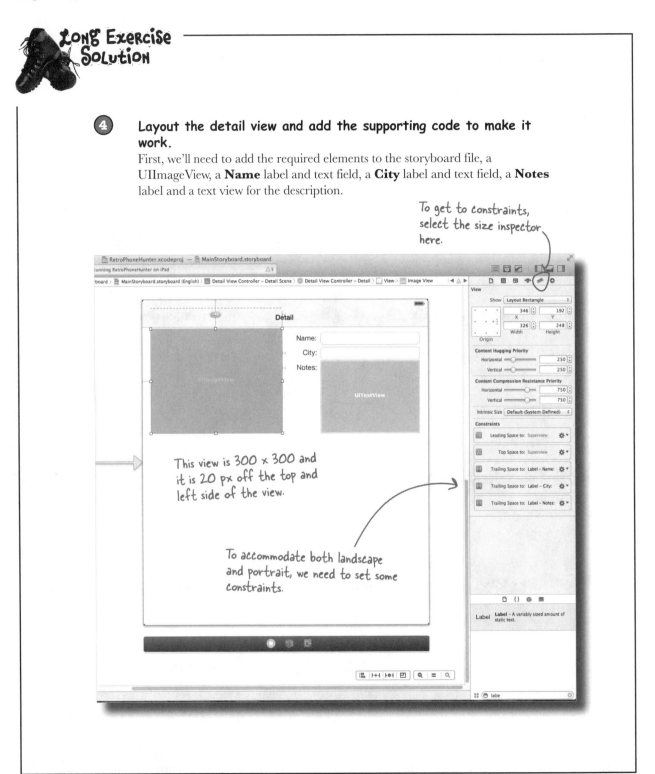

Long Exercise Solution

④ **Layout the detail view and add the supporting code to make it work.**

First, we'll need to add the required elements to the storyboard file, a UIImageView, a **Name** label and text field, a **City** label and text field, a **Notes** label and a text view for the description.

To get to constraints, select the size inspector here.

This view is 300 x 300 and it is 20 px off the top and left side of the view.

To accommodate both landscape and portrait, we need to set some constraints.

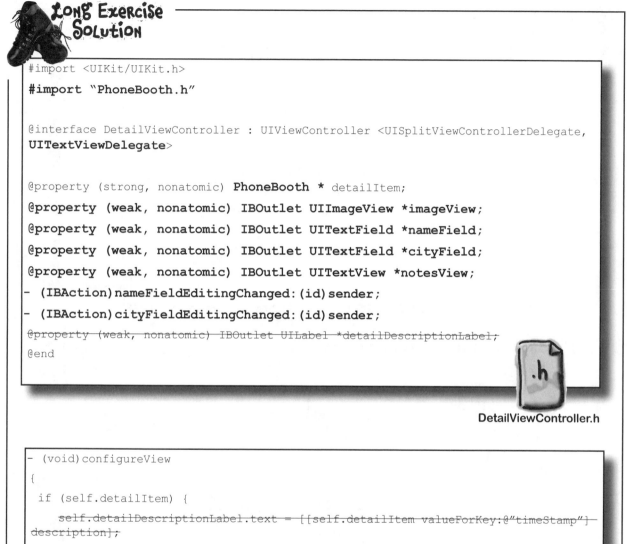

LONG EXERCISE SOLUTION

```objc
#import <UIKit/UIKit.h>
#import "PhoneBooth.h"

@interface DetailViewController : UIViewController <UISplitViewControllerDelegate,
UITextViewDelegate>

@property (strong, nonatomic) PhoneBooth * detailItem;
@property (weak, nonatomic) IBOutlet UIImageView *imageView;
@property (weak, nonatomic) IBOutlet UITextField *nameField;
@property (weak, nonatomic) IBOutlet UITextField *cityField;
@property (weak, nonatomic) IBOutlet UITextView *notesView;
- (IBAction)nameFieldEditingChanged:(id)sender;
- (IBAction)cityFieldEditingChanged:(id)sender;
@property (weak, nonatomic) IBOutlet UILabel *detailDescriptionLabel;
@end
```

DetailViewController.h

```objc
- (void)configureView
{
  if (self.detailItem) {
     self.detailDescriptionLabel.text = [[self.detailItem valueForKey:@"timeStamp"]
description];
     self.nameField.text = self.detailItem.name;
     self.cityField.text = self.detailItem.city;
     self.notesView.text = self.detailItem.notes;
     self.imageView.image = [UIImage imageWithContentsOfFile:self.
detailItem.imagePath];
  }
}
```

DetailViewController.m

Long Exercise Solution

```
- (IBAction)nameFieldEditingChanged:(id)sender
{
  self.detailItem.name = self.nameField.text;
}
- (IBAction)cityFieldEditingChanged:(id)sender
{
  self.detailItem.city = self.cityField.text;
}
- (void)textViewDidChange:(UITextView *)textView
{
  self.detailItem.notes = self.notesView.text;
}
@end
```

DetailViewController.m

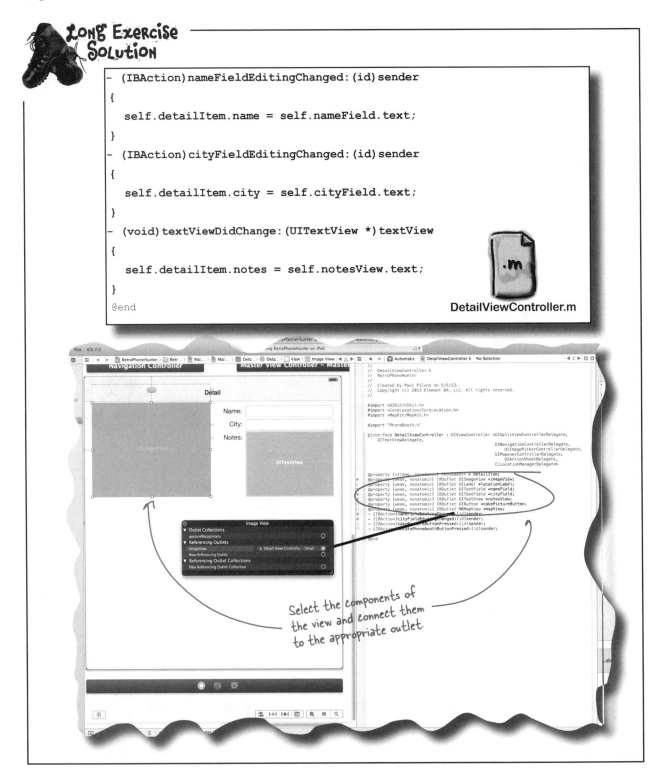

Select the components of the view and connect them to the appropriate outlet.

TEST DRIVE

Go ahead and try it out! It should launch in the iPad simulator
(the first time for us!) in portrait. To see it in landscape, go to
Hardware→Rotate Left or Rotate Right.

Since we don't have an image to
view, this area is blank. If you
wanted to see it in the simulator,
then go into the storyboard and
edit the background color away
from transparency. You'll see it!

Sharpen your pencil

Now that the views are working properly, what about the
image itself? Think about the data model when you fill in
the blanks below.

The UIImage will be stored in the ....

The .... has to know about the image and where to display it.

The image has to come from the .... or the ....

Sharpen your pencil Solution

Here's how we'll be getting at the image itself.

The UIImage will be stored in the ……… **documents directory** …………………… .

The ……… **DetailViewController** ……………… has to know about the image and where to display it.

The image has to come from the …… **camera** …………… or the …… **documents directory** ………… .

> And we should probably store the photos in a database, right?

Databases aren't one size fits all.

Newer iPhones and iPads are taking really nice pictures... and that usually means really big pictures. If you try and stuff that big image into your database, you're going to use up a lot of memory and space...fast.

But the image is already on your device... through the camera or in the user's Photo Library. So instead of copying it into your database, you can just reference the existing image that's on your phone.

But *where* is that image? What's the path to it? And where can you write the image once you've got it?

iOS apps are read-only (well, kind of...)

Since you won't be storing images in a database, you've got to get down and dirty with the iOS filesystem. Then, you can just write to that filesystem, whether it's the image itself or just a path to somewhere else on your device... right?

Well, sort of. Applications are installed on iOS devices as **read-only**. You can access resources that are bundled with your application, but you can't *modify* them. The only way to actually change data on the filesystem is to write that data to one of the special places iOS gives you...just for that purpose.

For example, the Core Data templates automatically takes care of this for you. Here's a short bit of code that creates a new database in one of those special writable places for your application:

Apple calls the directory structure that apps are written to—both the read-only and the writable parts—the "app sandbox."

```
NSURL *storeUrl = [NSURL fileURLWithPath: [[self
applicationDocumentsDirectory] URLByAppendingPathComponent:
@"retroPhoneHunter.sqlite"]];
```

retroPhoneHunterAppDelegate.m

The Core Data template looks in the application documents directory for the database, not the application bundle. That's because this section of the filesystem is writable, but the application bundle isn't.

You need to do something similar: figure out where you can write data to, grab the path to the image of a phone booth that a user wants to use, and write that path to the filesystem.

An iOS application structure defines where you can read and write data

For security and stability reasons, iOS locks down the filesystem pretty tightly. When an application is installed, the iOS creates a directory under */User/Applications* on your device using a unique identifier. The application is then installed into that directory, and a standard directory structure is created for the app, like this:

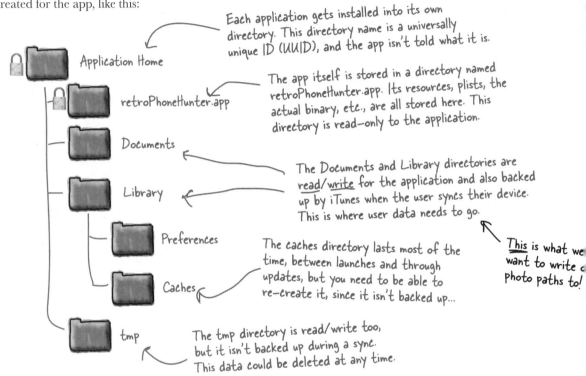

Each application gets installed into its own directory. This directory name is a universally unique ID (UUID), and the app isn't told what it is.

The app itself is stored in a directory named retroPhoneHunter.app. Its resources, plists, the actual binary, etc., are all stored here. This directory is read-only to the application.

The Documents and Library directories are read/write for the application and also backed up by iTunes when the user syncs their device. This is where user data needs to go.

The caches directory lasts most of the time, between launches and through updates, but you need to be able to re-create it, since it isn't backed up...

This is what we want to write photo paths to!

The tmp directory is read/write too, but it isn't backed up during a sync. This data could be deleted at any time.

Get the photo path and then write that path to the filesystem!

Now you know what to do... and even where you can write photo paths: the *Documents* and *Library* directories. But how do you actually get the path to the photo? That's what's next. Fortunately, iOS makes this a lot easier than it might seem...

Enter... UIImagePicker

The real mission here is to *pick* an image (after one is taken by the camera, or from the Photo Library), and then do something with that image...or at least that path to it. iOS implements image selection through `UIImagePicker`, which allows you to get your image from different places, like the camera or the Photo Library.

Even better, you can let `UIImagePickerController` handle all the user interaction. It lets users take a photo or select an existing one, and it hands you... the path to that image. Perfect!

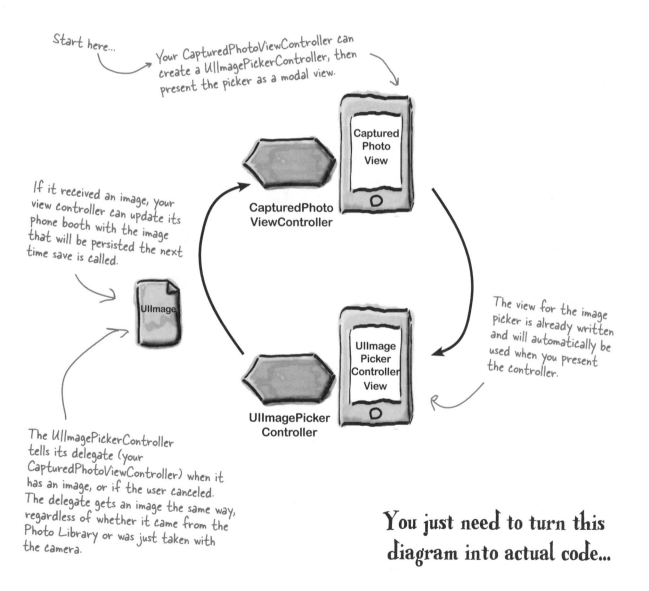

Start here...

Your CapturedPhotoViewController can create a UIImagePickerController, then present the picker as a modal view.

If it received an image, your view controller can update its phone booth with the image that will be persisted the next time save is called.

The view for the image picker is already written and will automatically be used when you present the controller.

The UIImagePickerController tells its delegate (your CapturedPhotoViewController) when it has an image, or if the user canceled. The delegate gets an image the same way, regardless of whether it came from the Photo Library or was just taken with the camera.

You just need to turn this diagram into actual code...

Ready Bake Code

Here is some of the code you'll need to tie the image picker together with your app. This code will go in your *DetailViewController.m* as part of the exercise on the next page.

```
#pragma mark UIImagePickerControllerDelegate methods

- (void)imagePickerController:(UIImagePickerController *)picker didFinishPickin
gMediaWithInfo:(NSDictionary *)info
{
  // Construct the path to the file in our Documents Directory.
  NSString *documentsDirectory = [NSSearchPathForDirectoriesInDomains(NSDocume
ntDirectory, NSUserDomainMask, YES) lastObject];
  NSString *uniqueFilename = [[NSUUID UUID] UUIDString];
  NSString *imagePath = [documentsDirectory stringByAppendingPathComponent:uni
queFilename];

  // Get the image from the picker and write it to disk.
  UIImage *image = [info objectForKey:UIImagePickerControllerEditedImage];
  [UIImagePNGRepresentation(image) writeToFile:imagePath atomically:YES];

  // Save the path to the image in our model so that it can be retrieved later.
  self.detailItem.imagePath = imagePath;

  // Update the image view.
  self.imageView.image = image;

  // Dismiss the picker.
  [self dismissViewControllerAnimated:YES completion:nil];
}

- (void)imagePickerControllerDidCancel:(UIImagePickerController *)picker
{
  // Dismiss the picker.
  [self dismissViewControllerAnimated:YES completion:nil];
}
```

↖ Remove the picker interface and release the picker object.

.m

DetailViewController.m

```
- (IBAction)takePictureButtonPressed:(id)sender
{
  NSLog(@"Taking a picture...");
  UIImagePickerController *picker = [[UIImagePickerController alloc] init];
  picker.sourceType = UIImagePickerControllerSourceTypeCamera |
UIImagePickerControllerSourceTypePhotoLibrary;
  picker.allowsEditing = YES;
  picker.delegate = self;


  [self presentViewController:picker animated:YES completion:nil];
}
```

DetailViewController.m

Exercise

Time to get some images! Using the code for the image picker on the previous page, as well as some of your Objective-C skills, it's time for you to get the image selection going.

1 Add the "Take Picture" button.
Edit the storyboard to create a button that covers the entire UIImageView and is then set behind it. Don't forget to connect it to your takePictureButton action. It should go right under the image view and be the same width as that image.

2 Add the code for the UIImagePickerController in the DetailViewController.m.
Now you can use that Ready Bake Code to finish up the UIImagePickerController. You'll need to say that your DetailViewController conforms to the UIImagePickerControllerDelegate and UINavigationControllerDelegate protocols in order to make it the delegate.

3 Add code for the takePictureButtonPressed action.
In *DetailViewController.m*, add the Ready Bake Code for the takePictureButtonPressed action above.

4 Wrap the whole thing up in a popover.
The image picker needs to be presented as a popover. Add a property for a UIPopoverController, make sure that *DetailViewController.h* conforms to the UIPopoverControllerDelegate, and implement popoverControllerDidDismissPopover in *DetailViewController.m*.

Exercise Solution

Getting that ImagePicker working isn't easy, but it's oh so sweet when that camera or Photo Library appears. Make sure your code matches the solution shown below.

① Add the "Take Picture" button.

Edit the storyboard to create a button that covers the entire UIImageView and is then set behind it. Don't forget to connect it to your takePictureButton action. It should go right under the image view and be the same width as that image.

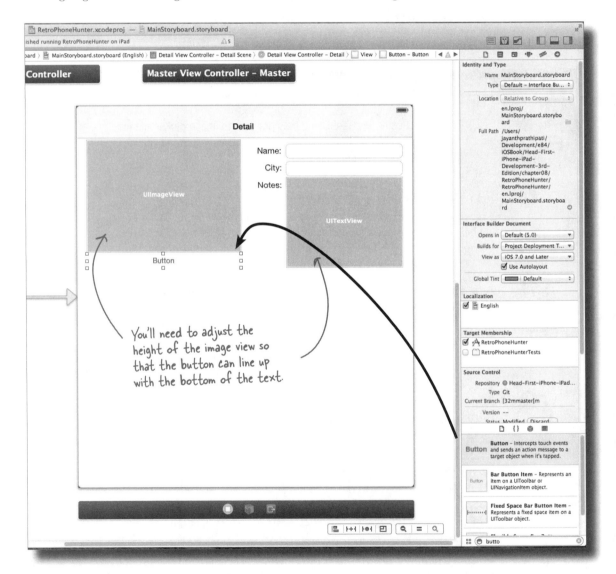

You'll need to adjust the height of the image view so that the button can line up with the bottom of the text.

2 **Add the code for the UIImagePickerController in the DetailViewController.m.**

Now you can use that Ready Bake Code to finish up the `UIImagePickerController`. You'll need to say that your `DetailViewController` conforms to the `UIImagePickerControllerDelegate` and `UINavigationControllerDelegate` protocols in order to make it the delegate.

```
@interface DetailViewController : UIViewController <UISplitViewControllerDelegate,
UITextViewDelegate, UINavigationControllerDelegate,
UIImagePickerControllerDelegate>
```

DetailViewController.h

3 **Add code for the takePictureButtonPressed action.**

In *DetailViewController.m*, add the Ready Bake Code for the takePictureButtonPressed action above.

Those should just be copying the code.

4 **Wrap the whole thing up in a popover.**

The image picker needs to be presented as a popover. Add a property for a `UIPopoverController`, make sure that *DetailViewController.h* conforms to the `UIPopoverControllerDelegate`, and implement `popoverControllerDidDismissPopover` in *DetailViewController.m*.

Wait. Why is this here? Why does it have to be in a popover?

This is one of those Apple-isms.

To conform with Apple standards, the image picker needs to be in a popover. If we don't, an exception is thrown (when you try and show the Photo Library).

Knock back all your Objective-C work with a tall glass of the storyboard editor. You're almost ready to run this thing!

4 **Wrap the whole thing up in a popover (continued).**

```objectivec
@interface DetailViewController ()
@property (strong, nonatomic) UIPopoverController *masterPopoverController;
@property (strong, nonatomic) UIPopoverController
*imagePickerPopoverController;

- (void)configureView;
@end
```

DetailViewController.m

```objectivec
#pragma mark -
#pragma mark UIPopoverControllerDelegate methods

- (void)popoverControllerDidDismissPopover:(UIPopoverController *)
popoverController
{
    self.imagePickerPopoverController = nil;
}

@end
```

DetailViewController.m

```objectivec
@interface DetailViewController : UIViewController <UISplitViewControllerDelegate,
UITextViewDelegate,
UINavigationControllerDelegate, UIImagePickerControllerDelegate,
UIPopoverControllerDelegate>
```

DetailViewController.h

TEST DRIVE

Go ahead and take it for a spin! The new button should be there and ready to click. If you go ahead and try to use it though...well...

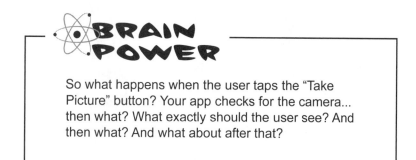

BRAIN POWER

So what happens when the user taps the "Take Picture" button? Your app checks for the camera... then what? What exactly should the user see? And then what? And what about after that?

Prompt the user with <u>action</u> <u>sheets</u>

Action sheets slide up from the bottom of the page and give the user options about how they want to continue. These sheets are similar to a modal view because the user *has* to address a sheet before they can move on to anything else. Action sheets are really straightforward to use, too: they take strings for each of their buttons and have built-in animations for appearing and disappearing.

Here's the code you'll need for a sheet that asks whether to take a new photo or choose from the Photo Library:

First, allocate the action sheet, and pass it a title.

```
UIActionSheet *photoSourceSheet = [[UIActionSheet alloc]
initWithTitle:@"Select PhoneBooth Picture"
  delegate:self
  cancelButtonTitle:nil
  destructiveButtonTitle:nil
  otherButtonTitles:@"Take New Photo",
  @"Choose Existing Photo", nil];
```

All action sheets need a cancel button, so you've got to include that for canceling the sheet.

Declare the other two buttons for your sheet, and you're done.

Action sheets frequently have a "Yes, I know this will delete all my stuff. Please do it" button, which is the destructive button. In this case, though, your app doesn't need that button.

Action sheets lead to...dactions!

You've got two actions in your sheet: "Take New Photo" and "Choose Existing Photo." Even better, it's pretty obvious what each choice should do:

Go to the camera, take a picture, and then come back and put the new image into the Phonebooth. In this case, you just need to hand over control to UIImagePickerControllerSourceTypeCamera, and it'll handle the rest.

Go to the Photo Library, pick an image, and then come back and stuff that image into the Phonebooth. Here, the UIImagePickerControllerSourceTypePhotoLibrary handles everything.

Cancel just goes back to the image view.

Sharpen your pencil

Time to implement the action sheet. There's a lot here to think
about since you're changing the flow of the app a bit... just take
your time, and you'll get it.

1 **Implement the delegate methods for the action sheet.**
Here's what you need to get started. Think about the different
options—including the default!

Don't forget to conform to the UIActionSheetProtocol in your header file!

```
- (void)actionSheet:(UIActionSheet *)actionSheet didDismissWith
ButtonIndex:(NSInteger)buttonIndex
{
    if (buttonIndex == actionSheet.cancelButtonIndex) {
        NSLog(@"The user canceled adding a image.");
        return;
    }
    UIImagePickerController *picker = [[UIImagePickerController
alloc] init];
    picker.delegate = self;
    picker.allowsEditing = YES;
    switch (buttonIndex) {
        case 0:
            NSLog(@"User wants to take a new picture.");
            picker.sourceType =
UIImagePickerControllerSourceTypeCamera;
            break;
```

2 **Modify the takePictureButtonPressed action in
CapturePhotoViewController.m to include the action sheet.**
retroPhoneHunter first needs to check for the camera. If there
is one, the user gets to pick whether to use the camera or an existing
picture. If not, the app should just go straight into the Photo Library.

The action sheet lets the user choose which of these to do.

3 **Add an outlet for the takePictureButton.**
We need this because we have to show the popover controller
from the button. Previously we used the 'sender' of the
takePictureButtonPressed method, but we can't do that in the
action sheet delegate method. So we need a new outlet!

Sharpen your pencil
Solution

Lots of code here... take your time and
make sure you got everything just right!

1 Implement the delegate methods for the action sheet.

```
@interface DetailViewController : UIViewController
<UISplitViewControllerDelegate, UITextViewDelegate,
UINavigationControllerDelegate, UIImagePickerControllerDelegate,
UIPopoverControllerDelegate, UIActionSheetDelegate>
```

DetailViewController.h

```
- (void)actionSheet:(UIActionSheet *)actionSheet didDismissWithButton
Index:(NSInteger)buttonIndex
{
  if (buttonIndex == actionSheet.cancelButtonIndex) {
    NSLog(@"The user canceled adding a image.");
    return;
  }

  UIImagePickerController *picker = [[UIImagePickerController alloc]
init];
  picker.delegate = self;
  picker.allowsEditing = YES;

  switch (buttonIndex) {
    case 0:
      NSLog(@"User wants to take a new picture.");
      picker.sourceType = UIImagePickerControllerSourceTypeCamera;
      break;
    default:
      picker.sourceType =
UIImagePickerControllerSourceTypePhotoLibrary;
      break;
  }
```

DetailViewController.m

```
    self.imagePickerPopoverController = [[UIPopoverController alloc] init
WithContentViewController:picker];

  self.imagePickerPopoverController.delegate = self;

  [self.imagePickerPopoverController presentPopoverFromRect:self.
takePictureButton.frame

inView:self.view

permittedArrowDirections:UIPopoverArrowDirectionLeft

animated:YES];

}
```

DetailViewController.m

2 Modify the takePictureButtonPressed action in
CapturePhotoViewController.m to include the action sheet.

DetailViewController.m

```
- (IBAction)takePictureButtonPressed:(id)sender
{
  NSLog(@"Taking a picture...");
  if ([UIImagePickerController isSourceTypeAvailable:UIImagePickerController
SourceTypeCamera]) {
    NSLog(@"This device has a camera. Asking the user what they want to
use.");
    UIActionSheet *photoSourceSheet = [[UIActionSheet alloc]
initWithTitle:@"Select PhoneBooth Picture"
      delegate:self
      cancelButtonTitle:nil
      destructiveButtonTitle:nil
      otherButtonTitles:@"Take New Photo",
      @"Choose Existing Photo", nil];
    // Show the action sheet near the add image button.
    [photoSourceSheet showFromRect:((UIButton *)sender).frame inView:self.
view animated:YES];
  }
```

Keep going...

Sharpen your pencil Solution ② Modify the takePictureButtonPressed action in CapturePhotoViewController.m to include the action sheet.

```
    else { // No camera. Just use the library.
    UIImagePickerController *picker = [[UIImagePickerController alloc]
init];
    picker.sourceType = UIImagePickerControllerSourceTypePhotoLibrary;
    picker.allowsEditing = YES;
    picker.delegate = self;


    self.imagePickerPopoverController = [[UIPopoverController alloc] ini
tWithContentViewController:picker];
    self.imagePickerPopoverController.delegate = self;
    [self.imagePickerPopoverController presentPopoverFromRect:((UIButton
*)sender).frame inView:self.view permittedArrowDirections:UIPopoverArrow
DirectionLeft animated:YES];

  }
}
```

DetailViewController.m

③ Add an outlet for the takePictureButton.

```
@property (weak, nonatomic) IBOutlet UITextView *notesView;
@property (weak, nonatomic) IBOutlet UIButton *takePictureButton;
- (IBAction)nameFieldEditingChanged:(id)sender;
```

Make sure it's wired up in the storyboard!

TEST DRIVE

Fire up your retroPhoneHunter and add a phone booth. Now try out your new code: select a photo of a phone booth (or take a new photo). If you've used the SourceTypePhotoLibrary in the takePictureButtonPressed code, everything should work, and you'll see your new action sheet.

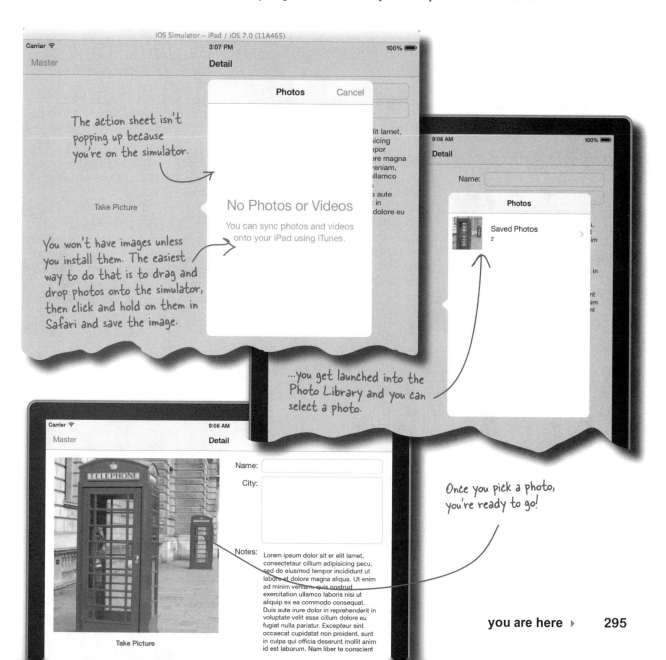

The action sheet isn't popping up because you're on the simulator.

You won't have images unless you install them. The easiest way to do that is to drag and drop photos onto the simulator, then click and hold on them in Safari and save the image.

...you get launched into the Photo Library and you can select a photo.

Once you pick a photo, you're ready to go!

there are no
Dumb Questions

Q: Don't newer iPhones and iPads support video now? How do I get to that?

A: Video is another media type you can access when you use the UIImagePickerController. By default, the controller uses still images, which is what you probable want for retroPhoneHunter.

Q: What about the whole augmented reality thing with the camera? Can I do something like that?

A: Yup. You can give the UIImagePickerController a custom overlay view to use if the camera is invoked. There are still limitations on what you can actually do in the camera view, but you can overlay it with your own information if you want.

Q: What's with the allowEditing thing we turned on in the UIImagePickerController?

A: The picker controller has built-in support for cropping and zooming images if you want to use it. The allowEditing flag controls whether or not the user gets a chance to move and resize their image before it's sent to the delegate. If you enable this, and the user tweaks the image, you'll be given editing information in the callback.

Q: Do I really have to worry about devices that don't have cameras?

A: Absolutely! When you submit your application to Apple for inclusion in the iTunes App Store, you specify the devices your application works with. If you say it works, Apple is going to test your app on both types of devices—with and without a camera. They also run tests where your application doesn't have network access to ensure you handle that properly as well. Think defensively! Apple is going to test your application in all kinds of scenarios.

Q: Is there any way to test the camera in the simulator?

A: No. The Test Drive on the last page is about as close as you can get, which is to implement the code for the camera and test it out with the Photo Library. You've learned a lot so far, and lots of the functionality that you're moving into has outgrown the simulator. GPS functionality, the accelerometer, speaker capabilities... all of these things can't be tested in the simulator. To really make sure they all work, you'll need to install your apps on your own device.

Q: What's the deal with Apple's Developer Program again?

A: In order to install an app on your device or to submit an app to the App Store, you need to be a registered iOS developer with Apple. The fee (currently) is $99. Even if you want to just install an app for your own personal use, you'll need to be registered.

Geek Bits

It might be time to register with Apple's Developer Program. If you do, you can install the retroPhoneHunter app on your actual iPad and test it for yourself.

So now this works...
with the camera or the
Photo Library...

And these are easy.
Just some properties in
your app...

...but what about maps?
Seems like a pretty big
deal, right?

Where
~~Who~~... are you? ~~Who, who?~~ Where

OK, you get the idea
by now, right? It's
about the "where"...

The map view is important here because it will tell us where the phone booths are
spotted. There are two pieces of information that we need to get there. We need to
display the phone booth location if we know it and we also need to figure out where you
are, so that when we show a location we have it's relative placment to you; and when
we take a picture the location of the phone booth is saved. Adding the view is actually
pretty easy; it's making it all go that is a little trickier.

So now the real question: how can an iOS device figure out that all-important location?

Core Location can find you in a few ways

GPS is often the first thing most people think of for getting location information, but the first-generation iPhone didn't have GPS, and neither do current iPod Touches or WiFi iPads. That doesn't mean that you're out of options though. There are actually three ways available for iOS to determine your location: GPS, cell tower triangulation, and WiFi positioning service.

GPS is the most accurate, followed by cell towers and WiFi. iPhones can use two or three of these, while iPod Touches and WiFi iPads can only use WiFi...which is still better than nothing. If your head is starting to spin, don't worry! Core Location actually decides which method to use based on what's available to the device and what kind of accuracy you're after. That means you don't have much to do; the iOS will handle it for you with the **LocationManager**:

```
- (CLLocationManager*) locationManager {
  if (locationManager_ == nil) {
   locationManager_ = [[CLLocationManager alloc] init];
   locationManager_.desiredAccuracy = kCLLocationAccuracyNearestTenMeters;
   locationManager_.delegate = self;
  }
  return locationManager_;
}
```

Allocate the CLLocation Manager.

Once the locationManager has the position, it will start sending it back to the delegate.

Set the accuracy to 10 meters. Higher accuracy can take longer to get a fix, and can really slow down the performance of your app.

Core Location relies on the LocationManager

To use Core Location, you simply need to create a LocationManager and ask it to start sending updates. It can provide position, altitude, and orientation, depending upon the device's capabilities. In order for it to send you this info, you just need to provide it with a delegate as well as your required accuracy.

The CLLocationManager will notify you when positions are available or if there's an error. You'll want to make sure you're also properly handling when you *don't* get a position from the location manager. Even if the device supports it, the users get asked before you collect location information, and can say "No" to having their position recorded (either intentionally or by accident).

BRAIN POWER

Where should you implement this code in your app?

I guess we're going to need a new header file for some Core Location constants, right?

You got it... and a new framework, too.

To keep the size of your app small, Apple breaks apart different features and functionality into **frameworks**. As you start adding new functionality, like Core Location, you'll need to start adding in these new frameworks.

Since the Core Location framework isn't included by default, you'll need to explicitly add it.

Do this!

Add the CoreLocation Framework.

Select the project in the naviagator and then select the
RetroPhoneHunter target, with the Build Phases tab. Then
add the CoreLocation Framework.

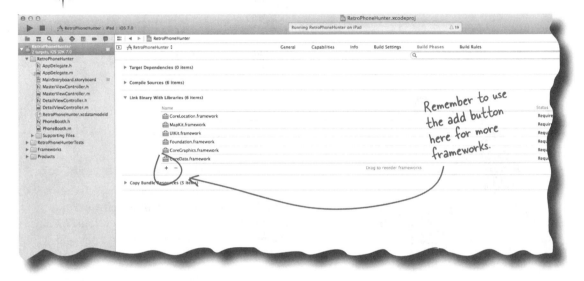

Remember to use the add button here for more frameworks.

Watch it!

Core Location is a battery killer.

*Making frequent API calls from your app that checks for
a location will quickly drain batteries, since it turns on the
GPS/cellular/WiFi receiver. That'll lead to upset users and
cranky iTunes reviews. Keep these calls to a minimum!*

BE the application flow

Your job is to be the application, and figure out where Core Location fits into the flow of action between and through the application views. Assume that finding a new phone booth requires a location, date, and time.

1 What method will be used to kick off Core Location when we take a picture?

....

2 What happens when the location is returned to the view controller?

....

....

3 What happens if Core Location can't get a position, or the user disables it?

....

....

4 What about other devices? What should happen with them?

....

....

BE the application flow solution

Your job was to be the application, and figure out where Core Location fit into the flow of action between and through the application views. Assume that finding a new phone booth requires a location, date, and time.

1 What method will be used to kick off Core Location when we take a picture?

The code to initialize Core Location could go into viewWillAppear for the detail view on an iPhone, but since it's an iPad, the detail view is always visible. To keep things simple, we'll add a button to get the location at user request.

BE the application flow solution

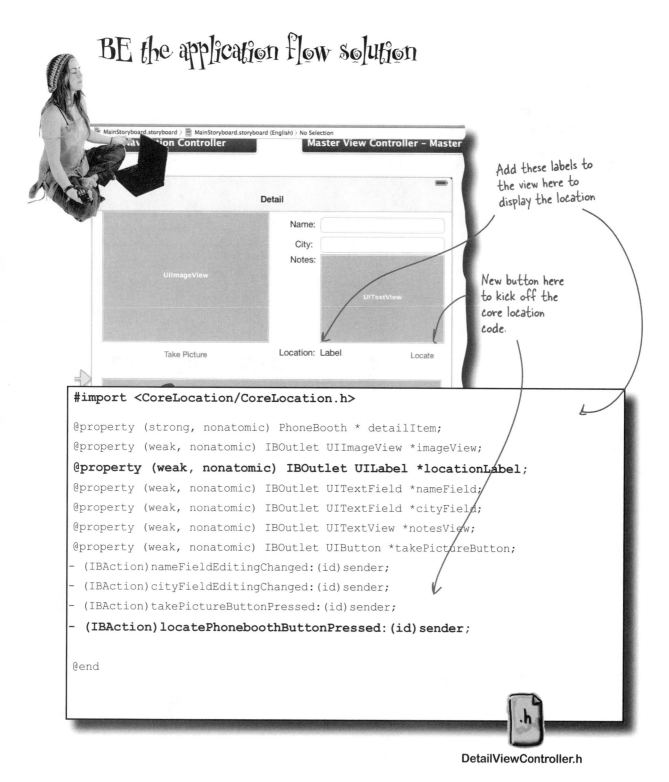

MainStoryboard.storyboard › MainStoryboard.storyboard (English) › No Selection

Navigation Controller | Master View Controller – Master

Detail

UIImageView

Name:
City:
Notes:

UITextView

Take Picture

Location: Label   Locate

Add these labels to the view here to display the location

New button here to kick off the core location code.

```
#import <CoreLocation/CoreLocation.h>

@property (strong, nonatomic) PhoneBooth * detailItem;
@property (weak, nonatomic) IBOutlet UIImageView *imageView;
@property (weak, nonatomic) IBOutlet UILabel *locationLabel;
@property (weak, nonatomic) IBOutlet UITextField *nameField;
@property (weak, nonatomic) IBOutlet UITextField *cityField;
@property (weak, nonatomic) IBOutlet UITextView *notesView;
@property (weak, nonatomic) IBOutlet UIButton *takePictureButton;
- (IBAction)nameFieldEditingChanged:(id)sender;
- (IBAction)cityFieldEditingChanged:(id)sender;
- (IBAction)takePictureButtonPressed:(id)sender;
- (IBAction)locatePhoneboothButtonPressed:(id)sender;

@end
```

DetailViewController.h

BE the application flow solution

① What method will be used to kick off Core Location when we take a picture? (cont.)

```objc
- (IBAction)locatePhoneboothButtonPressed:(id)sender
{
    [self.locationManager startUpdatingLocation];
}
```

DetailViewController.m

② What happens when the location is returned to the view controller?

It'll mean that the location manager can get the current position. If the user is adding a phone booth, the app needs to get the current position from the location manager and update the phone booth info.

```objc
@interface DetailViewController ()
@property (strong, nonatomic) UIPopoverController *masterPopoverController;
@property (strong, nonatomic) UIPopoverController *imagePickerPopoverController;
@property (strong, nonatomic) CLLocationManager *locationManager;

- (void)configureView;
end
```

DetailViewController.m

BE the application flow solution

2 What happens when the location is returned to the view controller? (cont.)

```objc
- (CLLocationManager *)locationManager
{
  if (!_locationManager) {
    _locationManager = [[CLLocationManager alloc] init];
    _locationManager.desiredAccuracy =
kCLLocationAccuracyNearestTenMeters;

    _locationManager.delegate = self;
  }


  return _locationManager;
}
```

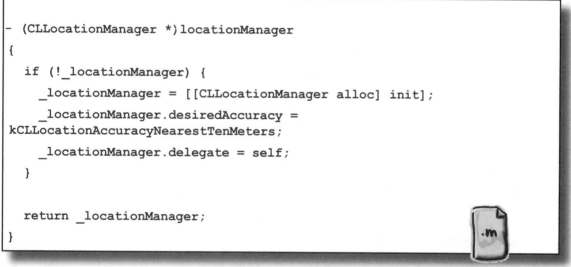

DetailViewController.m

BE the application flow solution

③ What happens if Core Location can't get a position, or the user disables it?

It's not ideal, but a location isn't 100% required for this app. So the user can manually enter a city, but no location from Core Location... and no map.

```objc
          #pragma mark -
        #pragma mark CLLocationManagerDelegate methods

- (void)locationManager:(CLLocationManager *)manager didUpdateLocations:(NSArray *)locations
{
  NSLog(@"Core location claims to have a position.");
  CLLocation *location = [locations lastObject];

  // Update the phonebooth and view.
  self.detailItem.lat = [NSNumber numberWithDouble:location.coordinate.latitude];
  self.detailItem.lon = [NSNumber numberWithDouble:location.coordinate.longitude];

  [self configureView];

  // Stop monitoring locations. In a real application, you would probably to keep updating
  // the location to get the most accurate position.
  NSLog(@"Shutting down core location.");
  [self.locationManager stopUpdatingLocation];
}

- (void)locationManager:(CLLocationManager *)manager didFailWithError:(NSError *)error
{
  NSLog(@"Core location can't get a fix!");

  // Update the view to alert the user that we can't get a location.
  self.locationLabel.text = @"Can't get a location.";
}

@end
```

DetailViewController.m

4 What about other devices? What should happen with them?

It's OK. Just tell Core Location the accuracy desired and it will deal with the rest. So, the iPod Touch gets the best data it can, and what's returned to the app. Perfect!.

TEST DRIVE

Implementing Core Location really wasn't that hard, but making it work in the user flow required a bit more work. Now that it's all done, you should be up and running...

iOS Simulator – iPad / iOS 7.0 (11A465)

Carrier 📶   4:34 PM   100% 🔋

Master   **Detail**

Name:

City:

Notes: Lorem ipsum dolor sit er elit lamet, consectetaur cillium adipisicing pecu, sed do eiusmod tempor incididunt ut labore et dolore magna aliqua. Ut enim ad minim veniam, quis nostrud exercitation ullamco laboris nisi ut aliquip ex ea commodo consequat. Duis aute irure dolor in reprehenderit in

Take Picture   Location: Label   Locate

Clicking the "locate" button, which tries to find the current location (presumably where the phone booth is)..

Saskatoon

Calgary   Regina

Winnipeg   ONT.

Choose stack frame 53.844 RetroPhoneHunter[10675:70b] Core location claims to have a position.
53.844 RetroPhoneHunter[10675:70b] Shutting down core location.

All Output ⏷

there are no
Dumb Questions

Q: Is starting and stopping Core Location in viewWillAppear and viewWillDisappear normal?

A: It's normal to start and stop Core Location as you need it. It uses a fair amount of power while it's running, so it's best to shut it down when you don't need it. This gets a little tricky, though, because Core Location can require some time to get its initial position information. To make that a little smoother for the user, you should enable it as soon as the view appears, which gives it a head start before the user needs the location. It's a balancing act, for sure.

Q: Is there any way to speed up getting that initial position?

A: Core Location will try to cache previous position information so it can give you something as quickly as possible. Because of this, if you're really concerned about accuracy, you should check the timestamp sent along with the position information to make sure the position is recent enough for your app's needs.

Q: Does location accuracy impact things like startup time or battery usage?

A: Absolutely. The more accurate a position you ask for, the more battery Core Location will consume, and it will potentially take longer to figure out that position, too. Lower-fidelity information tends to come to you faster. Use whatever accuracy you need for your application, but be aware of the implications of high-resolution information... and only ask for it if you really need it.

Q: Is there a way to just wait for Core Location to have a

position rather than having it call back to the delegate?

A: Unfortunately, no. Core Location, like a lot of other frameworks in iOS, calls back asynchronously as data is available. Network access generally works this way as well. You need to make sure you keep your users informed of what's going on in the application and what they can and can't do at the moment. For example, you could display a wait indicator (like a spinning gear) or display position status with a disabled indicator like an icon, button, or label.

Q: Why did we have to move the code around and do all that refactoring?

A: To follow the DRY principle (Don't Repeat Yourself). That meant cleaning up the code and eliminating duplication by pulling that common code out into a separate method and calling that method from the two places that need it. Otherwise, you'd have the same code in two different places in the app.

Q: What's the deal with private interfaces again?

A: Remember that your header file captures your public interface or API. But with refreshPhoneboothInformation, you don't want this internal method to be part of your API (in other words, you don't want other people to call it). You want to declare it so the compiler can check that you're calling a valid method, but can just add a private set of methods to your interface in the implementation file. Some people actually put an _ (underscore) before their private method names so that it's obvious that you shouldn't be calling this from anywhere but the class's own implementation. Apple, however, reserves this convention for their own private methods.

That location is great, but how about the map? Time for another framework.

Map Kit comes with every iOS device

When Apple opened up the API for the Map Kit in iOS 3.0, developers gained access to Apple's maps, including satellite imagery.

There's lots of customization that you can do with the maps, too. You can specify how wide an area should be shown, the initial view start width, and even add pins and annotations. Basically, you've got everything available that you see when you use Apple Maps yourself.

In previous versions of iOS, Map Kit used Google Maps. Since iOS 6, though, Apple provides their own maps. You still get satellite imagery, but it's no longer the same as what Google provides.

Depending on the information you want to show on the map, you can create your own views for annotations and show anything you want, like pictures, formatted text, etc.

MKMapView is a control that pulls map information from Apple's Maps. You can configure it for the normal road display, satellite imagery, or a hybrid, like you see here.

Map Kit comes with built-in support for pushpins at specified locations, called <u>annotations</u>.

City: London
Zip: [This may not make sense worldwide]
Notes: How retro is this? It's a phonebooth, and it's very Tardis!

The location of a phone booth can finally be shown on a nice map next to the phone booth's picture in the app.

Map Kit <u>requires</u> a network connection.

Since Map Kit pulls imagery information from Apple, apps have to have a network connection for it to be useful. That's not a problem for the simulator (assuming your Mac is online), but it could be an issue for any device with limited connectivity, depending on their location. Map Kit handles this gracefully, but it's something to be aware of.

Watch it!

there are no
Dumb Questions

Q: What's the difference between Core Location and Map Kit?

A: Map Kit is about displaying a map, position-sensitive information, and the app's user interface. Core Location is about getting information about where a device **is**. You can drag and drop a map onto your view in GUI editor, pass it some values, and everything will just work.

Core Location, on the other hand, returns values to the delegate, and you'll need to decide what to do with them. You're going to take that information from Core Location and give it to Map Kit to show a map of the location of a phone booth, for example.

Q: Where do all these frameworks come from? What if I want one that's not on the list?

A: The frameworks are included as part of the iOS SDK. The actual path to the frameworks varies by version and what platform you're developing for. For example, the Map Kit framework you're using is here: */Developer/Platforms/iPhoneOS.platform/Developer/ SDKs/iPhoneOS7.0sdk/System/Library/Frameworks/MapKit. framework*. In general, you should be able to add frameworks using Xcode and not worry about a specific location. However, if a framework isn't listed or you're adding a custom one, you can point Xcode to the actual path.

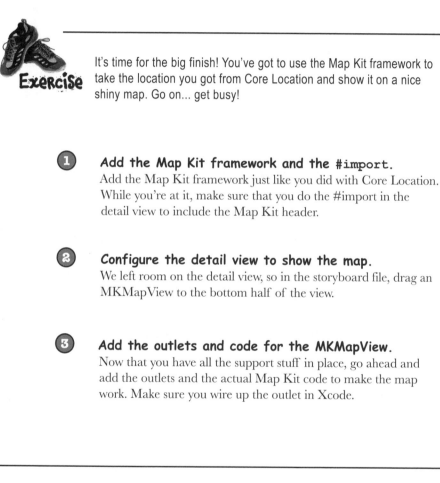

It's time for the big finish! You've got to use the Map Kit framework to take the location you got from Core Location and show it on a nice shiny map. Go on... get busy!

Exercise

1 **Add the Map Kit framework and the #import.**
Add the Map Kit framework just like you did with Core Location. While you're at it, make sure that you do the #import in the detail view to include the Map Kit header.

2 **Configure the detail view to show the map.**
We left room on the detail view, so in the storyboard file, drag an MKMapView to the bottom half of the view.

3 **Add the outlets and code for the MKMapView.**
Now that you have all the support stuff in place, go ahead and add the outlets and the actual Map Kit code to make the map work. Make sure you wire up the outlet in Xcode.

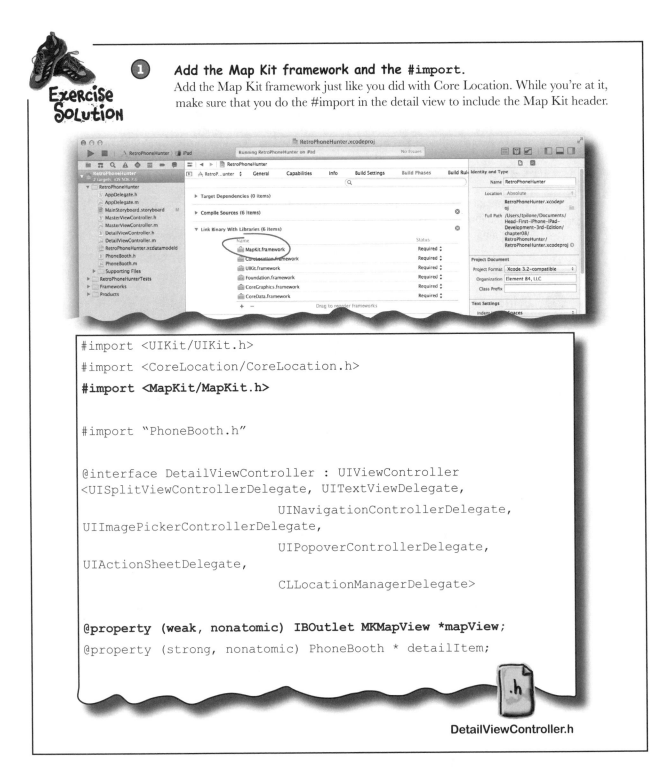

Add the Map Kit framework and the #import.

Add the Map Kit framework just like you did with Core Location. While you're at it, make sure that you do the #import in the detail view to include the Map Kit header.

```objc
#import <UIKit/UIKit.h>
#import <CoreLocation/CoreLocation.h>
#import <MapKit/MapKit.h>


#import "PhoneBooth.h"


@interface DetailViewController : UIViewController
<UISplitViewControllerDelegate, UITextViewDelegate,
                        UINavigationControllerDelegate,
UIImagePickerControllerDelegate,
                        UIPopoverControllerDelegate,
UIActionSheetDelegate,
                        CLLocationManagerDelegate>


@property (weak, nonatomic) IBOutlet MKMapView *mapView;
@property (strong, nonatomic) PhoneBooth * detailItem;
```

DetailViewController.h

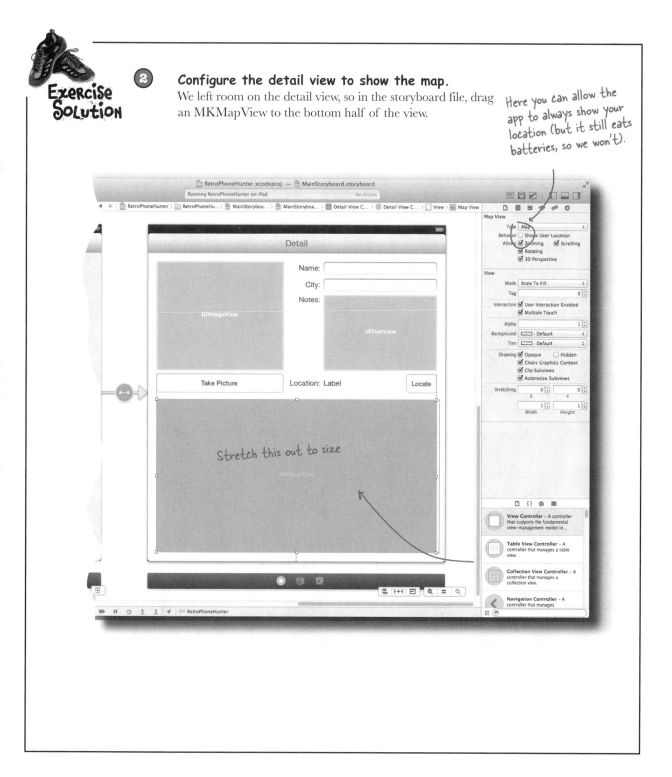

② **Configure the detail view to show the map.**
We left room on the detail view, so in the storyboard file, drag an MKMapView to the bottom half of the view.

Here you can allow the app to always show your location (but it still eats batteries, so we won't).

Stretch this out to size

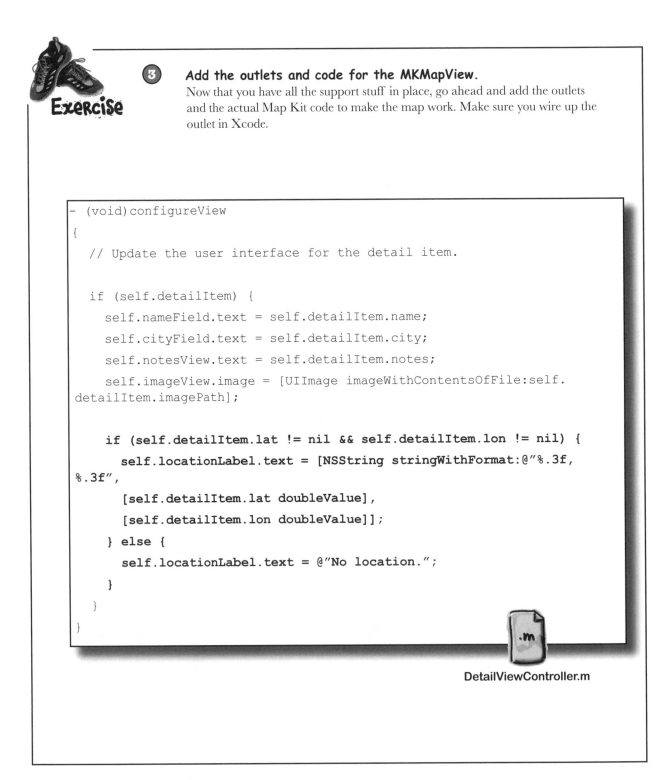

③ **Add the outlets and code for the MKMapView.**
Now that you have all the support stuff in place, go ahead and add the outlets
and the actual Map Kit code to make the map work. Make sure you wire up the
outlet in Xcode.

Exercise

```objc
- (void)configureView
{
  // Update the user interface for the detail item.

  if (self.detailItem) {
    self.nameField.text = self.detailItem.name;
    self.cityField.text = self.detailItem.city;
    self.notesView.text = self.detailItem.notes;
    self.imageView.image = [UIImage imageWithContentsOfFile:self.
detailItem.imagePath];

    if (self.detailItem.lat != nil && self.detailItem.lon != nil) {
      self.locationLabel.text = [NSString stringWithFormat:@"%.3f,
%.3f",
      [self.detailItem.lat doubleValue],
      [self.detailItem.lon doubleValue]];
    } else {
      self.locationLabel.text = @"No location.";
    }
  }
}
```

DetailViewController.m

Test Drive

It's time for the big finish! Try out what you have and see the map view working!

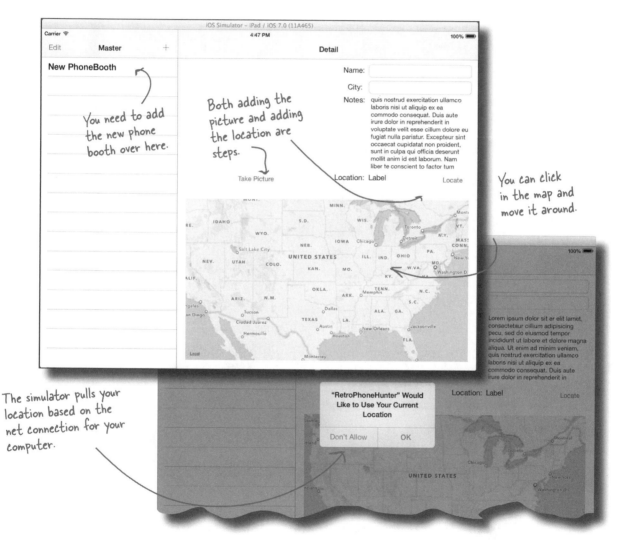

You need to add the new phone booth over here.

Both adding the picture and adding the location are steps.

You can click in the map and move it around.

The simulator pulls your location based on the net connection for your computer.

But there's no pin showing where it is!

Annotations require a little more ~~work~~ finesse

Annotations are the little flags that come up when you see a point of interest, represented by a pin. The catch? Incorporating annotations means conforming to the Map Kit annotation protocol. Map Kit uses an annotation protocol so that you can use your existing classes and provide them directly to Map Kit. The downside is that means you need to add just a *little more* code to your Phonebooth class:

```objc
#import <Foundation/Foundation.h>
#import <CoreData/CoreData.h>

#import <MapKit/MapKit.h>

@interface Phonebooth : NSManagedObject <MKAnnotation> {
@private
}
@property (nonatomic, retain) NSString * city;
@property (nonatomic, retain) NSString * name;
@property (nonatomic, retain) NSString * notes;
@property (nonatomic, retain) NSString * imagePath;
@property (nonatomic, retain) NSNumber * lat;
@property (nonatomic, retain) NSNumber * lon;


@property (nonatomic, readonly) CLLocationCoordinate2D
coordinate;

- (NSString *) title;
- (NSString *) subtitle;

@end
```

The MKAnnotation protocol is a little odd in that it defines a property and two getters. These are used by the MapView to position the pin and populate the overlay if a pin is tapped.

Phonebooth.h

Watch it!

If you use automatic NSManagedObject file generation again, you'll wipe out these customizations.

Fully implement the annotation protocol

The protocol requires you to have a coordinate property, a title, and a subtitle. Instead of synthesizing that coordinate property, you should implement it yourself and just return the phone booth's position, name, and so forth.

For an application in which you expect to have to do more data migration, you should implement a separate class conforming to the protocol that has a reference to its Phonebooth (through composition) rather than adding code to the Phonebooth class directly.

Your app conforms to the protocol by implementing the property getter and methods. Simply map these to data you already have about the phone booth.

```objc
- (CLLocationCoordinate2D) coordinate {
  return CLLocationCoordinate2DMake(
   [self.lat doubleValue],
   [self.lon doubleValue]);
}

- (NSString *) title {
  return self.name;
}

- (NSString *) subtitle {
  return self.notes;
}
@end
```

Phonebooth.m

Test Drive

That's it! Everything should be working now. Time to start adding phone booths, and let your friends do the same!

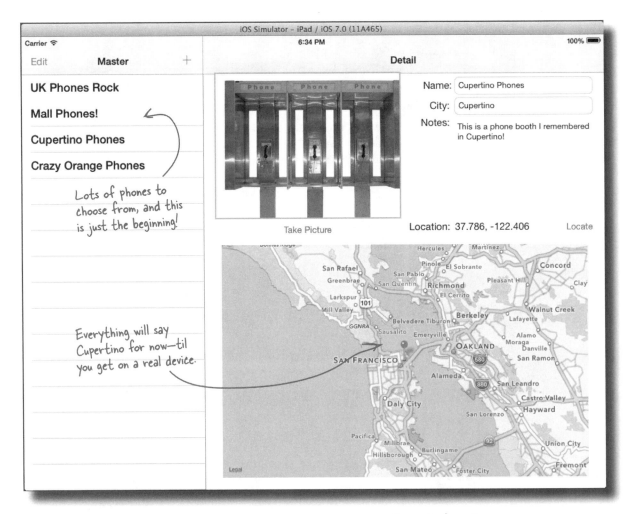

Lots of phones to choose from, and this is just the beginning!

Everything will say Cupertino for now—til you get on a real device.

Thanks to all the free help from Core Data, you can quit the app and restart, and everything is still there, ready to roll!

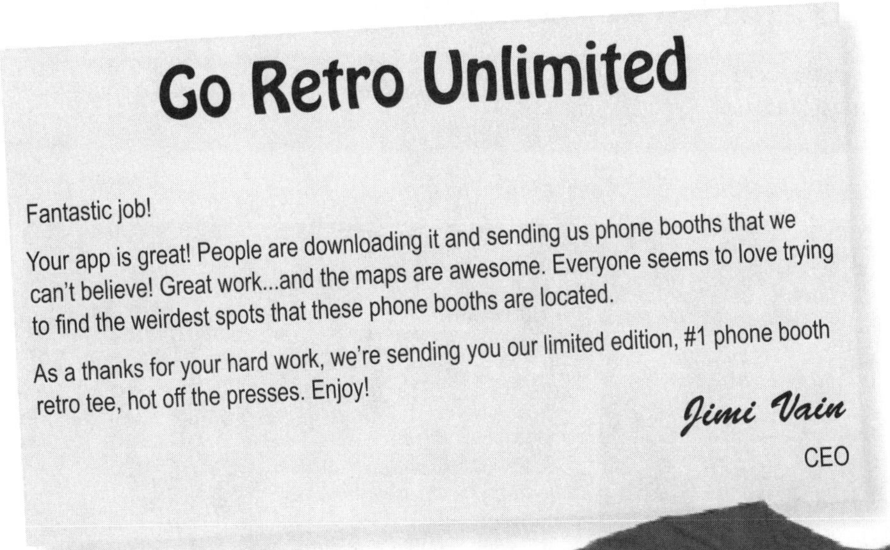

Go Retro Unlimited

Fantastic job!

Your app is great! People are downloading it and sending us phone booths that we can't believe! Great work...and the maps are awesome. Everyone seems to love trying to find the weirdest spots that these phone booths are located.

As a thanks for your hard work, we're sending you our limited edition, #1 phone booth retro tee, hot off the presses. Enjoy!

Jimi Vain
CEO

My mobile phone...

POLICE 'UBLIC BOX

...is a tardis.

iOS Hardware Cross

Go ahead and flex some of those new vocab words that you've learned.

Across

2. Core _____ enables you to access location information from your devices.
3. Map Kit allows you to access _____ maps, not Google's!
8. We're using a _____ to hold the descriptions of the phone booths.
9. For hierarchical data, iPad use _____ controllers.
11. Applications are installed on iOS devices as _____.
12. Use _____ sheets to prompt the user.

Down

1. _____ helps manage images and photos.
4. _____ are used only in iPad apps.
5. iPad apps need to support both portrait and _____ orientations.
6. You _____ test the camera in the simulator.
7. Using _____ makes it easier to build multiple orientations.
10. Location services use a lot of _____.

Your kit Toolbox

You've got Chapter 8 under your belt and now you've added hardware funcitonality to your toolbox.

UIImagePickerController

- Manages taking pictures.
- Works with the Photo Library on the device.
- Comes with built-in views.
- Works with video, too.

Core Location

- Uses WiFi, GPS, and cell tower triangulation to determine device location.
- Is resource (battery) intensive.
- Will ask for permission before it finds your location.

iPad

- Needs support for mulitple orientations.
- Uses real estate differently.
- Universal apps come with two storyboard files for tablet and phone views.

BULLET POINTS

- iOS apps are primarily read-only in their interactions with the device.

- iOS apps are sandboxed by application in the device file structure.

- Apps are allowed to read and write to the tmp and cache directories in the app sandbox.

- The cache and tmp directories aren't backed up by the system.

iOS Hardware Cross Solution

Go ahead and flex some of those new vocab words that you've learned.

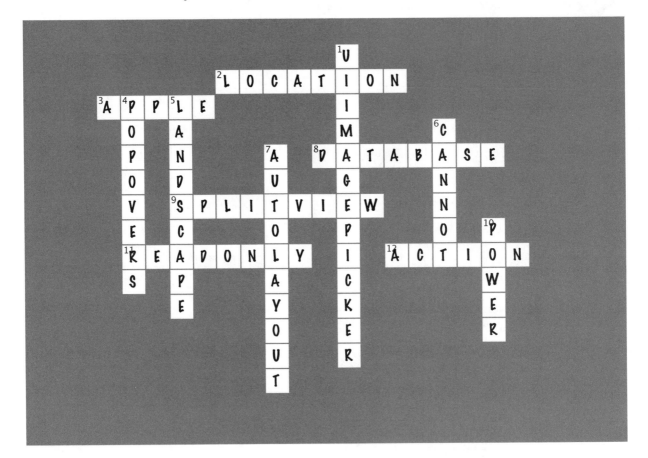

Across

2. Core _____ enables you to access location information from your devices. [LOCATION]
3. Map Kit allows you to access _____ maps, not Google's! [APPLE]
8. We're using a _____ to hold the descriptions of the phone booths. [DATABASE]
9. For hierarchical data, iPad use _____ controllers. [SPLITVIEW]
11. Applications are installed on iOS devices as _____. [READONLY]
12. Use _____ sheets to prompt the user. [ACTION]

Down

1. _____ helps manage images and photos. [UIIMAGEPICKER]
4. _____ are used only in iPad apps. [POPOVERS]
5. iPad apps need to support both portrait and _____ orientations. [LANDSCAPE]
6. You _____ test the camera in the simulator. [CANNOT]
7. Using _____ makes it easier to build multiple orientations. [AUTOLAYOUT]
10. Location services use a lot of _____. [POWER]

Index

Symbols

* (asterisk), preceding pointer variables 82

@ (at sign)

    preceding keywords. *See* specific keywords

    preceding string literals 58

[ ] (brackets), enclosing messages 88

: (colon), in method arguments 88

- (minus sign), indicating instance methods 83, 90, 93

+ (plus sign), indicating static methods 90, 93

A

accessor methods. *See* getters; setters

actions 52, 55, 83

    compared to methods 70

    creating 47–50

    events associated with 47, 49, 51–52

action sheets 290–295

Android apps, development process for 198–200

annotations for maps 309, 316–318

Apple Developer Program 26, 296

apps (Android) 198–200

apps (iOS)

    Apple logos in 186

    designing

        HIG for 101, 181, 190–192

        iOS 7 characteristics for 193–195

        on paper 36, 38, 45

        in Xcode 39–43, 47

    examples of. *See* examples

    external links in 185

    files for 13, 22, 281–282

    icons for

        changing 21–24

        resolution requirements 182

    initial content downloaded by 183

    installing on a device 13, 26, 29

    iOS versions supported by 183

    publishing to App store 3, 29, 181

    purchases in 182

    as read-only on devices 281

    testing 16, 187–189

    user expectations for 2

App store 181

    publishing apps to 3, 29

    rejections from

        appealing 185

        reasons for 182–186

        resubmitting apps after 185

ARC (automatic reference counting) 4

arrays 15, 119–121. *See also* plists

asset catalog 22

Assistant Editor 48, 158–159

asterisk (*), preceding pointer variables 82

atomic properties 86

at sign (@)

    preceding keywords. *See* specific keywords

    preceding string literals 58

Attributes Inspector 42, 46

attributes, property 84–86

augmented reality 296

automatic reference counting (ARC) 4

awakeFromFetch method 220

B

battery, Core Location using 300, 308

brackets ([ ]), enclosing messages 88

buttons 43, 46

C

Caches directory 282

Calendar app, navigation controller with 105

Y

Have it your way.

O'Reilly eBooks

- Lifetime access to the book when you buy through oreilly.com
- Provided in up to four, DRM-free file formats, for use on the devices of your choice: PDF, .epub, Kindle-compatible .mobi, and Android .apk
- Fully searchable, with copy-and-paste, and print functionality
- We also alert you when we've updated the files with corrections and additions.

oreilly.com/ebooks/

Safari Books Online

- Access the contents and quickly search over 7000 books on technology, business, and certification guides
- Learn from expert video tutorials, and explore thousands of hours of video on technology and design topics
- Download whole books or chapters in PDF format, at no extra cost, to print or read on the go
- Early access to books as they're being written
- Interact directly with authors of upcoming books
- Save up to 35% on O'Reilly print books

See the complete Safari Library at safari.oreilly.com

O'REILLY®

Get even more for your money.

Join the O'Reilly Community, and register the O'Reilly books you own. It's free, and you'll get:

- $4.99 ebook upgrade offer
- 40% upgrade offer on O'Reilly print books
- Membership discounts on books and events
- Free lifetime updates to ebooks and videos
- Multiple ebook formats, DRM FREE
- Participation in the O'Reilly community
- Newsletters
- Account management
- 100% Satisfaction Guarantee

Signing up is easy:

1. **Go to: oreilly.com/go/register**
2. **Create an O'Reilly login.**
3. **Provide your address.**
4. **Register your books.**

Note: English-language books only

To order books online:

oreilly.com/store

For questions about products or an order:

orders@oreilly.com

To sign up to get topic-specific email announcements and/or news about upcoming books, conferences, special offers, and new technologies:

elists@oreilly.com

For technical questions about book content:

booktech@oreilly.com

To submit new book proposals to our editors:

proposals@oreilly.com

O'Reilly books are available in multiple DRM-free ebook formats. For more information:

oreilly.com/ebooks

O'REILLY®

Spreading the knowledge of innovators   oreilly.com